D0958886

WINKELSTERN

THE NEW YORK TIMES . . . CHICAGO TRIBUNE . . . TIME MAGAZINE . . . PHILADELPHIA BULLETIN . . . CLEVELAND PLAIN DEALER . . . LOS ANGELES TIMES . . . SATURDAY REVIEW . . . HOUSTON POST . . . ASSOCIATED PRESS . . . JOHN BARKHAM REVIEWS . . . BOSTON GLOBE . . . NATIONAL OBSERVER . . . PUBLISHERS WEEKLY . . . WALL STREET JOURNAL . . . JOSEPH HELLER . . . WILLIE MORRIS . . . IRWIN SHAW

ALL HAIL JAMES JONES' WW II

"SUPERB . . . the sights, sounds and smells of the war, as well as the feelings of the men who fought it . . . WWII will bring the memories flooding back; for the student of that global conflict and for the general readers . . . a vivid, highly instructive capsule course in what happened during those dramatic 44-plus months."

—*Philadelphia Bulletin*

"A book that really matters . . . What Jones has done . . . is quite simply to make the event come fully alive again."

—*The New York Times*

"AMAZING . . . with his inimitable bent for realism, his perception and his combat infantry experiences in the South Pacific, he has somehow managed to write about the whole war, in all its far-flung theatres, and with its entire cast of combatants . . . brilliantly illuminated with samples of the finest combat art to come out of the war . . . SHOULD BE MADE REQUIRED READING."

—*Cleveland Press*

"AN EXPERT, ELOQUENT PERSONAL REMEMBRANCE OF BATTLES PAST, what it felt like to live each day as possibly one's last, what it felt like to go into battle, and finally what it felt like to get hit . . . WRITTEN BY ONE OF THE BEST COMBAT NOVELISTS OF OUR TIME."

—*San Francisco Examiner & Chronicle*

"OPULENT DESIGN . . . STRIKING GRAPHICS . . . JONES' BEST WRITING IN YEARS."

—*John Barkham Reviews*

"Spectacular and revealing."

—*National Observer*

"COMBAT, AS IT APPEARED TO GIs WHO DODGED BULLETS AND WATCHED THEIR COMRADES DIE, IS BRILLIANTLY PORTRAYED . . . pictures, almost all done on or near the scenes of action, dominate the book . . . an antidote to the hundreds of books about the war which have been written by generals and politicians."

—*New York Daily News*

"Anyone who truly wants to better understand [our] civilization ought to read it."

—*Providence Journal*

"ANYTIME HE WRITES OF WAR YOU CAN SMELL THE GUNSMOKE. A book like this was needed to remind us 35 years later what it was like . . . A REMARKABLE ACHIEVEMENT."

—*James Michener*

"THIS MAY BE JONES' GREAT CONTRIBUTION TO THE HISTORY OF WAR."

—*New Haven Register*

WW II

A Chronicle of Soldiering

James Jones

Graphics direction Art Weithas

BALLANTINE BOOKS • NEW YORK

 Published in the United States by Ballantine Books, a division of Random House, Inc., New York and simultaneously in Canada by Ballantine Books of Canada, Ltd., Toronto, Canada.

An excerpt from this book first appeared in the September 1975 issue of *Playboy* magazine.

Library of Congress Catalog Card Number: 74-27944

ISBN 0-345-25428-7

This edition published by arrangement with
Grosset & Dunlap Publishers

Manufactured in the United States of America

Illustrated format:
First Ballantine Books Edition: October 1976

Mass market format:
First Printing: August 1977

ACKNOWLEDGMENTS

It would have been impossible to do this book without the keen interest and intense dedication of the people below, who work and do battle in the much neglected field of military history in Washington.

My thanks are hereby tendered to all of them.

ARMY

Center of Military History

Brigadier General James L. Collins, Jr., Commander
Colonel R. W. Argo, Jr., Deputy Commander
Colonel Walter L. McMahon, Chief, Historical Services Division
Ms. Marian R. McNaughton, Chief Art Curator, Army Art Activity
Ms. Marylou Gjernes, Art Curator, Army Art Activity
Ms. Hannah Zedlick, Archivist and Historian, General Reference Branch, Army Historical Records Society
Lieutenant Colonel, GS, Hugh G. Waite, Chief, News Branch Public Information Division

Audio-Visual Agency

Major Ralph K. Anderson, Director, Pentagon Audio-Visual Operations
Ms. Viola De Stefano, Chief of the Reference Library

AIR FORCE

Air Force Art Collection

Lieutenant Colonel George R. Hockett, Chief, Art and Museum Branch, Community Relations Division, Office of Information
Ms. Leora Maybelle Stanley, Deputy Chief, Art and Museum Branch
Mr. Robert Arnold, Administrative Services Assistant
Ms. Ethel Forrest, Secretary

Lieutenant Colonel J. Robert King, Chief, Pictorial/ Broadcast Branch, Public Information Division, Office of Information

Air Space Audio-Visual Service

Ms. Margaret Livesay

COAST GUARD

Captain Adrian L. Lonsdale, Chief, Public Affairs Division

Commander J. L. Webb, Assistant Chief, Public Affairs Division

Mr. Brian Norris, Chief of Media Relations Branch, Public Affairs Division

MARINE CORPS

Colonel F. B. Nihart, Deputy Director, Marine Corps Museums

Mr. John T. Dyer, Head Curator, Marine Corps Art and Exhibits Unit

NAVY

Office of Chief of Naval Information

Mr. Charles Lawrence, Curator, Navy Combat Art Collection

Mr. John D. Barnett, Assistant Curator, Navy Combat Art Collection

Ms. Bonnie Kay Uhrich, PH3, USN

U.S. Naval Photographic Center

THE LIBRARY OF CONGRESS

Mr. George S. Hobart, Curator of Documentary Photography

A special thanks to General Fred C. Weyand, Army Chief of Staff, for his persistent interest and help when it counted.

And thanks to Eugene Clarence Braun-Munk whose valuable assistance helped to bring this book about.

James Jones

CONTENTS

WW II

INSIGNIA

(See pages 1-11 of first color section)

ARMIES

SHAEF

Supreme Headquarters, Allied Expeditionary Force

Sixth Army Group

Consisted of U.S. Seventh and French First Armies

Fifteenth Army Group

Made up of U.S. Fifth and British Eighth Armies

First Army

Fought in Normandy, took Paris, first to cross Rhine

Second Army

Trained tactical units

Third Army

Exploited Normandy breakthrough, fought in France, Germany

Fourth Army

Trained tactical units

Fifth Army

Landed at Salerno, took Rome and rest of Italy

Sixth Army

Fought in New Guinea, invaded Philippines, took Manila

Seventh Army

Invaded Sicily, southern France, fought up Rhône, took Munich

Eighth Army

Fought in New Guinea, invaded Philippines, took Mindanao

Ninth Army

Captured Brest, Aachen, northern Ruhr and reached the Elbe

Tenth Army

Saw its first action in the bloody battle of Okinawa

Fifteenth Army

It was the Army of Occupation for the U.S. zone in Germany

WW II

INFANTRY, AIRBORNE AND CAVALRY DIVISIONS

1st
Tunisia, Sicily, Normandy, the Bulge, Germany
2nd "Indian Head"
Normandy, the Ardennes, Leipzig
3rd "Marne"
Sicily, Cassino, Anzio, Colmar pocket, Munich
4th "Ivy"
Cherbourg, Bastogne
5th "Red Diamond"
Metz, Luxembourg, Mainz, Worms bridgehead
6th
Sansapor in New Guinea, northern Luzon
7th "Sight-Seeing"
Attu, Kwajalein, Leyte, Okinawa
8th "Pathfinder"
Brittany, Düren, Cologne plain
9th
El Guettar, Bizerte, Sicily, Cotentin Peninsula, Germany
10th Mountain
Arno River, Po Valley
11th Airborne
Leyte, Manila, Cavite
13th Airborne
France, Italy, the Ardennes
17th Airborne
Parachuted across Rhine
24th "Victory"
New Guinea, Leyte, Corregidor, Verde Island, Mindanao
25th "Tropic Lightning"
Guadalcanal, New Georgia, Philippines
26th "Yankee"
Battle of the Bulge, Siegfried Line

WW II

27th "New York"
Makin Island, Saipan, Okinawa
28th "Keystone"
Paris, Hürtgen Forest, Colmar pocket
29th "Blue and Gray"
D-Day in Normandy, Siegfried Line, Aachen
30th "Old Hickory"
St. Lô, Aachen, Malmédy, Stavelot, Rhine crossing
31st "Dixie"
Davao in southern Mindanao
32nd "Red Arrow"
Buna, Aitape in New Guinea, Leyte
33rd "Prairie"
Baguio in northern Luzon
34th "Red Bull"
Tunisia, Cassino, Leghorn, Bologna
35th "Santa Fe"
Metz, Nancy, Ardennes, Ruhr
36th "Texas"
Salerno, Cassino, France, Germany
37th "Buckeye"
Munda, Bougainville, Lingayen Gulf, Manila
38th "Cyclone"
The recapture of Bataan
39th
Inactivated
40th "Sunshine"
Los Negros, Luzon, Panay Island in Philippines
41st "Sunset"
Salamana, Marshalls, Mindanao, Palawan
42nd "Rainbow"
Schweinfurt, Munich, Dachau
43rd "Red Wing"
New Georgia, New Guinea, Luzon
44th
The Saar, Ulm, Danube River

WW II

45th "Thunderbird"
Sicily, Salerno, Cassino, Anzio, Belfort Gap
63rd "Blood and Fire"
Bavaria, Danube River
65th
Saarlautern, Regensburg, Danube River
66th "Black Panther"
Lorient, St. Nazaire, Army of Occupation
69th
First link up with Russians in Germany
70th "Trailblazers"
Saarbrücken, Moselle River
71st
Hardt Mountains, southern Germany
75th
Battle of the Ardennes Bulge, Westphalia
76th
Luxembourg, Germany
77th "Statue of Liberty"
Guam, Leyte, Okinawa
78th "Lightning"
Aachen, Roer River and the Ruhr
79th "Lorraine"
D-Day, Normandy breakthrough, Vosges Mountains
80th "Blue Ridge"
Normandy, Moselle River, relief of Bastogne
81st "Wildcat"
Angaur, Peleliu and Ulithi
82nd Airborne "All American"
Sicily, Normandy, Nijmegen, Ardennes
83rd "Ohio"
Italy, France, Düsseldorf, Magdeburg
84th "Railsplitters"
Ardennes, Hanover
85th "Custer"
Rome, Po Valley

WW II

86th "Black Hawk"
Dachau, Ingolstadt, southern Germany
87th "Acorn"
Ardennes, Germany, Czech border
88th "Blue Devil"
Liri Valley, Volterra, northern Italy
89th "Middle West"
Bingen, Eisenach, central Germany
90th "Tough 'Ombres"
Normandy, Metz, Czechoslovakia
91st "Wild West"
Arno River, Pisa, Bologna
92nd "Buffalo"
Arno River, Po Valley, Genoa
93rd
Bougainville
94th
Brittany, Siegfried Line, Moselle River, Saar
95th
Metz, Moselle River, Siegfried Line, Saar
96th
Leyte, Okinawa
97th
Central Germany, Neumarkt
98th
Hawaii
99th
Ardennes, Remagen bridgehead
100th
Bitche, Remagen bridgehead, Saar
101st Airborne "Screaming Eagle"
Normandy invasion, Bastogne
102nd "Ozark"
Siegfried Line, Ruhr, München-Gladbach
103rd
Wissembourg, Stuttgart, Austria

104th "Timber Wolf"
Rhine crossing, Cologne, Ruhr
106th
St. Vith, Battle of the Bulge
Americal
Guadalcanal, Bougainville, Cebu Island in Philippines
1st Cavalry "Hell for Leather"
2nd Cavalry
3rd Cavalry
Inactivated
24th Cavalry
Inactivated
61st Cavalry
Inactivated
62nd Cavalry
Inactivated
63rd Cavalry
Inactivated
64th Cavalry
Inactivated
65th Cavalry
Inactivated
66th Cavalry
Inactivated

ARMY AIR FORCES
(See last 13 pages of last color section)

Army Air Forces
Headquarters insignia is basic design for other AAF patches
Mediterranean Allied Air Force
Composed of U.S. and British air comands, fought over southern Europe
U.S. Strategic Air Force
Made up of U.S. 8th, 15th Air Forces, directed heavy bomber raids over Europe
First Air Force
Headquarters at Mitchell Field, N.Y., protected Atlantic Seaboard
Second Air Force
Headquarters at Colorado Springs, protected western U.S.
Third Air Force
Headquarters at Tampa, Florida, protected southeastern U.S.
Fourth Air Force
Headquarters at San Francisco, protected U.S. Far West

Fifth Air Force
Headquarters in the Philippines, patrolled Southwest Pacific
Sixth Air Force
Headquarters in Canal Zone, protected Caribbean area
Seventh Air Force
Headquarters in Marianas, covered Central Pacific
Eighth Air Force
Headquarters in England, carried out heavy bomber raids over Europe
Ninth Air Force
Headquarters in England, carried out tactical raids over Europe
Tenth Air Force
Headquarters in India, covered India-Burma area
Eleventh Air Force
Headquarters in Aleutians, covered Northern Pacific
Twelfth Air Force
Headquarters in Italy, carried out tactical Mediterranean raids
Thirteenth Air Force
Headquarters in Southwest Pacific, covered this area
Fourteenth Air Force
Headquarters in Chungking, covered China
Fifteenth Air Force
Headquarters in Italy, carried out strategic Mediterranean raids
Twentieth Air Force
Headquarters in Washington, D.C., was superbomber force against Japan

ARMORED DIVISIONS

1st
Oran, Bizerte, Cassino, Anzio, Rome, Milan
2nd "Hell on Wheels"
Morocco, Sicily, Normandy, Houffalize, Westphalia

3rd "Spearhead"
St. Lô, Battle of the Bulge, Cologne, Ruhr pocket
4th
Normandy breakthrough, Nancy, Coblenz, the Saar
5th "Victory"
Normandy, Hürtgen Forest, Trier
6th "Super Sixth"
Brest, Normandy breakthrough, Bastogne, the Saar
7th "Lucky Seventh"
Metz, St. Vith, the Ruhr
8th "Thundering Herd"
Cologne, Duisberg, northeast across Germany
9th
Battle of the Bulge, St. Vith, Remagen bridgehead
10th "Tiger"
Bastogne, Trier, Ulm, Bavaria, Tyrol
11th
Bastogne, Siegfried Line, Leipzig, Austria
12th
Colmar, Nuremberg, Danube, Munich
13th
Ruhr pocket, Regensburg Danube and Isar Rivers
14th
Southern France, Siegfried Line, Austria, Czechoslovakia

ARMY SERVICE FORCES

Army Ground Forces
Trained, organized and equipped Ground Force units
Armored Center and Units
Insignia for Armored Forces Headquarters and Headquarters Company
AGF Replacement Depots
Handled troop replacements
Replacement and School Command
Trained Infantry, cavalry and artillery personnel

WW II

Antiaircraft Command
Trained AA personnel
Airborne Command
Trained airborne units
Army Service Forces
Provided services and supplies for all Army units
Ports of Embarkation
Served units embarking for overseas duty
1st Service Command
Administered New England
2nd Service Command
Administered New York, New Jersey
3rd Service Command
Administered Middle Atlantic States
4th Service Command
Administered southeastern U.S.
5th Service Command
Administered Kentucky, Ohio, Indiana, West Virginia
6th Service Command
Administered Michigan, Illinois, Wisconsin
7th Service Command
Administered North Central States
8th Service Command
Administered South Central States
9th Service Command
Administered Far West
Northwest Service Command
Administered Alcan Highway and Alaskan supply route
Military District of Washington
Under ASF for supply and administrative functions
ASF Training Center Units
Trained ASF personnel
Army Specialized Training Program
Trained men in colleges
Army Specialized Training Program Reserve
For 17-year-olds

DEPARTMENTS

Antilles Department
Controlled units in western Caribbean
Alaskan Department
Controlled units on Alaskan mainland
Panama Canal Department
Controlled units in Canal Zone
Hawaiian Department
Controlled units in Hawaii

SPECIAL INSIGNIA

1st Special Service Force
U.S.-Canadian commando unit
U.S. Military Academy
Army personnel attached to West Point
Allied Force Headquarters
Allied staff in North African invasion
Combat Team 442
Japanese-Americans attached to the Fifth Army in Italy
Tank Destroyer Units
Attached to all Ground Force divisions
Persian Gulf Service Command
Moved Lend-Lease supplies to Russia
Rangers
Specially trained battalions which fought in Italy and France
Army Personnel Amphibious
Assigned to Amphibian Units
Army Personnel
Assigned to Veterans Administration

CORPS

1 Corps
Landed on Luzon with Sixth Army
II Corps
Fought in North Africa, joined Fifth Army in Italy

WW II

III Corps
With First Army. Fought in Ruhr
IV Corps
With Fifth Army. Its elements took Rome
V Corps
Helped take Cherbourg. Fought across Europe
VI Corps
Fought in Sicily, Italy, France, Germany
VII Corps
Aided V Corps on Cherbourg peninsula, fought in Germany
VIII Corps
Brest, Belgian Bulge, Leipzig, Elbe bridgehead
IX Corps
Hawaii, Philippines, with Army of Occupation in Japan
X Corps
With Sixth Army on Leyte
XI Corps
With Eighth Army in Philippines
XII Corps
With Third Army at Metz, in Saar
XIII Corps
With the Ninth Army across Germany
XIV Corps
Solomon Islands and Philippines
XV Corps
With Seventh Army in the Vosges Mountains
XVI Corps
With Ninth Army in Ruhr, at Essen
XVIII Airborne Corps
Jumped into Normandy on D-Day, jumped into Germany
XIX Corps
Fought across the Rhine, helped seal off Ruhr pocket
XX Corps
Spearheaded Third Army drive across France

XXI Corps
Fought in Sicily and Anzio, invaded southern France
XXII Corps
Occupation force in Germany
XXIII Corps
Occupation force in Germany
XXIV Corps
With Sixth Army in Philippines, with Tenth Army on Okinawa
XXXVI Corps
With Second Army and Fourth Army

DEFENSE AND BASE COMMANDS

Atlantic Base Commands
Under Eastern Defense Command
Eastern Defense Command
All U.S. except Far West
Antiaircraft Artillery Command, Western Defense Command
Antiaircraft Artillery Command, Eastern Defense Command
Iceland Base Command
Administered Iceland
Greenland Base Command
Administered Greenland
Bermuda Base Command
Administered Greenland
Labrador, Northeast and Central Canada Command
Caribbean Defense Command
Defended Caribbean

THEATERS

European Theater of Operations
U.S. Army Forces South Atlantic
Headquarters Southeast Asia Command
China-Burma-India Theater
U.S. Army Forces Pacific Ocean Area
U.S. Army Forces in Middle East
North African Theater of Operations

The Proposition

Do a picture book of World War II graphic art? I should write a text for it? I could write anything I wanted to write? Say anything I wanted to say?

Art Weithas, the head art director of *Yank*, had come up with the initial idea. There was a lot of good art about World War II, Weithas maintained. It was a shame that it should be sitting in Washington in the various archives where nobody but a few researchers knew about it and saw it. Much of this was work done expressly for the army, the navy, or the Marine Corps collections, by professional artists hired or in some cases actually enlisted to do just that. There was the Abbott Collection, commissioned by Abbott Pharmaceuticals and done on medical subjects alone. There was also the fine *Life* Magazine Collection, an interesting story in itself. In addition, there were the captured German and Japanese collections which the U.S. Army still possessed. Some of this total was excellent art work in its own right. Much, if not "great art," was intensely moving about the period, the men and the events—highly graphic depiction of the epoch. This material ought to be made available to the public, Weithas felt. Put it where it could be seen and enjoyed.

On the other hand, what could I write about World War II, in this historical fashion, that had not already been written? What could anyone write new about it? It had about been done to death, by historians, by commentators, by analysts, by novelists. At the same time, I was deep into the writing of an intensely personal novel about World War II, one that would make a trilogy with *From Here to Eternity* and *The Thin Red Line*. A trilogy conceived twenty-seven years ago, and very dear to my ambition. I had been digging away at the third volume for years, and then laying it aside to do something else.. Only a year before I had laid it aside once again to go out to Vietnam for the *New York Times*. Now it was much further along, and going well. I hated to put it aside again.

But as I looked through examples of the World War II art work (photographic copies of oils, watercolors, sketches, drawings) with which Weithas had surrounded himself in his New York apartment, I began to get excited. A week's trip to Washington to look at the paintings themselves, and at the huge files of photographs of the paintings and drawings available, excited me even more. Weithas was right that this material should be put where people could see and enjoy it.

If enjoy is the right word. And I suppose it is. Such are we humans, such is our nature, that we can look back on moments when we very nearly died and remember them with nostalgia, and pleasure. At the very least, some of the best of this work should be put where people could see it, and think about it. As Weithas said, our problem (if we did the book) was going to be an embarrassment of riches, so much material was available.

The truth is, thirty-five years has glossed it all over and given World War II a polish and a glow that it did not have at the time. The process of history always makes me think of the way the Navahos polish their turquoise. They put the raw chunks in a barrel half filled with birdshot, and then turn the barrel and keep turning it until the rough edges are all taken off and the nuggets come out smooth and shining. Time, I think, does the same thing with history, and especially with wars.

To Us Old Men

History is always written from the viewpoints of the leaders. And increasingly, in our age, war leaders do not get shot at with any serious consistency. Leaders make momentous, world-encompassing, historical decisions. It is your average anonymous soldier, or pilot, or naval gunnery rating who has to carry them out on the ground. Where there is often a vast difference between grandiose logic and plans and what takes place on the terrain. What it is that makes a man go out into dangerous places and get himself shot at with increasing consistency until finally he dies, is an interesting subject for speculation. And an interesting study. One might entitle it, THE EVOLUTION OF A SOLDIER.

The Evolution of a Soldier

Almost all war art is by definition propaganda. No government is going to commission its nation's artists to go out in the field and paint and draw the awful animal indecencies to which war subjects its citizens. Any government will want to make its cause and its action look as palatable as possible. Thus, there is a tendency to depict and perpetuate the good and let the bad get conveniently lost, which became increasingly apparent in the collections we looked at. If one is to believe the complete collections of *Yank* and *Stars and Stripes,* there *were* no bitter American soldiers in the whole of World War II. Even the death shown (and one must show a little death, if one is doing a war) is generally "good" death, meaningful death, clean death. All of this has given rise today to the idea, particularly among the veterans of the Vietnam War, that World War II should be thought of as a good war, a "pure" war. (So strong still is our American's firm and steadfast Puritan need for a "purity" in everything of value.)

And yet every now and then, poring through the collections, one sees a given artist, as though pressed beyond his official commitment by his own emotions, suddenly breaking out momentarily from this more or less unstated conspiracy to tell the folks back home only the "meaningful"; and then the work can rise to the level of greatness in art, which in the end can probably be defined simplistically as telling the whole truth beautifully, to create catharsis.

But there is an even greater power than government at work here. Physiologically we are so constructed that it is impossible for us to remember pain. We can remember the experience of having had pain but we cannot recall the pain itself. Try it sometime. In your next meditation session, reflect on your last dental appointment. In the same way our psychic memory is constantly at work winnowing out the bad and the unpleasant from our remembered experience, to leave and file away only the good parts and the pleasant. A summer day from childhood is remembered for the way the sun fell like greenish gold through the leaves of the maple trees and for the hot still quiet of anticipation in the air, not for the way one's mother cried out harshly across the back yard to get back to work weeding the tomatoes. It would seem the internal Universe as well as the external is built on the principle of letting the dead past bury its dead.

Thus we old men can in all good conscience sit over our beers at the American Legion on Friday nights and recall with affection moments of terror thirty years before. Thus we are able to tell the youngsters that it wasn't all really so bad. Perhaps fortunately for us all, there appears to be a psychic process one might label THE DE-EVOLUTION OF A SOLDIER, as well as the process I called THE EVOLUTION OF A SOLDIER.

And perhaps because of it, perhaps the hardest thing is to try to recreate it as it really was.

In the Beginning

Illustrations 1 and 2

There was never any question about the beginning of World War II for the United States. Pearl Harbor began it crisply and decisively and without discussion.

Absolutely nobody was prepared for it. At Schofield Barracks in the infantry quadrangles, those of us who were up were at breakfast. On Sunday mornings in those days there was a bonus ration of a half-pint of milk, to go with your eggs or pancakes and syrup, also Sunday specials. Most of us were more concerned with getting and holding onto our half-pints of milk than with listening to the explosions that began rumbling up toward us from Wheeler Field two miles away. "They doing some blasting?" some old-timer said through a mouthful of pancakes. It was not till the first low-flying fighter came skidding, whammering low overhead with his MGs going that we ran outside, still clutching our half-pints of milk to keep them from being stolen, aware with a sudden sense of awe that we were seeing and acting in a genuine moment of history.

As we stood outside in the street huddled back against the dayroom wall, another fighter with the red suns on its wings came up the boulevard, preceded by two lines of holes that kept popping up eighty yards in front on the asphalt. As he came abreast of us, he gave us a typically toothy grin and waved, and I shall never forget his face behind the goggles. A white silk scarf streamed out behind his neck and he wore a white ribbon around his helmet just above the goggles, with a red spot in the center of his forehead. I would learn later that this ribbon was a *hachimaki,* the headband worn by medieval samurai when going into battle, usually with some religious slogan of Shinto or Emperor worship inked on it.

One of the first rules Weithas and I made for this book was that we would use no art work that was not done at the time by the original combat artists, and here I am breaking my own rule right at the beginning. But the painting shown here, done by Robert T. McCall in 1971, was so like my Jap pilot over Schofield on December 7 that I simply had to include it.

There weren't many American artists standing around waiting to paint Pearl Harbor, since the Japanese had not informed us of their plans. Lieutenant Commander Coale's panorama shows clearly the destruction the Japanese achieved. On the left the battleship *Nevada* is steaming away with three near-misses geysering around her. Behind the capsized minelayer *Oglala* the *California* has already settled. On the right the *Oklahoma* has capsized hull up, the *Maryland* burning behind her. Far right the *Arizona* (now the monument), afire and under explosive attack, is settling. Lieutenant Commander G. B. Coale did this painting in 1944. Coale was in a large measure responsible for creating the whole navy art program, which is one of the most beautiful of all the collections, if perhaps a bit depersonalized. You have to try and imagine yourself standing on one of those flaming decks with explosions going up all around you and the water ablaze with burning fuel.

Battleship Row was turned into a living inferno and men there, precipitated into full-scale war without previous experience and with no preparation, performed feats of incredible heroism and rescue that seemed unbelievable later. Men dove overboard from red-hot decks to try to swim a hundred yards underwater beneath the oil and gasoline fires that spread over the surface. Some made it, God knows how. One sailor told of seeing a bomb land beside a buddy who was just starting to climb an exterior ship's ladder. When the fumes cleared, he saw the concussion had blown the buddy completely through the ladder and into neatly rectangular chunks the size of the ladder openings. "But I don't think he ever knew what hit him," the sailor said with a shaky smile.

Looking at Coale's painting, it seems to me that he minimized the vast amount of smoke from the fires. Later that Sunday in mid-afternoon, when in the confusion and shock my unit, along with several hundred others, finally pulled out of Schofield for our defensive beach positions, we passed Pearl Harbor. We could see the huge rising smoke columns high in the clear sunny Hawaiian air for miles before we ever got near Pearl. I shall never forget the sight as we passed over the lip of the central plateau and began the long drop down to Pearl City.

Down toward the towering smoke columns as far as the eye could see, the long line of army trucks, each with its splash of "OD"—the olive-drab field uniform shirts—wound serpentlike up and down the draws of red dirt through the green of cane and pineapple. Machine guns (MGs) were mounted on the cab roofs of every truck possible. I remember thinking with a sense of the profoundest awe that none of our lives would ever be the same, that a social, even a cultural watershed had been crossed which we could never go back over, and I wondered how many of us would survive to see the end results. I wondered if I would. I had just turned twenty, the month before.

I expect most of us felt about the same, if many

were less able to verbalize it. It was one of the first, tiniest steps in what I've labeled THE EVOLUTION OF A SOLDIER. Many had taken multiple giant strides along the path that day. And many had gone right on out the other end of the tunnel, without taking any steps at all.

WHISTLING DIXIE

Illustrations 3–6

In later days a theory has been advanced that the Japanese sneak attack was a colossal blunder, that it served only to weld the American people into one, destroy our isolationism, and replace it with a single-minded determination to win the war. This theory holds that the attack was not even much of a success militarily, since American plans in case of war called only for a most cautious advance into the western Pacific. I do not agree. Militarily, five of eight battleships were sunk or ruined; three cruisers were put out of action for over a year; three destroyers were smashed up; four other ships sunk, and innumerable shore installations destroyed. Some 2,400 men were dead, half that many wounded.

I cannot call that a blunder, or militarily valueless. And luckily for us our carriers were out at sea that day. It is true that it welded Americans together into a single strong and determined unit, at least for a while, especially when viewed from the distance of historical perspective. But it welded them in different ways, with different solders. While many poor, middle-class, and even rich young men were crowding army and navy recruiting stations to enlist, many others were calculating, with equally fervid patriotism, how they might make fortunes from the upcoming social and industrial change-over from peace to war. Or wangling jobs or commissions from their senators and representatives which would keep them out of combat and put them where the high living would be taking place. And the high living wasn't long in coming, as the nation geared up and Washington, D.C., became the officer's and serviceman's mecca.

And in addition, the attack had gained for the Japanese an enormous psychological advantage that lasted a full six months. The United States had been dumped and dumped hard. We were shaken by the catastrophe. The United States had been scared. True, it would take six months in any case to convert our massive industrial potential, and to raise and train a wartime army. But did we have the kind of men who could stand up eyeball to eyeball and whip the Jap? A sort of nervous inquietude and malaise of near-despair and insecurity set in.

We were a peace-loving nation, had been anti soldiering and soldiers since the end of World War I. And we were taking on not only the Japs in the Far East, but the Germans in Europe as well. The Japanese, with their warrior code of the bushi, had been in active combat warfare for ten years; the Germans almost as long. Could we evolve a soldier, a *civilian* soldier, who could meet them man to man in the field? Did we have enough crazies and suicidals? Enough weird types of our own, to do that? Not everyone was sure we did.

The historians have seen fit to slide over this period and not dwell on it.

But the good old U.S.A. was whistling Dixie, all right, all right.

And during that six-month period our bastions in the Pacific and those of our allies were falling with the regularity of bowling pins in a bowling alley filled with three hundred–shooters rolling strikes. Malaya. Thailand. The Gilberts. Guam. Northern Luzon. North Borneo. Mindanao. Wake. Hong Kong. Manila. Borneo. The Bismarcks. New Britain. Bougainville. Sumatra. Singapore. Flores. Java. New Guinea. The rest of the Solomons. And finally the whole of the Philippines. Quite a long list. All of them rank defeats. And, with the exception of the Philippines, most Americans didn't even know where most of these places were.

It was not until the Battle of the Coral Sea on May 7–8, 1942, that the United States and her allies in the Pacific achieved a victory over the Japanese, and then it was a questionable one because we lost the carrier *Lexington* in it, in the first sea battle of carrier forces. But the Jap invasion fleet bound for Port Moresby to take over Papua, the Australian half of New Guinea, was forced to turn back. On the day before, however, May 6, Bataan had fallen and the United States's mighty Philippines had become Japanese. And it was not until June 3–6, when a U.S. carrier fleet sank four Jap carriers in the great Battle of Midway (though losing the carrier *Yorktown* and a destroyer in the process), that the United States gained a decisive, course-of-the-war-changing victory in the Pacific.

It was a long six months. Only the Japanese could possibly justify to themselves and to their inviolable Bushido code of honor the unprovoked, undeclared-war attack on Pearl Harbor and Clark Field. But perhaps they didn't need to justify it. Perhaps the events of the next six months were justification enough. There were not many American artists working abroad during this period. But a lot of Japanese artists recorded it.

Meantime, in America, the United States was trying to convert its industrial potential to war and its young civilian men into types who might evolve (when the time arose, and it would soon) into the kind of combat soldier that was needed.

I Didn't Raise My Boy . . .

Illustration 7

Mothers, at least American mothers, are a weird lot. Some sea-change seems to happen in a woman as soon as she becomes a mother. If she gives up enjoying sex with her boyfriend when she finally marries him and becomes a wife, she gives up even dreaming about it when she becomes a mother. All sorts of virtues claim her, and she claims them. Things she would not have blinked an eyelash over when she herself was young and hungry for security become nightmarish horrors when contemplated for her darling offspring. Ideals suddenly become more important to her than any reality. I am not at all sure this is not equally true today, for the vast majority of American mothers. But it was certainly true then. While most nations were spending young fortunes preparing for wars, and indeed often already engaging in them in one area or another, we were teaching our young that war was immoral, and evil, and that, in fact, it was so costly in both treasure and spirit that mankind simply could no longer afford it. All conditions devoutly to be wished, but hardly a realistic description of the 1930s.

Thus, to teach a young American male to love war and to enjoy killing his fellow man—even a Jap or a Nazi—was about comparable to teaching his fresh, dewy-eyed, virginal sister to love the physical aspects of simple fucking and that fellatio could be an enjoyable form of high art. These were the young men who hastened joyously to enlist in the early days after Pearl Harbor, and for some months after. One wonders, looking back on it, if perhaps a great part of their joy was not a result of being able legitimately to get away from homes filled with mothers and/or wives like those described above.

There is always that exciting feeling about the beginning of a war, or even of a campaign. I guess the closest way to depict the feeling is to liken it to a sudden, unexpected school holiday. All restraints are off, everyday life and its dull routines, its responsibilities are scratched and a new set of rules take over. True, some people are going to die, but probably it will not be oneself. And for a while at least, adventure will reign.

In any case, the new enlistees, and new draftees (on December 19, Roosevelt extended the draft law to men aged twenty to forty-four, and set up our first Office of Censorship under somebody named Byron Price), got a pretty rude awakening. With the induction ceremony the honeymoon got over pretty quickly. Men who had been raised to believe, however erroneously, in a certain modicum of individual free-thinking were being taught by loud, fat, devoted sergeants to live as numbers, by the numbers. Clothes that did not fit, when they could see clothes on the shelves that did fit. Personal and dedicated harassments over wrinkles in blankets and blemished polishments of shoes and rifle barrels, when it was perfectly clear that neither wrinkle nor blemish existed. Living in herds and schools like steers or fish, where men (suddenly missing deeply the wives or girlfriends they left so adventuresomely two weeks before) literally could not find the privacy to masturbate even in the latrines. Being laughed at, insulted, upbraided, held up to ridicule, and fed like pigs at a trough with absolutely no recourse or rights to uphold their treasured individuality before any parent, lover, teacher or tribune. Harassed to rise at five in the morning, harassed to be in bed at nine-thirty at night.

Some men thrived on it. Whether they thrived or not, all, all of it, was aimed at and directed toward that EVOLUTION OF A SOLDIER of which these were the first faltering child's steps, although the men did not know they were taking them yet. And which had as its purpose the sole concept of teaching each numbered individual, by the numbers, that he was a nameless piece of expendable matériel of a grateful government and its ideals of freedom just as surely as any artillery shell, mortar round or rifle bullet. And the men who thrived on it got promoted. Those who wept could write letters home. Censored letters, if that need arose, too.

Add to this the gross privilege accorded their sadistic sergeant overseers, which they were constantly having their noses rubbed in, and you had at least the beginnings, hopefully, of a soldier so bitter he would gladly take on both Jap and Nazi simultaneously.

A lot of humor grew out of this. Humor was the civilian soldier's catharsis and saving grace. In 1941, before Pearl Harbor, a man named Marion Hargrove wrote a shallow, humorous book called *See Here, Private Hargrove,* about this peculiar process of induction into the draft, and achieved fame and riches and a cushy job writing for some army paper. His book worked because humor, even shallow humor, was bearable to the folks back home, more acceptable than tragedy while they were worrying about their sons' lives. Later Hargrove went to work for *Yank*. Meanwhile, the sons themselves dreamed in their sleep nightly, and frequently daydreamed consciously, of killing their "sadistic" sergeants in cold blood. Dreamed of murder, as it was hoped they would. Another step in the EVOLUTION OF A SOLDIER.

It was as if a massive conspiracy had been put together, everybody conniving at it in secret accord, home-front civilian and serviceman alike, in a nation which had eschewed war as insanity, to keep the semblance of sanity through a semblance of humor and good will. Humor and good will, if pursued diligently enough, might keep back out of sight all the dark side of humanity which was now being let out, must be let out. Must be stimulated and used.

The men who reported to camp each arrived harboring in his secret core of cores his harrowing, never-shared knowledges and ignorances of himself. His panic terrors and his carefully held-in-check brutalities. Would he do well? Would he die? Would he be able to kill another man? Would he not be able to kill another man? Did he really know himself? These things could not be talked about. All that was taboo in America. And only the paradox of humor could function as a safety valve, pull together the split in the national personality.

The only real difference, the main difference, between World War II and later wars was the greater overall social commitment and, therefore, the greater social stigma attached to refusing to go. Besides, in World War II there was nowhere to run. Just about every nation was involved, one way or another. The whole world was caught up. Had some sanctuary existed, transportation to it would have been impossible under the government control being exercised. Conscientious objectors went to camps. The mere awareness of this was perhaps a further step in that EVOLUTION OF A SOLDIER.

The question remained, always, that if idealistic America had birthed a new breed incapable of killing his fellow humans, who was going to protect him from those nations that had not yet evolved such a type?

The Coral Sea and Midway

Illustrations 8–11

Historically the Battle of the Coral Sea was a type of milestone historians love, in that it was the first naval battle ever to be fought between two carrier fleets. All fighting was carried out by aircraft, without surface craft firing on each other at all. Tactically it was a Japanese victory. The sinking of our carrier *Lexington,* plus the U.S. naval tanker *Neosho* (yes, *Neosho* was an American ship, not Japanese) and the destroyer *Sims* far outweighed the sinking of the Japanese light carrier *Shoho.* Strategically, however, Coral Sea was an American victory. The Japanese invasion sortie to take Port Moresby had to turn back, the first such withdrawal of the war, and for the first time the United States had sunk a major Japanese ship. The navy thought enough of the *Shoho* sinking to commission a painting of it. In addition, the United States had forced two other big carriers, *Shokaku* and *Zuikaku,* to return to port for bomb damage repair and replacement of aircraft, which would keep them out of the Battle of Midway, where their presence might have been decisive.

WW II

I first heard of the Battle of the Coral Sea from a drunken sailor in a bar in Honolulu. If news of it had come out in the papers or over the radio, nobody in my outfit had heard it. We didn't see many newspapers out in the field, but we had radios. Wherever there was electricity available.

I was on my first pass since December 7. After six months of martial law and living in the field far from the fleshpots, guarding Oahu's beaches from invasion, my outfit had begun to receive a few daytime passes as restrictions were gradually loosened. The only difference from the old days was that we had to be back at six o'clock, before sundown and the nighttime curfew and blackout.

The sailor was sitting at the bar of the old Waikiki Tavern, now long gone, which used to sit east of the Moana Hotel on Waikiki. He was with two other salts, all three curiously sun-blackened and with deep hollow eyes. And though it was nine o'clock in the morning of a glorious sunshiny day, all three were already drunk as hoot owls. I knew the moment I walked in and saw the three of them by themselves there that I was looking at somebody different. Different from me.

The old Honolulu—as we were already calling it—had changed in the six months since Pearl, and yet at the same time it hadn't changed at all. Hordes of steel workers and construction workers and ship fitters had been imported to repair and rebuild Pearl Harbor.

Concertina and double-apron wire had been strung along all the beaches, including Waikiki, right after the Jap attack. Barbed wire road blocks were up at all the important junctions, guarded by soldiers. Later, the wire on Waikiki had had gates made in it which, though they were closed at night, allowed people through to swim in the daytime. But not many people took advantage of it. The sight of the wire was too depressing, probably. And there were no more tourists. But the palm trees were still there, and the lovely sunshiny weather, and the sea breeze. The bars and the whorehouses (such whorehouses as hadn't closed and gone home) were still there; they just opened much earlier in the day, because of the night curfew. That was why I was there so early myself. You had to start your serious drinking early, with a six o'clock curfew. But the three sailors looked as if they'd been there since five A.M.

They were not at all reluctant to talk. All three were off the carrier *Yorktown*. They had pulled into Pearl the day before, armor plate blackened and torn, to refit and repair bomb damage received in a sea battle off New Guinea and Australia. The area where the battle took place was called the Coral Sea. As soon as the *Yorktown* was in shape, they would be pulling right back out again, because "something was up." They did not know what. But right now they were putting away all the booze they could put away, and were going to drink themselves into a stupor, and when they couldn't stand up any more would get themselves driven back to the base. "Might not ever get another chance," the chief spokesman, a junior petty officer, said grimly. There was no self-pity in his voice. He had gone beyond that. It was a flat simple statement of fact, and with it he gave me a bleak look of knowledgeable resignation.

As I listened, fascinated, the story of the wild desperate battle slowly emerged. The sinking of an enemy carrier the first day, and the rise of hopeful elation. On the second day the "Lady Lex" taking two torpedoes on her port side while a dive-bombing attack developed overhead. The *Yorktown,* with her tighter turning circle, avoided seven or eight torpedoes, only to take an eight hundred–pound bomb hit that penetrated to her fourth deck. At that, they had almost saved the *Lex,* and except for a series of internal explosions caused by loose fuel, they would have.

"Listen, we better not be telling him all this," one of the sailors said anxiously.

"Aw, shit," the petty officer snarled. "Look at him. You think he's some Jap spy?"

"What about that bartender?" the sailor said.

"Fuck it," the petty officer said. "I've known that bartender for ten years."

I stayed with them through the morning and the first part of the afternoon. When I left them, they were well on their way to fulfilling their promise to themselves, particularly the petty officer, who was no longer able to walk by himself. But the other two, though rolling well themselves, were looking after him, and would take care of him till the taxi got them all back to their ship, and I had an old friend in one of the whorehouses I wanted to see once more. At the moment, women did not seem to be one of my sailors' problems. It was as if, for now, women no longer meant anything to them.

With their sun-blackened faces and hollow haunted eyes, they were men who had already passed on into a realm I had never seen, and didn't particularly want to see. As the petty officer said, factually, it wasn't the going there the one time, but the going back again and again, that finally got to you.

A few days later when the news of the victory at Midway came in, and with it the news of the sinking of the *Yorktown,* I wondered if any of the three of them got off, or if all three of them had gone down with her. I never saw any of them again, to find out. I was very young then, and the whole encounter had been intensely romantic for me. More than anything in the world I wanted to be like them.

I had no idea what the date was that day. Years later, after the war, I learned that it must have been May 28. The *Enterprise* and *Hornet* had come in on May 26, the *Yorktown* on May 27. On May 28 Task Force Sixteen sailed with *Enterprise* and *Hornet* for Midway. The *Yorktown,* incredibly, was repaired and ready to sail on May 29, and did sail with Task Force Seventeen on the thirtieth, to join her sisters. The broken Japanese code, unbeknownst to all of us, had informed our Intelligence of Yamamoto's plan to draw our carriers into a last-ditch fight.

The Battle of Midway has been almost universally acclaimed as the turning point of the Pacific War against the Japanese. In four days from June 3 to 6, the outnumbered torpedo-bomber and dive-bomber squadrons from the three U.S. carriers accounted for four of Japan's fleet carriers, sinking the *Akagi, Kaga, Hiryu* and the *Soryu,* over half of the entire Japanese elite carrier strike force. It was a crippling loss, which would force Japan back from a highly successful offensive strategy onto a defensive strategy for the rest of the war.

Most of this near-ruinous damage was done in a single flaming five-minute attack begun at 10:22 A.M. on June 4, by the dive-bomber squadrons from *Enterprise* and *Yorktown,* after the torpedo squadrons from the three U.S. carriers had tried, and failed, and been shot down. Coming on high overhead, unnoticed by the Japanese, who were occupied with the U.S. torpedo-bombers making their runs, the dive-bombers were able to swoop down like avenging hellions and deliver their loads on the *Akagi, Kaga* and *Soryu,* without losing a single plane. The three Jap carriers, turning into the wind with their flight decks crowded with rearmed and refueling torpedo planes and bombers readying for a second takeoff, were reduced to blazing shambles in seconds, setting off the same dread series of internal fires and explosions that had done in the *Lexington.* So the suicidal attacks of the U.S. torpedo-bomber squadrons were not in vain.

There is no doubt that the three torpedo-bomber attacks were suicidal. The first two, by the *Hornet's* planes and by those of the *Enterprise,* were delivered singly, unaided and totally alone, without expectation of help. Of the fifteen TBDs off the *Hornet* only one pilot survived, by clinging to a rubber cushion from his crashed plane. Of the fourteen from the *Enterprise,* the commander and nine others of his force were shot down. It was sheer luck that the dive-bombers of the *Enterprise* and the dive-bombers and torpedo-bombers of the *Yorktown,* these last already veterans of the

Coral Sea, arrived just minutes later. Of the *Yorktown's* twelve TBDs two survived. The few torpedoes that got launched at all were easily avoided by the Japanese carriers. No Japanese kamikaze pilot later in the war ever went to his death more open-eyed or with more certain foreknowledge than these men.

It is hard to know what was in the depths of these men's minds. It is plain, though, that the suicidal nature of their mission was clear to them. We can only speculate about the rest. Certainly professionalism was a factor. Many were regular navy men, and the rest had the benefit of the semi-professionalism of the U.S. Naval Reserve. A certain sense of sacrifice would help. But they could not be sure their sacrifice would aid anything; and indeed, those who died in the attacks almost certainly did not know whether their deaths had helped their cause. *Esprit de corps?* Surely; they were America's elite: the flyboys, and naval carrier pilots in addition. Then too, personal vanity and pride are always important factors in situations of this kind, and the sheer excitement of battle can often lead a man to death willingly, where without it he might have balked. But in the absolute, ultimate end, when your own final extinction is right there only a few yards farther on staring back at you, there may be a sort of penultimate national, and social, and even racial, masochism—a sort of hotly joyous, almost-sexual enjoyment and acceptance—which keeps you going the last few steps. The ultimate luxury of just *not giving á damn* anymore.

Of course, patriotism has to be taken into account, too. Despite the overmilking of that word to death. And perhaps some of them had wives they didn't care about anymore, and were glad to get rid of. Though probably they were all too gentlemanly to say so openly. But whatever it was, these men went on in and died, and they were relatively healthy young Americans with no tradition of medieval warrior Bushido, and with good fortune their sacrifice was a big factor in the Midway victory. They were probably not the first, and certainly they were not the last, to carry out a deliberately suicidal mission, but they were the first large group whose suicides were blessed with success. Much was made over them in the press and in the national propaganda services. They were given about the fullest coverage the media of the time allowed. At least one movie was written about them. And in its secret heart America heaved a sigh of relief to know that its humping parents could still produce men like them. None of this detracted from what they did. Or from what they gained for themselves, in their own private satisfactions.

Meantime the battle wasn't over. And even in battle, perhaps especially there—as the torpedo-bomber men may have learned conclusively in those last few fiery minutes—the principle of the dead past burying its dead still applied. The *Yorktown* was hit by three bombs in a dive-bomber attack from the fourth Jap carrier *Hiryu,* which had been cruising alone, separately from the others. Then the *Hiryu's* torpedo planes caught her and she took two torpedoes on her port side. Abandoned, she continued to float. Her remaining planes, transferred to the *Enterprise,* joined with the *Enterprise* dive-bombers in attacking *Hiryu,* and at 2:30 A.M. that night *Hiryu,* burning and dead in the water, was abandoned. She was sunk by her own destroyers and sent to join her sisters. The Japanese heavy cruiser *Mikuma,* which had collided with her sister ship *Mogami* and had to be left behind, became another, and easy victim. The *Mogami,* heavily damaged, miraculously survived and managed to reach the base at Truk.

On June 6 the *Yorktown,* still incredibly afloat and now taken in tow with a navy salvage crew put aboard, was hit by torpedoes from a Japanese submarine sent after her by Yamamoto, which was able to penetrate her antisubmarine screen; she finally sank the next day.

Later on that summer of '42, on other passes when my turn came up again, I watched the victorious carrier pilots of Midway drunk and having fist fights on the lawns of the Royal Hawaiian, or in the parking lot of the dinky little filling station across the street from the Moana. The flyers mixed indiscriminately among themselves, Marine Corps, navy, and army, and although they had various little partisan cliques and special groups among themselves, they turned a fairly well united, closed front toward all other types of servicemen. At the same time, the flying officers were the kindest and least snotty or superior to all kinds of enlisted men. Hundreds and hundreds of new flyers of all the services were being shipped to Hawaii, way-stationing there before moving on west into the Far East, and their hard, cruel, laughing bitterness was about equal already to that of the veterans. They were America's elite, all right; but somehow they had passed along on through their own EVOLUTION OF A SOLDIER, and had already written themselves off. None of them expected to come back, and they wanted everything they could get of living on the way out, and that included fist fighting. God knows what all the drunken or half-drunken fights were about (we ground forces were having a few of our own, time to time) and as often as not the two bloody participants would march back into the Royal bar arm in arm while their seconds and fans cheered. Once I saw two Air Corps officers (it hadn't been renamed Air Force yet, then) come out of the Moana and have one hell of a fight over a hooker I knew from the New Senator Hotel, whom one of the flyers had brought to the Moana to dinner.

The authorities always looked the other way, of course, when it was flyers. Each time I came to town the faces had all changed. Except of course for the carrier pilots, if the carriers happened to be in. But then suddenly one day all the carrier faces disappeared at once. *Enterprise* and *Hornet* had pulled out. To where? Australia? Noumea, in New Caledonia? Nobody knew.

WAITING

Illustrations 12 and 13

My outfit had won a battle star for Midway. So had every other outfit serving in Hawaii at the time. Because of some geographical technicality, Hawaii had been included in the theater of operations. So that earned us the little bronze battle star—which, somebody or other told us, was to go on the orange, red-striped Asiatic-Pacific Campaign medal and ribbon; not on the yellow American Defense ribbon, where the battle star for Pearl Harbor was to be worn.

But, as somebody else pointed out, it appeared unlikely any of us would see any of those medals, or even the official campaign ribbons, for quite some little time. Maybe never. No one appeared scheduled to come around and bestow them. The same did not hold true for the commercial army-navy stores on the island, however. Almost before the news of Midway could be digested, the army-navy stores began displaying for sale, along with the American Defense ribbon and star, commercial copies of the Asiatic-Pacific ribbon with a star on it. None of us had even seen it. How they got them over from California, with all the severely restricted priority wartime shipping, no one knew. Somebody suggested maybe they made them on the island.

Around us Honolulu continued to grow and expand into a boom town. Troops, ships, workers, clerks, boatloads of supplies and matériel. Then it was announced the marines had invaded Guadalcanal in the Solomon Islands, and we knew where the carriers had gone.

On through the summer we had continued to maintain our anti-invasion guard on the beaches, with our puny .30-caliber watercooled MGs. (Nobody had had to tell us how ineffectual they would be against a serious invasion.) And as the hypothetical invasion threat shrank and then disappeared entirely with the victory at Midway, our guarding and guard inspections shrank in efficiency in direct ratio to the slackening of tension. We began to agitate for more passes. Some of the guys, who were lucky enough to be on beach positions which had suburban homes nearby, had found themselves wahine girlfriends in the neighborhood. We were settling in. But that heavy cloud of waiting and wondering where we were going hung over us. Some of us who were not so lucky were on beach positions out of town farther east, in a string all the way to Makapuu Head where the southern exposure of Honolulu turns the corner to become the famous Windward Side, over which the easterly wind from the Mainland never ceases to blow, day or night.

But even we had our little windfalls. One day, when some of us were sitting on the wall of the scenic overlook in that wind, speculating on just when there would be tourists again, especially women tourists, to drive out in their rented cars to our scenic overlook, a half-Hawaiian gentleman with a good eye for business drove up in a pick-up truck with four wahines in the back. While our lieutenant and his staff sergeant looked the other way, the four girls, utilizing one of our five pillboxes and a sheltered ledge open to the wind directly behind it, managed to take care of the whole thirty-seven of us on the position in just over forty-five minutes. The lieutenant timed it, while ordering five men who had already been to go and relieve the five men on post in the pillboxes so they could go. The fee was ten bucks a man, and everybody was happy with the price.

But windfalls like that were rare. Word somehow got back to the company headquarters, and the man didn't come again. We went back to our more constant though less favorite pastime. Speculating on what was going to happen to us. Some rumors going around said we were going to Australia. That would mean combat against the Japanese, somewhere down there. Very few were really looking forward to that. Other, more hopeful rumors were that we were going to stay right there in Hawaii for the duration, as a former part of the old Hawaiian Division, and continue to take care of, guard and protect our dear friends the Islanders. Nobody quite believed that one.

And yet, strangely, if we had really found out we were actually going to stay on in Hawaii for the duration, we would not have been happy about it. We wanted to get into the act. On the other hand, if we had really found we were going to go south to combat, we would not have liked it at all. Thus, waiting, we teetered and swayed, pulled one way, then pulled another.

Then quite suddenly in mid-September we got orders to move back to Schofield Barracks for a period of reorganization and intensive training. Our beach positions would be taken over by a new, "green" division recently arrived from the States. We wondered what they thought we were, a "weathered" division, after our brief excitement of Pearl Harbor?

While we were at Schofield, whenever we had a free minute, which was seldom, we did what we had done all the past six months. We wondered, and we waited. Our training was neither intensive nor complete. It was woefully inadequate, and we knew it. But then these were the early days of the war. And perhaps it was impossible really to train a man for combat, without putting him actually in it. We jumped off some antique barges, already obsolete, and waded through shallow water and sand. We crawled on our bellies through mud under machine gun fire which was coming from MGs fixed between posts. We practiced throwing hand grenades, and practiced firing our rifles and various weapons. All this we had already done, except the barge part, innumerable times. For a week we had an hour of jiu-jitsu a day, and tried throwing each other on the ground. The rumor was still Australia.

Then, equally suddenly, the rest of our training schedule was cancelled, and we were loaded onto transports inside Pearl Harbor. The transports sailed out into the wastes of the trackless Pacific. We sat on the transports, and did what we had done at Schofield, in our few spare moments, the same as we had done all during the six months before. The rumor was still Australia.

While Waiting . . .
A Look at Europe

Up to this point in time there had been damned little American war art done. Nobody had much thought about it. If they had, there wouldn't have been the time, and probably not the inclination, to do it. Everyone was too busy just getting this war started.

The Europeans, on the other hand, had been at it three full years by now. They had had time to get collections started. The Europeans, in actual fact, had been at it a lot longer than that. The Europeans had been at it something like two thousand years. The history of their internecine warring went back at least as far as the Romans. The idea that war—modern war—might be an insanity, a racial evolutionary hangover, could only seem ridiculous to them. Survival meant fighting, spitting, clawing what you needed away from those who needed it as badly as you. War was a legitimate means of adding to your territory and of settling political disputes, had been all through their bloody history, had been in 1812, in 1870, in 1914, and was in 1940. In a way they were hardly to be blamed. It had been their tradition and their heritage for a hundred generations. And as nations they all enthusiastically subscribed to Clausewitz' theorem.

In this current episode of European games-playing, by September, 1942, they had been through the phony war, the blitzkrieg and Dunkirk, the fall of France, the air battle of Britain, the abortive Italian attack on Greece, the fall of Greece and Yugoslavia to the Germans, the fall of Crete, the first, the second, the third and fourth North African campaigns, Hitler's first Russian campaign. War by now was practically a way of life to Europeans. And they were still at it, still going strong. At an unthinkable cost in blood and lives and treasure.

Denmark had fallen to Germany. Norway had fallen to Germany. The Low Countries had fallen almost unnoticed in the greater debacle: the incredible, unbelievable fall of France. With the other bits and pieces she had picked up along the way, as when Hungary and Rumania decided (near forcibly) to join the Axis, Germany now held almost the whole of the European continent. Only Britain across the Channel still held out against her, helped by her overseas empire and by the United States, now after Pearl Harbor no longer "neutral." Together they were fighting the battle of the Atlantic to keep the shipping lanes open, and if they had not won a thorough victory, they had at least achieved an open stalemate. In the East, Communist Russia fought her own war against Germany, mainly to save herself after being attacked. And by September, 1942, was fighting it well, while complaining loudly that Britain and America should open a second front for her.

Luckily for the Allies, Germany had Italy as an Axis partner. Unfortunately for Germany, she had as an enemy the British, a people equally as arrogant, supercilious, stiff-necked and warlike as her own. England, this time, appeared to be on the side of right. This seemed to be proven by Hitler's insane ambitions (such as taking on Russia to conquer), his murderous treatment of the already conquered peoples, his mad policy to exterminate Europe's Jews, and by the simple fact that he had won too much and gotten too big. Anyway, wrong or right—whatever—on they went, whaling hell out of each other. When they finished, Europe would be ruined, a collection of empireless, petty little states in the world eye.

There had to be something somewhere in all of them, in all of us, that loved it. Some dark, aggressive, masochistic side of us, racial perhaps, that makes us want to spray our blood in the air, throw our blood away, for some damned misbegotten ideal or other. Whether the ideal is morally right or wrong makes no difference so long as the desire to fight for it remains in us. Fanatics willing to die for ideals. It was territory, back when we were animals. Now that we have evolved into higher beings and learned to talk, territoriality has moved up a step higher with us, and become ideals. We like it. Cynical as it sounds, one is about led to believe that only the defeated and the dead *really* hate war. And of course, as we all know, they do not count.

And back then at least, in September, 1942, the Germans were still ahead.

German War Art

Illustrations 14–19

There is an interesting story, perhaps apocryphal, that Hitler personally ordered the beginning of the German war art program. Remember, Hitler was a painter himself. The story goes that the Führer was making some field inspection early on in the war and, walking along with some aides, saw a German soldier sitting out painting a landscape of the battlefield. "That man is good," he is reputed to have said. After reflection, he is supposed to have given orders to begin an official war art program which he personally sponsored.

The great bulk of this material was captured by the United States and brought back to Washington and housed with the Army Historical Division. After cataloging, which must have taken years, there were thirty-seven large volumes of it in eight-by-ten photos, often two to the plastic leaf. We went through all of them, and from the general lack of excellence among them, I can only suppose that the nephews of many Germans with political pull got themselves appointed as official artists in order to save their lives.

This is not just a joke. Since the Germans are not all that different from the rest of humanity, and corruption and nepotism reached a notoriously high level in the Nazi government, I think one is free to suppose that once the German art program became official, especially one sponsored by the Führer, people began to get on the bandwagon. One would assume anybody who got appointed official artist to some military outfit at least had to know how to draw a little. But one would suppose too that many close friends of colonels or sergeants major of the German army, if they knew how to draw a little, would get appointed official artists. Why go up with a line company when you didn't have to?

But even when the painters are not clearly somebody's nephew or pal, there is a curiously wooden, unfeeling quality about the paintings and drawings. In general they seemed to sort themselves out into two distinct categories. One was landscapes. The other was portraits of individual soldiers, usually in charcoal, pencil or ink, but occasionally in oils. The landscapes are particularly wooden and unfeeling. The great majority of them are somewhat impressionistic renderings of terrain and, from the names of them, were localities where some battle or smaller fight known only to a particular regiment or division had taken place. But they almost never contain any warlike qualities. There were no corpses lying around, no burnt-out tanks, no shattered trees, no bombed-out villages. In by far the most of them there were no people at all, only the terrain features. They weren't cheerful paintings, but neither were they gloomy. In each case it was almost as if the artist had set out to paint, impressionistically but factually, a field of battle which some German soldier who had served there might look at later and recognize affectionately. Not at all the usual stinking, rusting, rotting mess most battlefields are afterwards, as if no one wanted to be reminded of all that. Occasionally there might be a figure or two which might be soldiers walking. And once in a while one might turn up a watercolor or an oil that showed tanks moving up into battle in North Africa or in Greece or Russia. But they were rare, and if one did not know these were war paintings of battlefields, one would never have guessed it from the subject matter.

There were so many of them, by so many different painters, that it must have been an accepted style. But what could have been the reason? Had the directive come down directly from the Führer himself, or from some high-ranking aide? Did they not want the people back home to see the desolation and horror of war? Did they not want the soldier to see, later, and brood on it? Did they not want posterity to see? Was it guilt? Was it that these things simply didn't interest them, and that they just wanted to show the terrain features which, if studied accurately by one who had fought there, would show how the battle had been won?

Of course, as everyone knows, the Germans are a neat people. Almost compulsively so. And maybe the official artist (wisely) did not arrive on the scene until the Graves Registration men and the Quartermaster salvage crews had been over the area and cleaned it up?

Or was it simple German affection and sentimentality, that same national schizophrenia that could allow an extermination camp commander to grow flowers or weep over his sick cat, after ordering a thousand exterminations?

The soldier portraits had the same wooden, unfeeling quality about them. Almost never did the artist comment in his drawing. Once in a great while one would. But even in that rare one, the comment seemed enigmatic. Portraits in charcoal or pencil of Sgt. Hans So-and-So, Lt. Helmut Somebody, Pvt. Karl This-or-That. Page after page, string after string of them, interspersed among the landscapes. Their rumpled field uniforms were always meticulously drawn, some had Afrika Korps caps on, a few wore coal-scuttle helmets, some wore what we call overseas caps. Almost always they had the great bladelike noses we've come to associate with Germans, but not handsome noses. They were knotted, hooked, noses clearly once broken. A few had blue eyes. Most stared out at you with large, dark, limpid eyes that were totally noncommittal about everything. They were obviously tough professional soldiers. But they might have been farmers. You wondered what could make them go off carrying the red and black Nazi banners across the face of the earth of Europe. They weren't telling. Few looked young. The average looked about thirty. Almost all looked tired. But here again the painter made no comment on the tiredness. He just drew what he saw, as if some colonel had shouted an order at him, "Here. Draw that one. He looks a likely prospect," so he drew him.

These were the men the United States in September, 1942, would shortly be coming up against, somewhere across the Atlantic. In North Africa, as it turned out. They did not look as though they had gone through any EVOLUTION OF A SOLDIER. But surely they must have. Whether the artist saw it or not.

Japanese war art and American war art by comparison were much livelier, much more active, and gave a much better impression of what it was like to be there. The Japanese work, as might be expected, was more openly propagandistic, and more bloody. In every combat painting there was always some Japanese thrusting a sword or bayonet through the chest or guts of some Britisher or American. The British war art was very British.

In any case, what with the enormous wealth of material to choose from, any book I would do or want to do must concentrate on American.

GUADALCANAL

Illustrations 20–24

Long afterward, we found that our training schedule had been cut short because a big troop transport headed for Guadalcanal had run afoul of the Japs and been sunk, and men were urgently needed on Guadalcanal. But our original destination really had been Australia.

O, shades of splendid endeavor. Of youth's wild strenuous exertion and adventure. O, lost tropic beauty of sea and cocopalm and sand.

It is scarcely believable that I can remember it with pleasure, and affection, and a sense of beauty. But such are the vagaries of the human head. One can hardly credit that a place so full of personal misery and terror, which was perfectly capable of taking your life and on a couple of occasions very nearly did, could be remembered with such kindly feelings, but I do. The pervasive mud, and jungle gloom and tropical sun, when they are not all around you smothering you, can have a haunting beauty at a far remove. When you are not straining and gasping to save your life, the act of doing so can seem adventurous and exciting from a distance. The greater the distance, the greater the adventure.

But, God help me, it was beautiful. I remember exactly the way it looked the day we came up on deck to go ashore: the delicious sparkling tropic sea, the long beautiful beach, the minute palms of the copra plantation waving in the sea breeze, the dark green band of jungle, and the dun mass and power of the mountains rising behind it to rocky peaks. Our bivouac was not far from the ruined plantation house and quarters, and you could look at its ruin—not without awe—and imagine what it must have been like to live here before the armies came with their vehicles and numberless feet and mountains of supplies. Armies create their own mud, in actual fact. The jungle stillnesses and slimes in the gloom inside the rain forest could make you catch your breath with awe. From the mountain slopes in mid-afternoon with the sun at your back you could look back down to the beach and off across the straits to Florida Island and one of the most beautiful views of tropic scenery on the planet. None of it looked like the pestilential hellhole that it was.

The day we arrived there was an air raid, trying to hit our two transports. Those of us already ashore could stand in perfect safety in the edge of the trees and watch as if watching a football game or a movie. Around us marines and army oldtimers would cheer whenever a Jap plane went smoke-trailing down the sky, or groan when one got through and water spouts geysered up around the transports. Soon we were doing it with them. Neither transport took a hit, but one took a near-miss so close alongside it sprang some plates, and had to leave without finishing unloading. Almost immediately after, a loaded barge coming in took a hit and seemed simply to disappear. A little rescue boat set out from shore at once, to pick up the few bobbing survivors. It seemed strange and curiously callous, then, to be watching and cheering this game in which men were dying.

Later, after our first time up on the line, we would sit in our bivouac on the hills above Henderson Field and watch the pyrotechnic display of a naval night battle off Savo Island with the same insouciance, and not feel callous at all. They took their chances and we took our chances.

Guadalcanal was the first American offensive anywhere, and as such got perhaps more than its fair share of notoriety, both in history and in the media of the time; more than later, perhaps tougher fights such as Tarawa and Peleliu. Fought at an earlier period of the war, when the numbers and matériel enegaged were smaller, less trained and less organized, there was an air of adventure and sense of individual exploit about it (at least in the press) where small units of platoon and company strength still maintained importance, more than in the later battles of massed armadas, masses of newer equipment, and massed units of men in division and corps strength. It was still pretty primitive, Guadalcanal.

Everybody now knows, at least everybody of my generation, how the marines landed virtually unopposed on the 'Canal itself, after heavy fights on two smaller islands, Tulagi and Gavutu; how the Japanese, for reasons of their own deciding not to accept their first defeat, kept pouring men and equipment into the island; how Major General Vandegrift's tough First Marine Division, learning as they went along, fought them to a standstill, while the navy sank their loaded transports of reinforcements behind them—until in the end they were finally forced to evacuate it anyway. Not many, even of my generation, know that from about mid-November, 1942, on, U.S. infantry was doing much of the fighting on Guadalcanal, and from mid-December were doing it all. The doughty First Marine Division, dead beat, ill and tired, decimated by wounds and tropical diseases, but evolved into soldiers at last, had been relieved and evacuated.

The first elements of the Americal Division had landed in mid-October. The first elements of my outfit landed in late November, the rest in early December. No living soul looking at us, seeing us come hustling ashore to stare in awe at the hollow-eyed, vacant-faced, mean-looking First Marines, could have believed that in three months from that day we would be known as the famed Twenty-fifth Infantry Tropic Lightning Division, bearing the shoulder patch of the old Hawaiian Division Poi Leaf, with a streak of lightning running vertically through it. In the interim we had taken over from the First Marines, prosecuted the final offensive on the 'Canal, chased the Japanese to Tassafaronga in the whirlwind windup which gave us our name, and begun to move up to New Georgia for the next fight of our campaign. By then we would have had a fair amount of casualties and sick, and as a division and as individuals have made our own EVOLUTION OF A SOLDIER.

My own part in all of this was relatively undistinguished. I fought as an infantry corporal in a rifle company in a regiment of the Twenty-fifth, part of the time as an assistant squad leader, part of the time attached to the company headquarters. I went where I was told to go, and did what I was told to do, but no more. I was scared shitless just about all of the time. On the third day of a fight for a complex of hills called "The Galloping Horse" I was wounded in the head through no volition of my own, by a random mortar shell, spent a week in the hospital, and came back to my unit after the fight and joined them for the relatively little that was left of the campaign. I came out of it with a Purple Heart and a Bronze Star for "heroic or meritorious achievement" (not the V-for-Valor one), which was given to me apparently by a process as random as that of the random mortar shell that hit me. At least, I don't know anything I ever did to earn it. I was shipped out after the campaign for an injured ankle that had to be operated on.

It's funny, the things that get to you. One day a man near me was hit in the throat, as he stood up, by a bullet from a burst of MG fire. He cried out, "Oh, my God!" in an awful, grimly comic, burbling kind of voice that made me think of the signature of the old Shep Fields' Rippling Rhythm band. There was awareness in it, and a tone of having expected it, then he fell down, to all intents and purposes dead. I say "to all intents and purposes" because his vital functions may have continued for a while. But he appeared unconscious, and of course there was nothing to do for him with his throat artery torn out. Thinking about him, it seemed to me that his yell had been for all of us lying there, and I felt like crying.

Another time I heard a man yell out "I'm killed!" as he was hit. As it turned out, he was, although he didn't die for about fifteen minutes. But he might have yelled the same thing and not been killed.

One of the most poignant stories about our outfit was one I didn't see myself, but only heard about later. I was in the hospital when it happened. One of our platoon sergeants, during a relatively light Japanese attack on his position, reached into his hip pocket for a grenade he'd stuck there, and got it by the pin. The pin came out but the grenade didn't. No one really knows what he thought about during those split seconds. What he did was turn away and put his back against a bank to smother the grenade away from the rest of his men. He lived maybe five or ten minutes afterward, and the only thing he said, in a kind of awed, scared, very disgusted voice, was, "What a fucking recruit trick to pull."

A lot of the posthumous Medals of Honor that are given are given because men smothered grenades or shells with their bodies to protect the men around them. Nobody ever recommended our platoon sergeant for a Medal of Honor that I know of. Perhaps it was because he activated the grenade himself.

I think I screamed, myself, when I was hit. I thought

I could vaguely remember somebody yelling. I blacked out for several seconds, and had a dim impression of someone stumbling to his feet with his hands to his face. It wasn't me. Then I came to myself several yards down the slope, bleeding like a stuck pig and blood running all over my face. It must have been a dramatic scene. As soon as I found I wasn't dead or dying, I was pleased to get out of there as fast as I could. According to the rules, my responsibility to stay ceased as soon as I was hurt. It really wasn't so bad, and hadn't hurt at all. The thing I was most proud of was that I remembered to toss my full canteen of water to one of the men from the company headquarters lying there.

ARMIES

SHAEF

SIXTH ARMY GROUP

TWELFTH ARMY GROUP

FIFTEENTH ARMY GROUP

FIRST ARMY

SECOND ARMY

THIRD ARMY

FOURTH ARMY

FIFTH ARMY

SIXTH ARMY

SEVENTH ARMY

EIGHTH ARMY

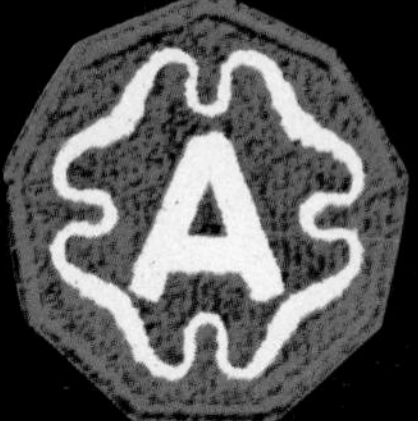

NINTH ARMY

TENTH ARMY

FIFTEENTH ARMY

INFANTRY, AIRBORNE AND CAVALRY DIVISIONS

1st

2nd "INDIAN HEAD"

3rd "MARNE"

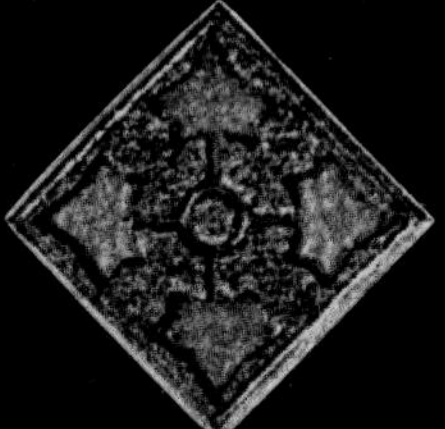

4th "IVY"

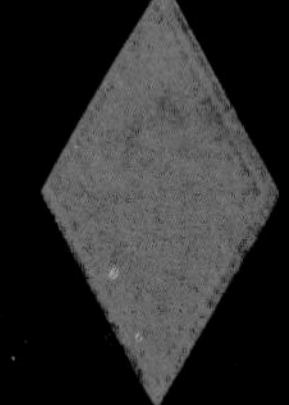

5th "RED DIAMOND"

6th

7th "SIGHT-SEEING"

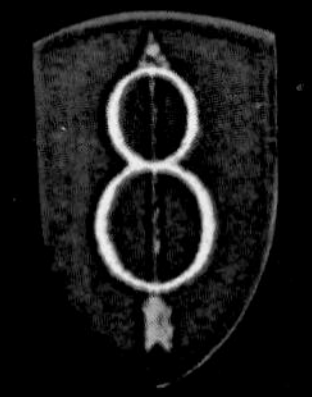

8th "PATHFINDER"

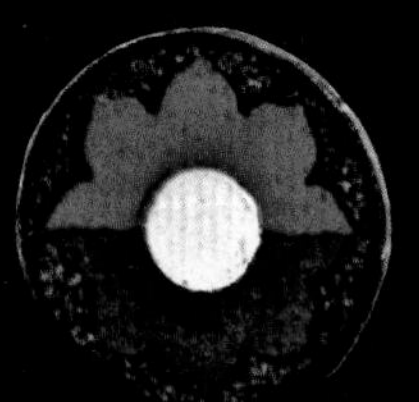

9th

10th MOUNTAIN

11th AIRBORNE

13th AIRBORNE

17th AIRBORNE

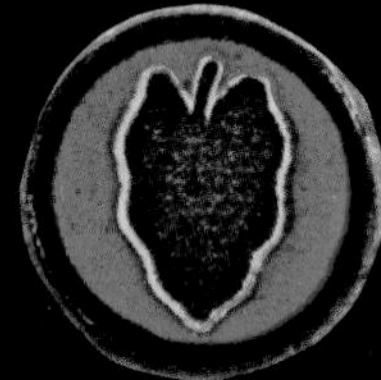

24th "VICTORY"

25th "TROPIC LIGHTNING"

26th "YANKEE"

27th "NEW YORK"

28th "KEYSTONE"

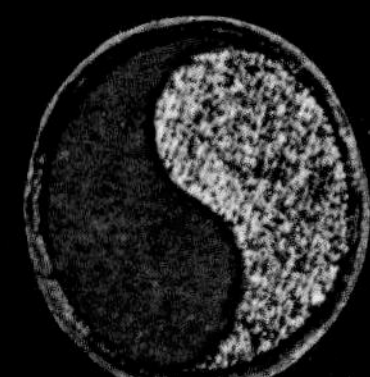

29th "BLUE AND GRAY"

30th "OLD HICKORY"

31st "DIXIE"

32nd "RED ARROW"

33rd "PRAIRIE"

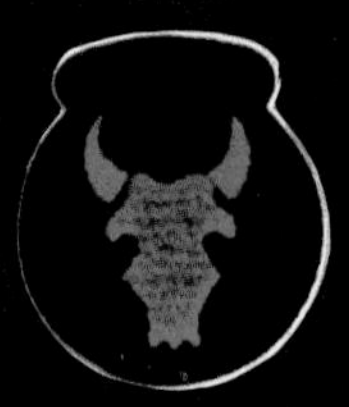

34th "RED BULL"

35th "SANTE FE"

36th "TEXAS"

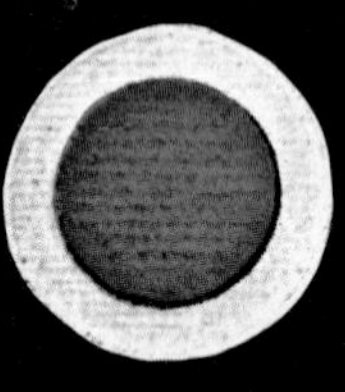

37th "BUCKEYE"

38th "CYCLONE"

39th

40th "SUNSHINE"

41st "SUNSET"

42nd "RAINBOW"

43rd "RED WING"

44th

45th "THUNDERBIRD"

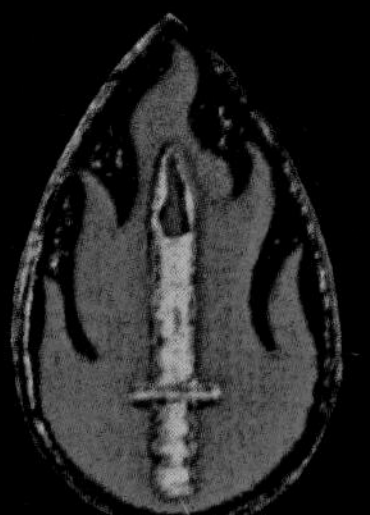

63rd "BLOOD AND FIRE"

65th

66th "BLACK PANTHER"

69th

70th "TRAILBLAZERS"

71st

75th

76th

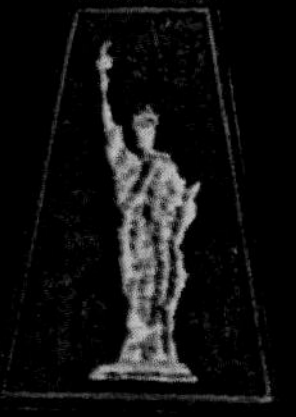

77th "STATUE OF LIBERTY"

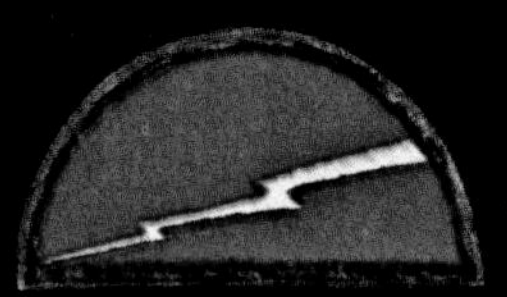

78th "LIGHTNING"

79th "LORRAINE"

80th "BLUE RIDGE"

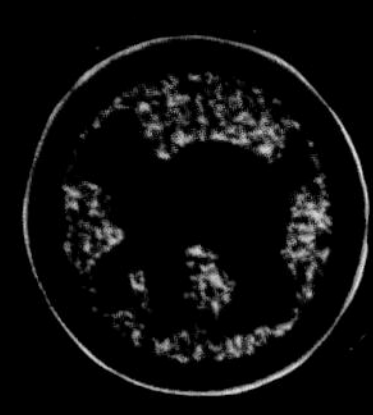

81st "WILDCAT"

82nd AIRBORNE
"ALL AMERICAN"

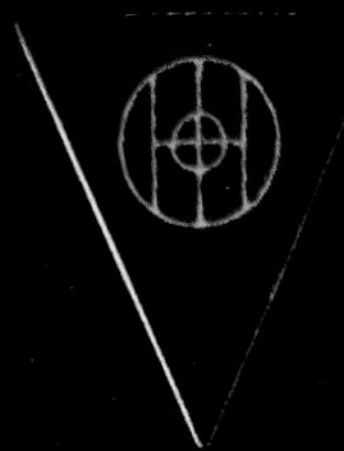

83rd "OHIO"

84th "RAILSPLITTERS"

85th "CUSTER"

86th "BLACK HAWK"

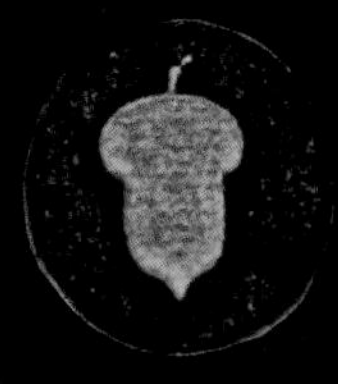

87th "ACORN"

88th "BLUE DEVIL"

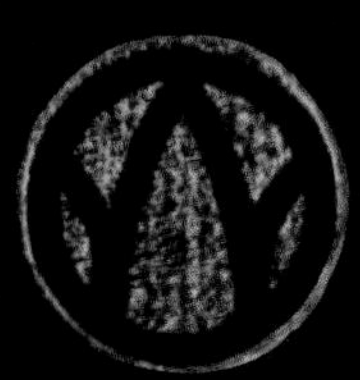
89th "MIDDLE WEST"

90th "TOUGH 'OMBRES"

91st "WILD WEST"

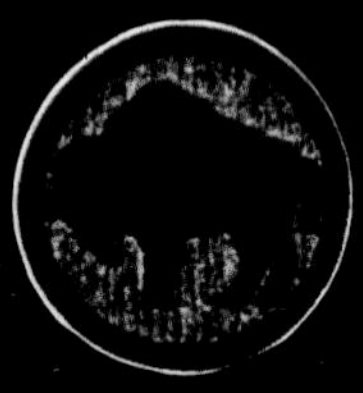
92nd "BUFFALO"

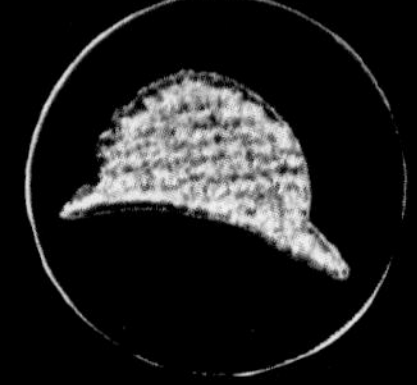
93rd

94th

95th

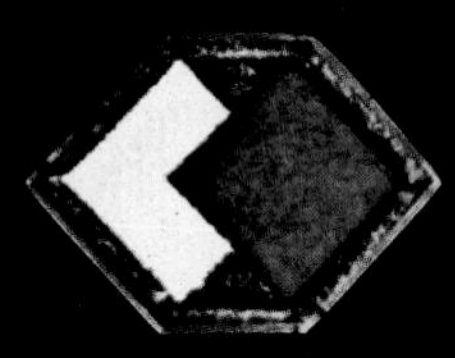
96th

97th

98th

99th

100th

101st AIRBORNE
"SCREAMING EAGLE"

102nd "OZARK"

103rd

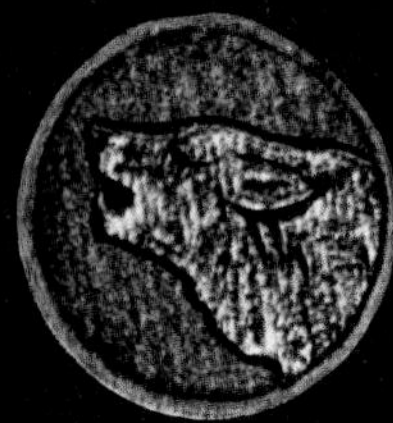
104th "TIMBER WOLF"

106th

AMERICAL

1st CAVALRY
"HELL FOR LEATHER"

2nd CAVALRY

3rd CAVALRY

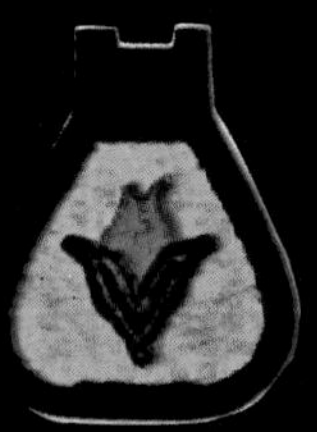

24th CAVALRY

61st CAVALRY

62nd CAVALRY

63rd CAVALRY

64th CAVALRY

65th CAVALRY

66th CAVALRY

"All the News That's Fit to Print."

The New Y

VOL. XCI No. 30,634. Entered as Second-Class Matter, Postoffice, New York, N. Y. NEW YORK, MON

JAPAN WARS ON
MAKES SUDDEN A
HEAVY FIGHTING

CONGRESS DECIDED

Roosevelt Will Address It Today and Find It Ready to Vote War

CONFERENCE IS HELD

Legislative Leaders and Cabinet in Sober White House Talk

By C. P. TRUSSELL

Special to THE NEW YORK TIMES.

WASHINGTON, Dec. 7—President Roosevelt will address a joint session of Congress tomorrow and will find the membership in a mood to vote any steps he asks in connection with the developments in the Pacific.

The President will appear personally at 12:30 P. M. Whether he would call for a flat declaration of war again Japan was left unannounced tonight. But leaders of Congress, shocked and angered by the Japanese attacks, were talking ... r on not only

TOKYO ACTS FIRST

Declaration Follows Air and Sea Attacks on U. S. and Britain

TOGO CALLS ENVOYS

After Fighting Is On, Grew Gets Japan's Reply to Hull Note of Nov. 26

By The Associated Press.

TOKYO, Monday, Dec. 8—Japan went to war against the United States and Britain today with air and sea attacks against Hawaii, followed by a formal declaration of hostilities.

Japanese Imperial headquarters announced at 6 A. M. [4 P. M. Sunday, Eastern standard time] that a state of war existed among these nations in the Western Pacific, as of dawn.

Soon afterward, Domei, the Japanese official news agency, announced that "naval operations are progressing ...

PACIFIC OCEAN: THEATRE OF WAR

Shortly after the outbreak of hostilities an America... sent a distress call from (1) and a United States Army tr... carrying lumber was torpedoed at (2). The most importan... was at Hawaii (3), where Japanese planes bombed th... ...l Harbor base. Also attacked was Guam (4). From...

rk Times.

LATE CITY EDITION
Increasing cloudiness with rising temperature today. Tomorrow cloudy, somewhat colder.
Temperatures Yesterday—Max., 34; Min., 25

Times Company.

CEMBER 8, 1941. THREE CENTS NEW YORK CITY and Vicinity

S. AND BRITAIN; TACK ON HAWAII; AT SEA REPORTED

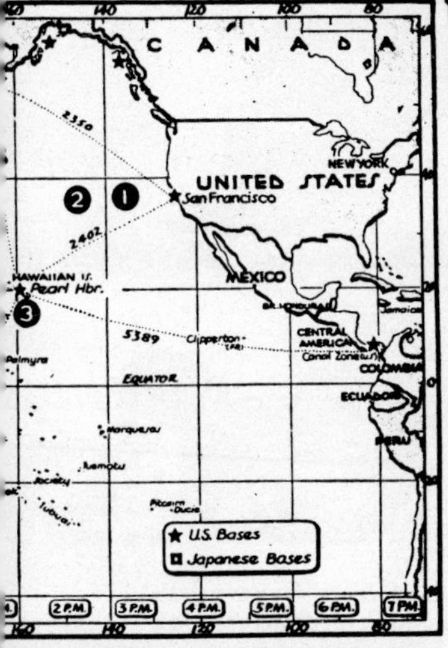

ING UNITED STATES AND ITS ALLIES

Philippines were raided, as was Hong Kong, to the northwest. Shanghai (5) a British gunboat was sunk and an American boat seized. To the south, in the Malaya area (7), the British bed Japanese ships, Tokyo forces attempted landings on Brit- itory and ... pore underwent an air raid. Distances

GUAM BOMBED; ARMY SHIP IS SUNK

U. S. Fliers Head North From Manila—Battleship Oklahoma Set Afire by Torpedo Planes at Honolulu

104 SOLDIERS KILLED AT FIELD IN HAWAII

President Fears 'Very Heavy Losses' on Oahu—Churchill Notifies Japan That a State of War Exists

By FRANK L. KLUCKHOHN

Special to THE NEW YORK TIMES.

WASHINGTON, Monday, Dec. 8—Sudden and unexpected attacks on Pearl Harbor, Honolulu, and other United States possessions in the Pacific early yesterday by the Japanese air force and navy plunged the United States and Japan into active war.

The initial attack in Hawaii, apparently launched by torpedo-carrying bombers and submarines, caused widespread damage and death. It was quickly followed by others. There were unconfirmed reports that German raiders participated in the attacks.

Guam also was assaulted from the air, as were Davao, on the island of Mindanao, and Camp John Hay, in Northern Luzon, both in the Philippines. Lieut. Gen. Douglas MacArthur ...

1.
"A Day That Will Live in Infamy" *is captured by navy artist Griffith B. Coale, who painted the attack on Pearl Harbor.*

2.

3.
Fall of American Guam *from the brush of ancient-style Japanese artist.*

4.
Clark Field and Manila *are bombed—a more modern Japanese painting.*

5.
The capture of Bataan *brought on the famous Death March of Americans.*

6.
General Wainwright *surrenders Corregidor before Japanese movie cameras.*

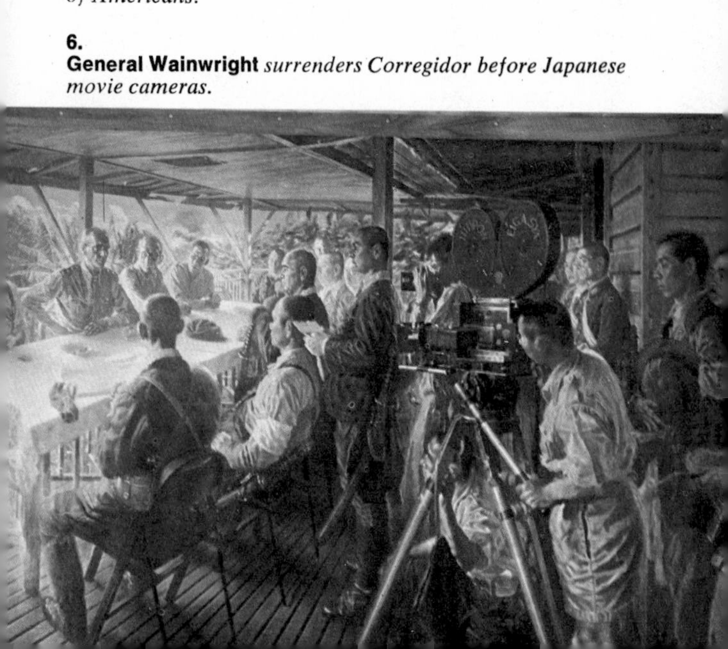

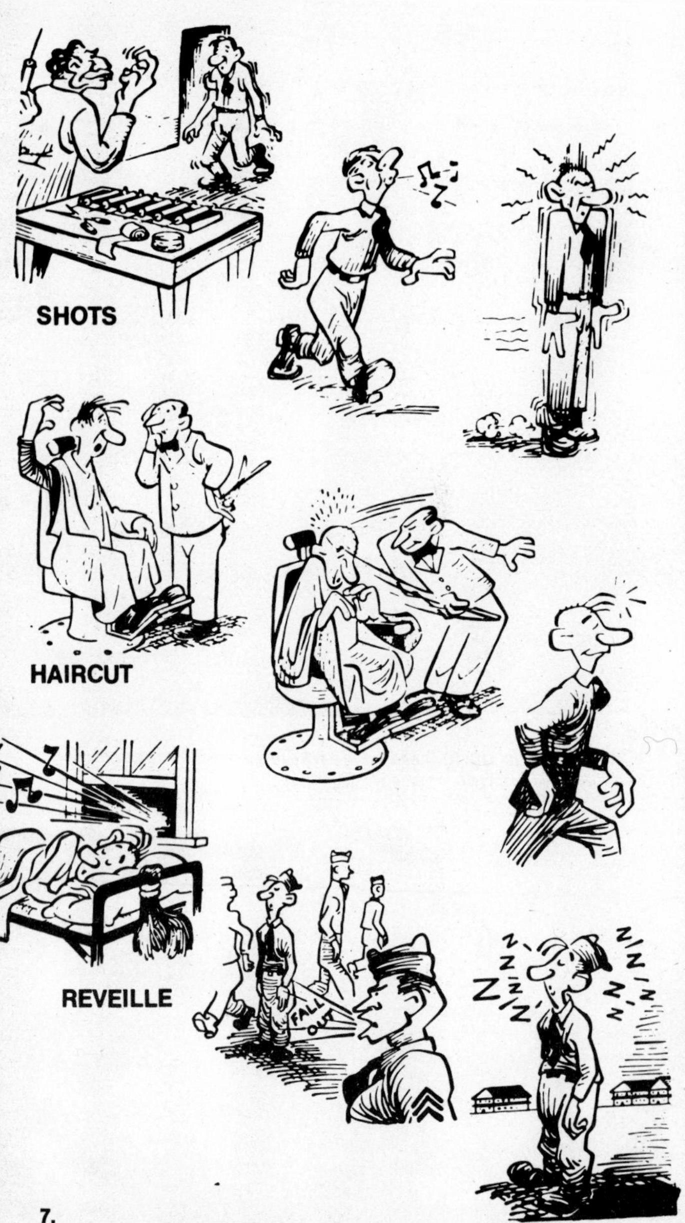
SHOTS
HAIRCUT
REVEILLE
FALL OUT
ZZZ
SGT. GEORGE BAKER

8.
Coral Sea *was the first sea battle where carriers fought carriers beyond the horizon by use of air power.*

9.
The Battle of Midway *was, perhaps, the decisive battle of the Pacific war.*

10.
Death of the Shoho *marked a turning point in the Pacific war as U.S. forces struck back and began to inflict costly losses on the Japanese Imperial Navy.*

11.
River Street *in Honolulu on a Saturday night provided almost any sort of "entertainment" a G.I. might dream about.*

12.

13.

14.
Trench positions *in the Masuren district on the East Prussian front, as seen by a German artist.*

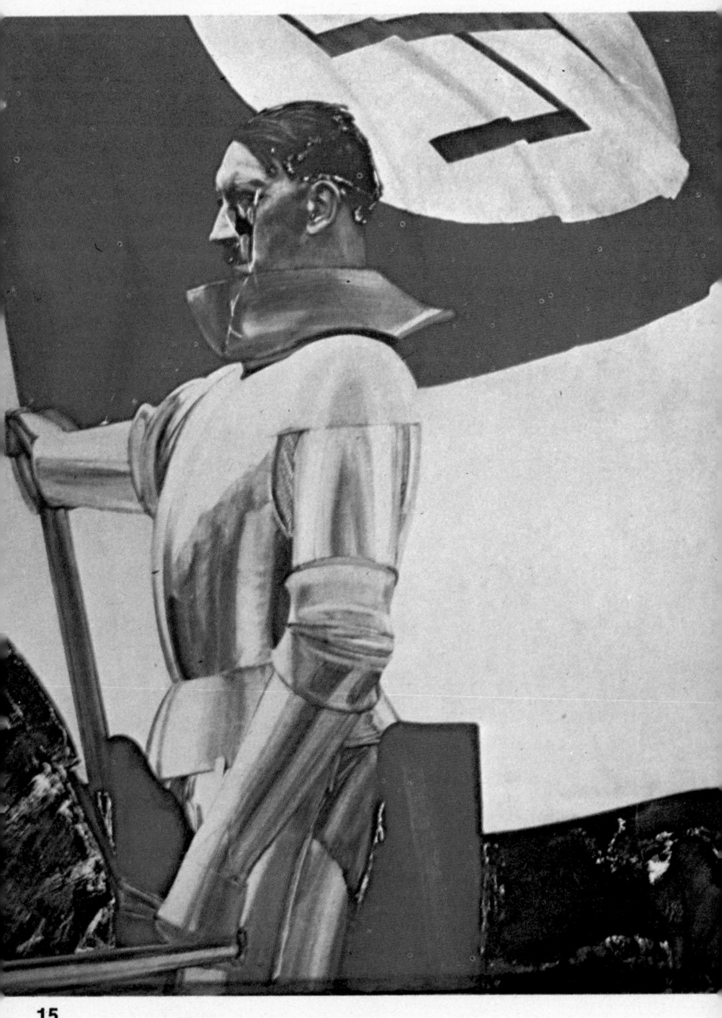

15.
Hitler as a crusading white knight *by a German artist. This painting was captured by G.I.'s and defaced.*

16.
Hitler painting *is one of a number the Führer allegedly painted in his early years.*

17.
German soldiers
as seen by
German portraitist.

18.
Dead Russians *beside a wrecked tank in this "victory scene" by a German artist.*

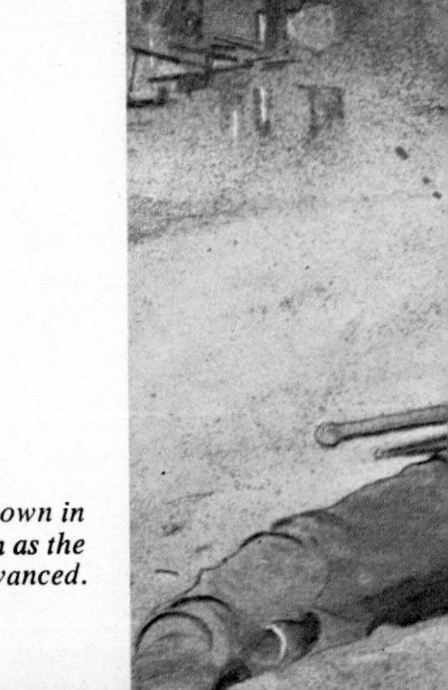

19.
Machine gun crew *is shown in street-fighting action as the Germans advanced.*

20.
Bullet Junction *was the nickname for a slope on Mt. Austin, Guadalcanal. Here a G.I. covers a buddy.*

21.
SGT. HOWARD BRODIE
GUADALCANAL
HOWARD
BRODIE
GUADALCANAL

22.
Stripped for action, *a bombardier aboard a "Flying Fortress" is ready for a low-altitude mission.*

SOLDIER'S EVOLUTION

What was it, really, this EVOLUTION OF A SOLDIER? What is it still? I've been talking about it all through this book, but I'm not sure I can explain or define it. I think that when all the nationalistic or ideological propaganda and patriotic slogans are put aside, all the straining to convince a soldier that he is dying *for* something, it is the individual soldier's final full acceptance of the fact that his name is already written down in the rolls of the already dead.

Every combat soldier, if he follows far enough along the path that began with his induction, must, I think, be led inexorably to that awareness. He must make a compact with himself or with Fate that he is lost. Only then can he function as he ought to function, under fire. He knows and accepts beforehand that he's dead, although he may still be walking around for a while. That soldier you have walking around there with this awareness in him is the final end product of the EVOLUTION OF A SOLDIER.

Between those two spectator episodes I described

earlier, that first air raid we watched and cheered albeit guiltily, and the naval night battle we watched and cheered with callous pleasure, something had happened to us. Between those two points in time, somewhere during our first long tour up on the line, we changed. Consciously or unconsciously we accepted the fact that we couldn't survive. So we could watch the naval battle from the safety of the hills with undisguised fun.

There is no denying we were pleased to see somebody else getting his. Even though there were men dying. Being blown apart, concussed, drowning. Didn't matter. We had been getting ours, let them get theirs. It wasn't that we were being sadistic. It was just that we had nothing further to worry about. We were dead.

Now, not every man can accept this. A few men accept it immediately and at once, with a kind of feverish, self-destructive joy. The great majority of men don't want to accept it. They can accept it, though. And do accept it, if their outfit keeps going back up there long enough. The only alternative is to ask to be relieved and admit you are a coward, and that of course is against the law. They put you in prison.

And yet, strangely, for everyone, the acceptance and the giving up of hope create and reinstill hope in a kind of reverse-process mental photo-negative function. Little things become significant. The next meal, the next bottle of booze, the next kiss, the next sunrise, the next full moon. The next bath. Or as the Bible might have said, but didn't quite, Sufficient unto the day is the existence thereof.

This is a hard philosophy. But then the soldier's profession is a hard profession, in wartime. A lot of men like it, though, and even civilian soldiers have been known to stay on and make it their life's work. It has its excitements and compensations. One of them is that, since you have none yourself, you are relieved of any responsibility for a future. And everything tastes better.

It is absolutely true, for example, that when you

think, when you *know,* you are going off to die somewhere soon, every day has a special, bright, delicious, poignant taste to it that normal days in normal times do not have. Another perversity of the human mechanism?

Some men like to live like that all the time. Some are actually sorry to come home and see it end. Even those of us who hated it found it exciting, sometimes. That is what the civilian people never understand about their returned soldiers, in any war, Vietnam as well. They cannot understand how we could hate it, and still like it; and they do not realize they have a lot of dead men around them, dead men who are walking around and breathing. Some men find it hard to come back from their EVOLUTION OF A SOLDIER. Some never come back at all, not completely. That's where the DE-EVOLUTION OF A SOLDIER comes in. Sometimes it takes at least as long to accomplish as its reverse process did.

Everything the civilian soldier learned and was taught from the moment of his induction was one more delicate stop along this path of the soldier evolving toward acceptance of his death. The idea that his death, under certain circumstances, is correct and right. The training, the discipline, the daily humiliations, the privileges of "brutish" sergeants, the living en masse like schools of fish, are all directed toward breaking down the sense of the sanctity of the physical person, and toward hardening the awareness that a soldier is the chattel (hopefully a proud chattel, but a chattel all the same) of the society he serves and was born a member of. And is therefore as dispensable as the ships and guns and tanks and ammo he himself serves and dispenses. Those are the terms of the contract he has made—or, rather, that the state has handed him to sign.

Most men in a war are never required to pay up in full on the contract for the life the state has loaned them. For every combat soldier there are about fifteen or twenty men required to maintain and service him who are never in much danger, if any. But everybody pays interest on the loan, and the closer to the front he gets the higher the interest rate. If he survives at all, it can take him a long time to get over the fact he isn't going to have to pay.

First War Art

Illustrations 25–29

To my knowledge, the first of any interesting American war art was done by the cartoonists (and later the combat sketch artists) of the army magazine *Yank*. This may or may not say a great deal about the art appreciation of the average American. In any case, the American men fighting the war, as the first draftee replacements and whole draftee units began to be siphoned overseas, did not give a whole hell of a great damn about art at the moment. They did care about their predicament and, perhaps depending on how far their own particular EVOLUTION OF A SOLDIER had advanced, the way the *Yank* cartoonists depicted their predicament delighted them, or at least gave them solace.

Yank, The Army Newspaper, as it was originally called, published its first issue of the day Rear Admirals Spruance and Fletcher were winding up the Battle of Midway: June 6, 1942. Its gimmick was that it was a paper done "by the men . . . for the men in the service." Nobody on its staff was more than a sergeant. But in its first issue it carried a message from Gen. George Marshall to the troops overseas, and in its second it displayed a full-page letter endorsement from Franklin Roosevelt, commander in chief, which extolled the reasons for which everybody was fighting, and the fact that our armed forces now had a paper in which they could freely express their own ideas—something, the C-in-C said, our enemies would never understand. Everybody apparently appreciated this, and the paper was a hit from the start. Nobody ever expressed any opinions anti the government's policies in it. (Such as, for example, the decision to concentrate on Hitler and Europe first and let the Pacific limp along on short rations.) But then probably nobody was anti the government's policies. If they were anti anything, they were anti the human race's policies, not the American government's.

Looking back on it, and poring over the yellowed old issues, one finds a curiously sophomoric quality and naive cheerfulness about it all, the whole of *Yank*. But perhaps we were all sophomoric—we were certainly young. Most of the articles are inane and offensively happy-sounding. Occasionally, there is one about some graphically bloody action, emphasizing bravery and courage. In every issue is an obligatory full-page "pin-up" of some known or unknown star or starlet (and so many oh-so-familiar names: Paulette Goddard, Ann Sheridan, Barbara Stanwyck, Jane Russell, the ubiquitous Betty Grable), but compared to the *Playboy* and *Penthouse* pictures of today they were innocent and ughsville, unattractive with their bare knees, half-thighs and carefully hidden breasts; to look at them you would not think the women of those days ever had crotches and tits, or even armpits. Although, of course, Hollywood producers knew different. (It wasn't that we weren't dirtier-minded; it was just all we could get. I remember a mean-faced first sergeant, on hearing the famous story which swept the South Pacific about some movie director going down on a famous actress in Ciro's or Romanoff's behind some screens that got knocked over by a waiter, grinning and saying, "Now, man, that's what I'm fighting this war for. That kind of freedom. Where could that happen but in the good old U.S. of A.?") There were sports items like the picture of Tommy Loughran exchanging his boxing gloves for a marine sun helmet. In addition to the regular letters column called "Mail Call," there was a regular column called "Words Across the Sea," in which a serviceman would send in his picture and a word or two to his brother or some former service buddy serving in some other theater—vapid comments usually, but curiously touching now. It was as if we all had on our faces this curiously fixed regulation smile, behind which seethed and swirled all the held-in misery and terror. A historian a hundred years from now, if he had no other research source but *Yank,* would think us all a bunch of whistling, happy-go-lucky grade school boys. And, maybe, we were. But of "bitterness" in *Yank* there was none. As might, I guess, be expected.

But down in amongst most of this material was the work of cartoonists like Ralph Stein, Dave Breger and George Baker which told artfully and well the real story of this mainly draftee army, who didn't like what they were doing but who were there because they had no choice, and told it, through humor, in a way it could not otherwise be told in an army publication.

Baker particularly, with his strip-cartoon of "The Sad Sack," reached the unsung souls of the hundreds of thousands of draftee "GIs" who never won a medal or earned a stripe. One of his strips was in the first June 6, 1942, issue and as far as I know he had one in every issue thereafter throughout the war, and his "Sack" became an internationally famous character. Strangely enough, a whole generation of civilians seem never to have learned where the term "Sad Sack" came from. I've had hundreds of them ask me and I've always delighted in telling them. The name derives from a term used everywhere in the army at the time: "You're a sad sack of shit," a sergeant might say, and usually did say, to the slobbiest, most worthless member of his platoon, and Baker's "Sad Sack" came to symbolize the army's and the war's "pore dumb fuck" of an eternal victim.

At this same time several non-humorous sketch artists began to emerge from the pages of *Yank.* Men like Howard Brodie, Robert Greenhalgh, and Pete Paris. All three of these men had distinctive styles, easily recognized at a glance. All three were fine sketch artists. Brodie in particular came to attention when he made a trip around the South Pacific with a *Yank* writer named Mack Morriss. The drawings he sent back from Guadalcanal were printed in a series of issues with articles by Morriss, and were a hit everywhere. Later, Brodie wound up on the Italian front, and still later in France, where he did some equally fine combat work.

As it happened, Brodie and Morriss were on Guadalcanal at the same time my outfit was. On one of these sketches Brodie had written that the scene occurred "on the 'Horse's Neck' front." What Brodie had called the "Horse's Neck" was in fact what we called the "Horse's Head," and got its name from the fact that the whole complex of hills was named "The Galloping Horse" by some bright young staff officer because that was what it looked like in an aerial photo—though apparently Brodie did not know this, and neither did we at the time.

I first saw these drawings in New Zealand, where I was in the hospital waiting to be shipped home, sometime in April, 1942. There were five or six of us there from my old company, scattered around the different wards. With that fierce sense of family feeling soldiers have for other members of the same unit, we all of us knew where each of the others were in that big nest of Quonset huts, and when one of us ran onto this back issue of *Yank* around the hospital, he rushed to get the rest of us together.

He had recognized it from one of Brodie's pictures on the cover. The cover caption carried the word

Guadalcanal, but that was not what interested him. We all saw the word *Guadalcanal* often enough—always attached to something about the marines. What had caught his attention were the two bluebirds tattooed on the chest of the man Brodie had drawn. In the old, prewar army, the two bluebirds tattoo was a distinguishing mark of a man who had served in the Hawaiian Department. Other places had other special signature tattoos—Manila in the Philippines had a couple, Panama had one or two—but the two bluebirds were one of the Honolulu tattoos. That had to be the Twenty-fifth Division. He had quickly pored over the drawings inside, noted the "Horse's Neck" reference, and come to find the rest of us. The rest of us pored over them too, less quickly. Brodie somehow had permanently captured on paper the filth and misery and fatigue we had lived through. He was using at the time (I would learn on my own, years later) a modification of the Renaissance "heroic-scale" figure, which was a body eight or nine head-lengths long, instead of the normal man's scale of seven head-lengths, and it fit perfectly with the subject matter. It accentuated the fatigue, the muscle-straining work, the sense of tension we all remembered. We kept poring over them till someone put them away. We were astonished. Somebody *had* understood. We *did* exist, after all. And in the next days we would get them out and pore over them again and again, there in the wilderness of the suburbs of Auckland, New Zealand.

The Battle of Auckland

Illustrations 30 and 31

Actually, it was called the Battle of Queen Street, Queen Street being the main street of Auckland. For a long time there were rumors that the senior commander of the Guadalcanal area was going to distribute a special campaign ribbon to Guadalcanal veterans of the Battle of Queen Street, and it became quite famous. Guys as far away as San Francisco and San Diego and Memphis, Tennessee, would ask about it. Well, we were in it, and if I didn't actually *see* the beginning of it, I was present at the beginning. I just happened to be looking the other way in the bar when the first fight started.

The whole thing began because a fresh young (young to us) regiment of marines had been shipped into Auckland for staging and for some final training before heading north. North, where we had been. The new marines were young, cocky, fresh-faced, and apple-cheeked. They had had no malaria at all, no mud, and no combat fatigue. They were camped somewhere outside the city, and they immediately began making a big play for all the New Zealand women.

Pitted against them were the rest of us. Army infantry, air force personnel, navy sailors, and our own contingent of sick, wounded, battle-weary marines; all of us down from the 'Canal haggard, hollow-eyed, yellow as lemons from malaria, ill, nervous, wounded and hurt. True, we weren't much, but the women of Auckland had taken to us very kindly, what with their men away overseas fighting in North Africa so many years; and lots of them were widows. But the new marines were younger, healthier, and better looking. To make it worse the new marine regiment was all decked out in new, fresh, tailored, well-cut marine khakis. We were dressed in the worst, most ill-fitting, GI khakis, which was all the hospital had to issue us.

But the last straw was when the young marines began buying up Purple Heart ribbons and campaign ribbons from the local army-navy stores, and sporting them around in the bars to attract girls. With their ribbons, they would impress the Auckland women with tales about how they had won the Battle of Guadalcanal. After that there was bound to be trouble.

Particularly so, since there had grown up a taboo at the hospital against wearing decorations or insignia of any kind. Nobody knew where it had started. Of course, the local army-navy stores did not sell our regimental or division insigna, anyway. And everyone refused to *buy* ribbons for medals they knew they had been awarded, but had not been presented yet. Noncoms even refused to sew their chevrons on their sleeves, unless they were hospital personnel and had to. And yet no one knew how or where or with whom this taboo had first grown up. Probably it was just some half-crazed pride we had.

On the night of the big battle I did not have a pass. That was another bone of contention. The hospital was very chary with its passes, while the young marines were in town every night. There had been rumors of a showdown, and that night two of the guys from our old company (with passes) sneaked out with me. I needed at least two to go with me because I had my leg in a cast. One would hold my crutches and help me over the fence on one side, and the other would stand and take the crutches and help me down on the other. The truth is I think we were very nearly a little crazy. We did not really give a shit for anything during that time.

There had been fights before in town, but never one that had gone all the way. When the fight began that night in the bar where we were sitting (with New Zealand girls), and then spread, and spread, and finally spilled over outside, my buddies got me out a side door and I stationed myself in one of those receding, narrowing store fronts. Whenever anybody wearing ribbons or a well-cut uniform stuck his head in, I would use one of my crutches like a bayoneted rifle, and jab him with the rubber foot or buttstroke him with the shoulder pad.

If I remember rightly, Queen Street was about five or six blocks long in the downtown honky-tonk area, and ran back flat from the dock area a couple of blocks, made a little turn, and then ran straight up a hill. And the whole five blocks of it were alive and flaming with fighting men and cartwheeling arms, as the battle spread from bar to bar. It was the young marines against the rest of us from the hospital, with the numbers about even. The MPs and SPs could do nothing to quell it. From the docks a flying wedge of British sailors tore in, hitting everybody, though they couldn't have known what it was about.

In my doorway I had laid out a couple of the young marines, who crawled away, presumably to begin again somewhere else.

Finally a battalion of Maori troops was called out. Half of them started at the top of the street, shoulder to shoulder with fixed bayonets, and the other half at the bottom. When they finally came together halfway up the hill, everybody was gone. Queen Street was empty. All of us fight-wise Americans had sneaked away up the side streets. My two buddies came charging by to collect me, and together we sneaked off back to the hospital fence, laughing and gasping over the great fun.

We must all have been half-crazy. When I started this little piece, I intended to do it humorously. Reading it over, I find that it's not, particularly. It seems more sad.

North Africa

Illustration 32

I am sure that every area of American incursion had its Battle of Queen Street or some similar name. I'm sure every major city had, wherever American troops proliferated. And in the autumn and early winter of 1942 American troops were proliferating just about everywhere. Greenland. Iceland. South America. The Caribbean. Australia. India. Burma.

Dwight Eisenhower's landings at Casablanca, Oran and Algiers took place in November. The British Isles were filling up with us. Some eighty-four thousand American troops and twenty-three thousand British made up Ike's three landing forces. Most of them, American and British, embarked from England. More Americans sailed to replace them. Thirty-five thousand Americans sailed directly to invade French Morocco from the United States, an unprecedented feat of logistics.

It had taken just about a year to get America moving. The direction she was moving in reflected the Churchill-Roosevelt strategy decision to get Hitler first. The handling of Eisenhower's mass landings made it clear that the age of massed, managerial, industrial-production technological warfare had been born—although probably nobody including Eisenhower and George Marshall knew that then, and the term "technology" hadn't been invented. A single infantryman in a war like that was about as noteworthy and important as a single mosquito in an airplane-launched DDT spray campaign: another fact the American soldier would take to sourly. More and more generals would become known by the names of their forces. Fewer and fewer individual soldiers would be known at all, or known only in larger and larger groups named for their generals.

Eisenhower's army was mainly composed of draftees and national guard outfits. As it moved across Morocco and Algeria it encountered somewhat the same problem as the first troops into combat in the Pacific. Untried, inexperienced infantry find it hard to do two things at first: Stand and hold ground in the face of fire or a frontal attack; and get up out of the safety of their holes and move forward in attack themselves. In Guadalcanal and New Guinea the marines and army troops jumped full tilt into their first combat experience in some of the tougher harder-fought campaigns of the early Pacific war. In Africa, Eisenhower's troops had the good fortune (or perhaps misfortune) to come up first against the fourteen hesitant divisions of French troops who still held Morocco and Algeria under the authority of the Vichy government. These fought only reluctantly against their former allies, and often didn't fight at all. The Americans (unlike the British along their left flank, who had fought the Germans) became afflicted with an overconfidence that didn't help much when they began to meet the Afrika Korps. In eastern Algeria they began to slow down and gradually came to a complete halt. In the south at El Guettar even Italian infantry stopped them. And finally at Kasserine Pass the Germans beat the hell out of them. It was their first serious face-to-face meeting with the German soldier.

The American armies in Morocco and western Algeria had been slow moving, even at the very first. Green, unused to daily war as the British and Germans had fought it for over two years across the top of Africa, they bogged down when they began to be hammered by Stuka divebombers and the exceptional German 88 artillery piece whose fire was both fast and deadly accurate. The Germans had reacted swiftly on the other hand and had occupied Tunisia and, utilizing its closeness to Sicily, had built up a powerful strength in troops and planes between America's western pincer and Montgomery's Eighth Army coming fast after Rommel from El Alamein and Benghazi, making the job of throwing them completely out of Africa harder day by day.

The series of engagements around Kasserine Pass cost the U.S. II Corps 6,500 men, 2,400 of them as surrendered prisoners. It also cost II Corps something like 240 tanks and 110 self-propelled guns and reconnaissance vehicles. General Fredendall, the U.S. II Corps commander, was relieved by Eisenhower, on the grounds that he did not inspire confidence in his troops. He was replaced by Maj. Gen. George S. Patton.

I was in the hospital for a while with a man who had fought at Kasserine. A piece of shell fragment had taken off most of the calf of his leg as though some animal with a large-sized mouth had bitten a half-moon piece right out, and he told me that his regiment of the First Infantry Division had been standing a full-field inspection in Kasserine Pass itself at the exact moment the Germans had broken into them. A by-the-numbers full-field inspection, with pup tents up, and everything laid out on the ground, cartridge belts and bandoliers of ammo included. Naturally, the Germans swept over them like some tidal wave. I've often wished I could remember what the number of the regiment was, and the name of the commanding officer. The man I knew in the hospital was very bitter about it.

Maybe his story was exaggerated. Anyhow, a lot of pros and cons have been written about the Kasserine fiasco. The truth is probably that without previous serious combat experience the U.S. II Corps troops at Kasserine could not have been expected to do better. Undoubtedly they were spoiled by their little bit of combat against the fading French, rather than helped by it, so that when they came up against the Germans the shock was twice as great. Then too, they were fighting against a relatively civilized enemy with similar cultural background, in the Afrika Korps. The marines and army in New Guinea and Guadalcanal didn't have that advantage to fall back on, and there was little thought of surrendering to the Japanese.

In any case, General Eisenhower had other problems than just creating an efficient American fighting force. Politics was also one of his sad duties. And his entire command was composed of British, American, Free French and ex-Vichy French units which had to be forced into a single functioning army. As if that wasn't bad enough, there was serious bitterness among the French toward the British. And the British army, no matter what their Prime Minister promised, did not wish or intend to take any backseat to a bunch of green Americans.

And the Americans were green, all right. Their level of training was seldom up to what it should have been, as happens so often in new large armies. Coordination between the branches of service was lumpy, to say the least. American planes bombing their own troops. American artillery falling on wrong coordinates. The individual fighting soldier hadn't yet acquired the stomach for head-on fighting.

When Monty chased Rommel and the Afrika Korps into Tunisia in late March, Ike was able to begin hitting the Axis forces from both west and south, forcing them into the extreme northeast corner of the Tunisian peninsula, from which only Rommel and maybe seven hundred other troops got away. The rest, some two hundred seventy-five thousand men, surrendered. Africa was over.

GRAND STRATEGY

Illustrations 33 and 34

Eisenhower's landings were on November 8, 1942. The lamentable Kasserine Pass battle began February 14, 1943. The last Germans in Tunisia (and therefore in Africa) surrendered on May 13. So a good six months had passed in securing French North Africa, an accomplishment the original planners of the "greatest amphibious invasion the world has known" hoped to see finished in six weeks.

Probably the planners' estimate was too hopeful. The arrival of unforeseen difficulties is probably the only absolute certainty in war. Certainly, the swiftness of the Germans in occupying Tunis, Bizerte and the rest of eastern Tunisia was unanticipated, and brought the Allied hopes way down. Certainly the split command of the Anglo-American forces slowed things down. By November 17 the Germans had stopped the British forward elements along the coast, and by the beginning of December the two-hundred-mile front from Bizerte south had stabilized into a kind of demi-trench warfare. And Tunis, the original main Allied objective of the entire invasion, was safely inside the German lines. A number of reasons for this failure were advanced by Monday-morning quarterbacks, and one of them was the greenness of the new American troops.

Strategically, the North African landings were intended to force Rommel (still fighting in the Libyan desert to the east, and now on the run from Montgomery and El Alamein in Egypt) into fighting a "two-front war" with the Anglo-American force behind him in Tunis. And this in fact they did do. An Allied army in French North Africa would make Rommel's whole position in Africa untenable, and this in fact it did. Fighting a stalled winter campaign in Russia at Moscow, Leningrad and Stalingrad simultaneously, Germany could not hope to reinforce and maintain a large enough German army in Africa. The mere fact of the landings alone just about guaranteed a German defeat in Africa. With the vast and superior American resources filling the beaches behind them, the Anglo-American forces could just keep pouring it on. Hitler was unwilling—or unable—to keep feeding men and matériel to Rommel on anything like equal terms. Sheer weight would grind out a win for Eisenhower. Which, after the failure of the first "swift" effort to capture Tunis, it did do, forcing Rommel to flee, leaving his Afrika Korps to surrender.

With North Africa in their hands the Anglo-American allies for the first time could pose a direct threat to Italy. It was Churchill's favorite "soft underbelly of Europe" theory and he had been plumping for it for quite a long time. One of his favorite analogies was to compare it to a prizefighter. If invasion on the Atlantic coast of France was the left hand, then invasion through Sicily and Italy was the right hand. Why use only one hand? Why not use both? An attack up through Sicily and Italy would force Germany to divide her European defenses, would open the Mediterranean and save a million tons of shipping by avoiding the Cape route to Australia, bring in a wavering Turkey and threaten southern France. Only then should France be attacked on the Atlantic coast. In addition, all Britain's Chiefs of Staff were worried and in some doubt over the unreadiness of the American soldier. By doing it this way the United States would have a chance to season itself an army before going into France.

As a matter of fact, all these things were decided in January, 1943, at the Casablanca Conference, before the Battle of Kasserine Pass was fought, or the North African campaign brought to a close. So it would seem the British Chiefs of Staff were right. In any case, by May, 1943, Americans stood poised on the northernmost tip of Africa, preparing to invade Sicily—at approximately the same time that Americans in Guadalcanal in the Solomons were preparing to invade New Georgia. And Generals Eisenhower and Marshall had themselves a toughened, seasoned nucleus for an American combat army with which to invade Europe.

As far back as December, 1941, and January, 1942, in a series of strategy talks called the "Arcadia" Conference, Churchill had talked about possible French North Africa landings and Marshall and Eisenhower and the other American generals had been against it. They wanted to hit Europe immediately, and they presented a plan which in all its strategic elements was the parent of the later "Overlord" plan of 1944. Their idea was to go right on into western France straightaway. Had they done so back then in 1942, they might well have been thrown right back out —a catastrophe that will hardly bear thinking about. But Roosevelt, cautiously, had decided in favor of Churchill and North Africa. With the result that he was called by many the toady of Churchill.

In all, the Allies during the seven months' "strategic" campaign in Africa had lost 41,133 killed and wounded; 9,310 of them had died; 2,156 Frenchmen, 2,715 British, and 4,439 Americans.

Of the Americans who were left, those who survived it, it could be said of just about every one that he had passed through his own private, special EVOLUTION OF A SOLDIER.

And it was said by observers that it showed on their faces.

One thing about the Americans, the British said, they learned fast and they learned well.

Green and Obscene

Illustration 35

The worst thing about being a seasoned soldier was they wouldn't let you go home. Your experience was needed, sorely needed, they told you. You yourself—that is, your body and its recently acquired skills—were at least ten times as valuable as when you were a green hand. So that the better you became, the less chance you had. About the only hope left was a serious wound.

It was probably simple vanity and pride which made Eisenhower, Marshall and company believe untested U.S. soldiers could go headlong straight on into the France of Hitler's "Fortress Europe" and win. The U.S. officer corps of those far-off days before the war lived in a sort of sealed-off plastic shell of their own making which could support such unrealistic dreams. The Great Depression years hurt them less than most citizens. Low-salaried though they were, their creature comforts were well seen to, by even lower-salaried enlisted slaves; and they could live well on their well-gardened, manicured posts and forts with booze and food at PX prices, and conduct their obsolete little training exercises with the same flair that they used to conduct the Saturday night Officers' Club dances. Polo was a great sport among them, for example, in those days when the use of horseless armor was just being understood. But they were brave men, and dedicated, and intelligent, great men a few of them, and with a Churchill and a Roosevelt to guide them, and some time in the field in a war to humble them a little, they could and would do great things to preserve the nation.

In the meantime, while the army leaders and the heads of state and their entourages gathered to debate the movement and the use of masses of lesser mortals and the millions of long tons of supplies needed to maintain them (gathered to decide, in fact, the actuarial statistics of death for tens and scores of thousands), the civilian soldier objects of this loving attention (and it was loving) themselves slogged on ahead, fighting and fearing one day, sleeping wet in mud the next. Gasping on the desert and in the hills (or puking and shaking with malaria in the jungles), his total horizon limited to from one to about five hundred yards in front of him, the private, noncom or junior officer knew little about what was going on or the grand design for his life for the next year. Or two years. Or three years.

There was no way for him to know. Strategic aims and planning, for simple reasons of security, could not be handed down to the rank and file. Even if he knew them, they wouldn't change his life much, or what he had to do. They might very well change his death date, but why tell him that. Anyway, he knew that (or suspected it) already.

The worst thing about being green was that he didn't know what to look for or listen for, or smell for. No amount of training behind his own lines could teach him what it was like to move out beyond them where there might be enemy. Where, eventually, there was sure to be enemy. But where? How did he look for them? What did he listen for? Those men seriously meant to kill him. Beyond the lines, a strange still breathlessness seemed to come down and settle on things: trees, roads, grass. Handling his fear was another problem. Learning to live with it, and to go ahead in spite of it, took practice and a certain overlay of bitter panache it took time to acquire. There were damned few fearless men. I knew, I think, two personally. But they were both crazy, almost certifiably so. That made them good soldiers.

But the human body, the animal human body, is incredibly adaptable. Did you ever begin using a new set of house and apartment keys? How you have to stop, and search, and look down till you find the right key for the right door? And how after several weeks or a couple of months, without any conscious participation on your part, you find that your hand itself is finding and selecting the right key by itself as the ring comes out of your pocket, without your even having to look? It was the same process which worked in the combat infantryman, almost entirely without conscious awareness, if he survived long enough to acquire it. (And the vast majority did survive: that was another thing he learned.) But there was no way to learn it except by actual practice on the actual ground under the actual fire. Meantime, he exhausted himself daily.

It's a pity the old men can't fight the wars. From the way they talk to the young we all know that they would love to do it. And they probably would be a lot more willing. At least, they have lived out a good part of their lives, and have some living chalked up behind them. But the truth is that physically they couldn't stand the gaff. I know from myself, now at fifty-three, that I couldn't possibly have stood the physical stresses I had to go through back then. And, secretly, I'm glad. But, of course, I won't admit it and will deny it with my last breath.

So there he stood—our once green, now obscene

infantryman or tanker. Filthy, grimy, bearded, greasy with his own body oils (body oils aided by a thin film of dirt could make a uniform nearly completely waterproof, if it was worn long enough), dedicated to his own survival if at all possible, and willing to make it as costly as he could if it wasn't possible. He knew by the sound of incoming shells whether they would land near enough to be dangerous. He knew by the arc of falling aerial bombs if they would light nearby or farther out. He had learned that when fire was delivered, being thirty yards away could mean safety, and that fifty or a hundred yards could be pure heaven. He had learned that when the other guy was getting it a couple of hundred yards away, it had nothing to do with him; and that conversely when he was getting it, the other guy two hundred yards away wanted nothing to do with him, either. He had learned, maybe the most important of all for survival, that danger only existed at the exact place and moment of danger, and not before and not after.

He was about the foulest-mouthed individual who ever existed on earth. Every other word was fucking this or fucking that. And internally, his soul was about as foul and cynical as his mouth. He trusted nobody but his immediate outfit, and often not them. But everybody else, other outfits, he would cheerfully direct straight into hell. He had pared his dreams and ambitions down to no more than relief and a few days away from the line, and a bottle of booze, a woman and a bath.

But the green man had all this to go through yet. He had yet to serve his apprenticeship, to be accepted. Smart replacements soon learned that they got the dirtiest most-exposed jobs in the squad or platoon or section. They prayed for newer replacements to come in behind them, so that they might be, if not accepted, at least less noticed. The lucky, the tough, and the smart survived, and the rest were forgotten, shipped home, or buried. For the green hand the worst quality was the uncertainty and the total unfamiliarity with everything. And only time and lucky survival would change it to skill. On to Sicily! On to New Georgia!

Is History Written by the Upper Classes for the Upper Classes?

It would seem that it is.

In every country the upper classes, if you can get to know them, are characterized by a high accretion of faith and belief. They have a high sense of personal honor and moral integrity the lower classes simply do not have, perhaps because the poor cannot afford them. But also because they have not had them ingrained in them. The upper classes have had these ideals like Honesty is the best policy, and the Golden Rule, inculcated in them almost from birth. Perhaps they do not always live up to them as well as they would wish, but they sincerely believe them. This, plus never having had to really live in the lower depths, makes it genuinely impossible for the upper classes to comprehend, let alone understand, the attitudes of the poor and the lower classes.

As in most wars, in the United States in World War II (and I assume in most of the nations) most of the commanding was done by the upper classes, and most of the fighting was done by the lower. You might find a Princeton or Harvard graduate leading a forward infantry platoon, but it was rare. And you almost never found a Princeton or Harvard grad serving as a private in such a platoon.

Thus, when an official army historian (almost always an educated member of the upper classes himself) came onto the field after a fight, it was usually the commanders and higher officers (themselves members of the upper classes) to whom he talked. He might talk to a few truck-driver privates for textural material. (How muddy it was. How scary the enemy charge was.) But when he wrote it, it was always filtered through the ideals system he and the other members of his class, the commanders, shared and adhered to.

And thus it is possible—it is even probable—that you can read the history of a campaign in which you served, and find the history doesn't at all tally with the campaign you remember. The private remembers it from the viewpoint of his lower class ideals, or lack of them, while the historian has written it from the viewpoint of the upper class commanders and their totally different ideals. That is why there can be such a glaring discrepancy between the history of a battle, and the way is was played out in reality on the field. And yet both views are (or believe they are) totally honest.

For example, I know a fight which was won pure and simple because two Pfcs who hated each other were bucking for the same sergeant's stripes. Because of casualties each of them was leading a group of around squad size. And each drove himself and his men so hard to outdo the other because of those vacant sergeant's stripes that the enemy position was broken open. Because the two of them were spearheading my company's drive, the company achieved its objective. Because the company was the leading company in a major attack, an important major breakthrough was won and exploited which opened up the whole rest of the campaign. Yet when the history was written up none of this was mentioned or even known. The battalion commander got the credit for the success. But my company and the company with us knew. And in the end, to finish out the story, both Pfcs made sergeant because other sergeants were killed. And both wound up as S/Sgts with platoons of their own. They still hated each other.

In a way, I was in a unique position in that I was born into the upper classes (such as they were, in my small town), and for personal and economic reasons of my own enlisted into the lumpen proletariat of the old Regular Army; and then, since then, have moved back in among the upper classes by reason of a certain success as a writer. But even back then I was always confused by the slippage and discrepancy between these two systems of ideals. No fight I know about personally (and perhaps, by extension, all battles—if they follow the same reason and rules) was ever written up historically as it really happened, but rather was written as filtered through the ideals systems of the historians and the officers who fought it wished that it might have been, and in fact believed that it was.

This is not to say that all field-grade officers and above were born with silver spoons in their mouths as members of the upper classes. We all know the humble antecedents of such high-ranking men as Eisenhower and Omar Bradley and Lesley J. McNair. But the upper classes have a way of adopting talent. They quickly and happily make room for it and then close ranks around it and take it unto themselves. Since the aim of just about every American (except for those who cannot hope to aspire) is to move up into these rarefied regions of power and privilege, the talented quickly take on the protective coloration and absorb (if they never had it before) or reabsorb (if they had temporarily lost it) the high-ideals system of this upper class who can economically afford to think liberally of their fellow humans.

And this is not to say that the ideals are not

eminently admirable. But they have almost no effect on your proletarian infantry soldier at all.

In my old age I have about come to believe that the whole of written history is miscreated and flawed by these discrepancies in the two ideals systems: the one of how we would all like to believe humanity might be, but only the privileged can afford to believe is; and the one of how we all really know humanity in fact is, but none of us wants to believe it.

So that one can perhaps honestly say that history is in fact written by the upper classes for the upper classes. And if that is so, then the whole history of my generation's World War II has been written, not wrongly so much, but in a way that gave precedence to the viewpoints of strategists, tacticians and theorists, but gave little more than lip service to the viewpoint of the hairy, swiftly aging, fighting lower class soldier.

HUMOR

Illustrations 36–47

It was the safety valve and saving factor of the "lower class" Fully Evolved Soldier. He wasn't really as lower class as all that, only comparatively so. America then as now has perhaps the biggest middle class in human history, mixed in there with its "proletarian" city-worker soldiers. But he was the kind of soldier who would never make an officer, let alone a colonel or a general. And his humor reflected his interest and preoccupation with the absurdities of privilege all around him, while he fought and died or lived in inconceivable daily misery in a war where he himself had none.

It was pretty rugged humor. And it got ruggeder and gruesomer as this middle period of a seemingly hopelessly long war wore on. There was the classic of the P-38 Lightning pilot shot down over the desert (or the jungle, or the Alaskan tundra) who, when rescue parties got to him, was clearly dying and a real mess. Both legs were twisted out at odd angles, both arms were smashed, his chest cavity was crushed

23.
G.I.'s in their jeep, *the hated but trusted little vehicle that was their workhorse.*

24.
Stretcher Party *is the title of this pencil sketch by an anonymous marine who drew it on cardboard on October 8, 1942, on Guadalcanal. It was later found in an ambulance.*

25.
Sex hygiene

26.
The Bayonet

THE SAD SACK
Cocktails
Bar
BAR
CHURCH BAZAAR
ADMISSION
$1
PER PERSON
SGT. GEORGE BAKER

27.
In town

28.

29.

30.
Pubs in Auckland *were frequently crawling with G.I.'s looking for some relaxation.*

31.
Auckland harbor *as seen from a transport.*

32.
Tank trap *was set up in a pass by the Allies to surprise German tank crews.*

33.
Leaders' meeting *in 1941 was planned to allow Churchill and Roosevelt to coordinate the Anglo-American war effort in face-to-face sessions. The ships in the picture are (l. to r.): the U.S.S.* Augusta *(Admiral King's flagship, bearing Roosevelt), the U.S.S.* Tuscaloosa, *the U.S.S.* Arkansas, *H.M.S.* Prince of Wales *(which brought Churchill).*

34.
Roosevelt press conference *depicts FDR at his confident best, his cigarette at a cocky angle, as he briefs reporters on the signing of the Atlantic Charter in 1941.*

35.
Marine marksman *in New Britain scans the jungle ahead in this dramatic charcoal drawn by Kerr Eby.*

36.
"Aw, go on back. What have you got to lose?"

37.
"My man are appoint me to offer surrendering—only under one condition—that we are not required to eat admirable American delicacy named spam."

38.
"I don't know, Hans, but I still say this won't get you a private room and bath."

39.
"And furthermore, I think your last picture stunk!"

40.
"Something big must be coming up; I haven't heard a rumor in three days."

41.
"Ain't been in long, have you, mate?"

42.
"TEN-SHUN!"

43.
Sometimes the most elaborate and attractive battle souvenirs are exceptionally hard to keep, if you know what we mean.

44.
"You're sure you are not just trying to get out of a detail?"

45.
"Hey, Rocco. Any sign of them yet?"

46.
Left:
"Merry Christmas to you, too. And on New Year's, knock before entering."

47.
"Nice thing about combat points is that they come in such big bunches."

48.

49.

50.

51.

52.

53.

54.
Murmansk Run *was cold and dangerous duty for coast guardsmen.*

55. *Right:*
Drydock *at Pearl Harbor ministered to our damaged ships.*

56.
The dollar *was always welcome in the honky-tonk bars of San Juan, Puerto Rico, as many American sailors and soldiers discovered.*

57. *Right:*
Grand Central Station *in New York City was the point of departure, night and day, for thousands of G.I.'s.*

PLEASE CALL ME
AT 1:15 AM
PLEASE CALL ME
AT 2:30 AM

58.
Staging base *in England handling the massive supplies received from America.*

59.
Awaiting departure, *a group of American soldiers is bound for combat in Europe.*

60.
Wounded man *is held by a worried buddy.*

61.
Litter-borne G.I. *being gently manhandled up a too-steep slope.*

62.
Plasma *was a life-saving gift from home.*

63.
A wounded marine *is lowered to waiting LST for transfer.*

64.
Waiting for the wounded, *an American hospital transport stands ready to evacuate casualties.*

65.
The end of a busy working day *comes for corpsmen.*

THE SATURDAY EVENING
POST
MAY 26, 1945
10¢
The Story of a
Fighting Destroyer
A NEW ROMANCE

66.

67.

The battle-wise
Infantryman..
..is CAREFUL
what he says or writes

68.

by the forward edge of the cockpit, his face a mess of bloody hamburger. Every time he breathed a bloody froth of foam came out of the ruined mouth. They dragged him away from the wreckage, but the medic could only look at him helplessly. Finally he bent down and said inanely, "How do you feel?" From the bloody hamburger of his mouth, through the froth of blood, the pilot answered, "It only hurts when I laugh."

This story ran like wildfire across the world, through every theater, through every homeland camp, through every navy ship. And it never failed to crack everybody up who heard it. There were other more gruesome ones.

Then there was the ubiquitous Kilroy, his long pathetic hungry-looking nose hanging over the wall with the two peering eyes above it, always the spectator, never inside. "Kilroy was here." It was marked on the standing walls of ruined buildings, on latrine walls, on bars and whorehouses from Seattle to Miami and from Italy to Australia. No one ever knew who started it. Everybody understood it. If something bad had happened, Kilroy was responsible. If something good had happened, Kilroy had been across that wall, outside looking in.

It could be pretty rough humor. But then isn't all humor essentially cruel? A bunch of us were standing on an open hill one day, winded, after just having taken it against only token resistance, when one of our men facing toward the enemy on the next hill across a jungle ravine was hit by a ricochet. He had taken off his helmet to cool his head, and the bullet, traveling flat instead of by the point, struck him square between the eyes in the forehead, and went screaming off exactly as if it had hit a rock. Nobody knew where it came from. Nobody had heard the shot. It must have come from far off or it would have killed him anyway. Instead, it only knocked him halfway out. After no more fire came and we all got back on our feet (excepting, of course, the wounded man) the man who had just been standing with him started to yell for a medic, but then began to choke up with laughter and couldn't. Choking and gasping, he tried two or three times and failed, and then fell down on the ground, curled up and gasping, roaring with laughter. By that time someone else had called the medic. But then the wounded man sat back up beside his laughing buddy and looked around at all of us with a hurt look on his face. The skin on his forehead was torn, but the hot bullet must have partially cauterized the tear, because only a trickle of blood ran down onto his nose. This, plus the look on his face, sent his buddy off into fresh roars. And by this time the rest of us were laughing. Finally the buddy got himself stopped enough to tell what had happened. Standing with his back to the enemy hill, he had been looking right at his friend, talking, when the bullet hit him with a loud smack and went twanging off. Slowly the hit man's eyes had crossed themselves until the irises nearly disappeared beside his nose, and he had sat down and then fallen flat. If we could only have seen those eyes going crossed, he groaned, breaking out again and hugging himself. The medic had come up now, and looked at the slight tear on the hit man's forehead with disgust. "Christ, is this what you guys got me up here for?" He got the casualty on his feet, "Come on, I'll take you back to battalion. They'll give you some aspirin." By now there were six or eight of us roaring and paralyzed, on our knees or squirming on the ground or holding onto each other, as the medic led the stunned man off. "You sons of bitches, I coulda been killed," he called back irately at us. And we all broke out afresh.

Naturally, when he came back an hour later, he was immediately nicknamed "Irondome" and "Steelhead" and "Helmethead." Finally his nickname settled permanently: "Skillethead." And Skillethead he remained until he finally left the outfit.

It could be pretty basic humor, too. A man on a bare hillside who had to take a crap could do no better for privacy than to take an entrenching shovel and scoop out a hole and squat above it on the uphill side, while the men in the hollow below would whistle and make cowlike moans of false passion. One day when my company's forward platoon had just repelled a light, half-hearted Japanese attack, wild shouts of laughter and exclamations fell on the wind from the hill crest above us where the line was. When we called up to see what had happened, a soldier yelled down, "Jerry Marti's got a hard-on, for Chrissake. Right in the middle of an attack. He showed us. Won a five dollar bet from So-and-So."

A Polack in our outfit (nicknamed "Polack," naturally), who bore an unfortunately comic resemblance to a rhesus monkey, came down with a dose of clap in the middle of the Guadalcanal campaign. We had all of us been away from women for at least three months. Nobody knew how he could have caught it. He was accused of everything from buggering dead Jap corpses to getting himself up in a disguise as a monkey, so as to get in with a band of jungle monkeys. But Polack had the last laugh. His case was so bad it refused to respond to treatment and he had to be evacuated to New Zealand. We never saw him again, but used to curse him roundly for having such good luck as to get sent out for a dose of clap in a womanless jungle campaign. Later, the battalion surgeon gave it as a considered medical opinion that it was an old case never quite cured which was brought back on by strain and exertion.

The resilience of the human body is perhaps only exceeded by the comeback abilities of the human psyche. Hours after terror, and the hot dry mouth of fear, men back out of a fight or back off the line could begin to wrinkle their eyes a little and smile again. If the cynicism of each man's EVOLUTION OF A SOLDIER and the rawness of his humor grew proportionately with the trips up front he made, he was still able (after a relatively short period of relief) to perk up enough so that whenever he saw a reporter with a pencil or a photographer with a camera, he could be ready with the wisecrack and make the toothy smile for the folks back home.

It was amazing how little of his secret bitterness (as well as how little of his private humor) he allowed to filter through to the people at home as they worried, worked, and grew rich and fat on his war.

The Art Programs

In February of 1943 the army established and organized an official war art unit in the Corps of Engineers. Thus the last half of Eisenhower's North African campaign was the first one where official war artists moved with the troops and various service units, and from that time on they were present in just about every campaign.

The army's brochure on the program says that the official army program, in which at one point forty artists participated, was discontinued in late 1943; and that "When the demands of the war terminated the funds for the continuation of the Army's war art program, the artists already in the war theaters were subject to recall."

That means the official program lasted something less than one year. It would be interesting to speculate on just why the official program was terminated like that. Government money was being spent like water on just about everything else at the time. Movie film units were beginning to work all over the globe on government funds. And God knows how many friends of senators and representatives were sitting in little (and not so little) offices all over Washington doing nothing and drawing down the salaries of majors and colonels. Perhaps one of those very senators, in a patriotic excess of good will, raised hell in the Congress about money being spent on "war art programs." The demands of the war were not all *that* stringent at home. I do not have any further information on its strange cancellation.

Anyhow, it was at this point that the then Executive Editor of *Life,* Daniel Longwell, stepped in and went to see Assistant Secretary of War McCloy and offered to hire the civilian artists in the program, of which there were nineteen. Seventeen accepted. "The Army, however," the brochure goes on to say, "continued to support the program by billeting the artist-correspondents and providing for their transportation." That would make it seem to sound as though only the salaries demanded by the artists were in question, since the army would already be billeting them and providing their transportation in the Corps of Engineers program. In any case, a lot of work that might never have been done on the war was saved by *Life.*

This special collection (called the *Life* Collection) forms the nucleus of the present army war art library. Presumably, the seventeen artists continued work throughout the rest of the war for *Life,* where their works were reproduced. In return for the billeting and transportation *Life* agreed to give the collection to the military establishment after the war.

Another special collection, called the Abbott Collection, was begun in 1944. Abbott Pharmaceutical Laboratories sponsored a program to build a pictorial record of Medical Department activities on the home front and in the various combat theaters. Twelve artists were selected and some two hundred forty-four paintings were put together out of it.

By far the largest single addition to the army's war art collection was the group of original drawings, sketches and cartoons published in *Yank* beginning in 1942, already referred to above.

The navy (within which of course was included the Marine Corps) and the Coast Guard began making their own collections at various times, the navy as far back as 1941. Lt. Cmdr. Griffith Bailey Coale, a muralist and expert on small boats and ship models, who painted the panoramic *Pearl Harbor Attack*, is credited with founding and organizing the navy's Combat Artists Corps.

Nothing but highest admiration can be given to these men who went ashore and into combat with the troop units, and who lived their intensely uncomfortable out-of-combat lives with them, to get the material for their work. Not a few of them died in the performance of it.

At the same time, it can probably be safely said that by spring 1943 "covering the war" had become a big proposition in a big war. Newspapers had over five hundred correspondents overseas with the armed forces. Magazines like *Time* and *Life* practically lived off of it. As *Time* said, and could easily say, it was the best-reported war in history.

Life, with its platoons of correspondents and photographers, and its seventeen army-organized war artists, could have said the same. Because by May of 1943 it really was a big war. By May of 1943, after the fall of North Africa, the war had come into its own.

The Big War

Illustrations 48–59

Admiral Yamamoto is supposed to have said before Pearl Harbor that he could raise havoc with the United States for a year or perhaps even eighteen months, but that after that he could not give any guarantees. He was referring of course to the U.S. industrial potential, and what it could do when it got converted to war production.

Yamamoto was shot down and killed over Bougainville on April 18, 1943—in a prearranged sneak attack by U.S. P-38 Lightnings from Guadalcanal: a nicely ironic end for the planner of Pearl Harbor. Yamamoto's hope for both Pearl Harbor and the Battle of Midway six months later had been to inflict quickly on the United States one single defeat so huge that the United States would have to negotiate a peace before her war machine got moving. (It is possible that he underestimated the United States's tenacity and resilience.) In any case, both plans failed. And just about exactly at the same time as his own death (by the guns of a group of one of the newer American planes he had envisioned), the thing Japan's greatest strategist had feared most about the United States was coming to pass. The massive U.S. industrial war power was getting going.

In 1939 only 2 per cent of the gross national product of the United States was in armaments. By 1944 U.S. plants were putting out 50 per cent more armaments than the whole of the Axis. In 1943 the U.S. standard of living had jumped to one-sixth higher than what it had been in 1939. On July 10, 1943, 160,000 troops, American and British, landed on Sicily's beaches. There were nearly 3,000 landing craft and warships, 14,000 vehicles, 600 tanks, 1,800 artillery pieces. Britain agreed to put up 80 per cent of the naval cover and 45 per cent of the air cover needed; the United States put up all the rest. In 1944 some 3.5 million U.S. women stood on the assembly lines alongside the 6 million men workers. Between them they could turn out an entire cargo ship in 17 days. They reduced the time required to make a bomber from 200,000 man-hours to 13,000.

The big war had arrived, all right. Finally. As Yamamoto had predicted. And, almost incidentally, it had killed the Great Depression, and put the national economy back on its feet. In fact, most people were making more money than they had ever made in their lives. And if meat, sugar, butter and gas were rationed, nobody really suffered; there always seemed to be enough booze, and enough steaks in the restaurants, on the home front. In fact, the whole of America seemed to have become one vast boom town.

In March of 1943 the biggest single convoy battle of the Battle of the Atlantic ended with twenty-one Allied ships lost, sunk by U-boats operating in packs. If people read about that in their papers (if, in fact, it was even in the papers), nobody paid much attention or cared much.

In June of that year, in Memphis, Tennessee, where I was in the hospital, I rode home on a street bus and heard one tired plant-worker say to another, "If this son-a-bitching fucking war only lasts two more years, I'll have it made for life."

I couldn't get angry at him for it. I understood him. He didn't really mean he wanted the war to continue. He meant he was another working stiff who remembered the Depression. As for the rest, it was too big for a single mind to try to encompass. Ordinary citizens were lost in the almost incomprehensible boom and mass movement, trying to pick their way uphill through the crush to some island of security, in a new world that seemed to have gone crazy with both destruction and a lavish prosperity.

This wrenching social upheaval and realignment, as much as the fact of the war itself, accounted for an almost total breakdown of the moral standard of prewar U.S. living. And nothing would ever quite be the same again.

In Miami Beach, where I spent a brief furlough with my brother after getting home from overseas in the hospital, platoons and companies of young-looking OCS cadets marched through the golf courses and ritzy shopping areas shouting out old army rhymes to the command "Count off!" In marching rhythm and at the top of their lungs they sang songs like "I've Been Working on the Railroad" and "Roll A Silver Dollar" and "For Me and My Gal." The government had taken over most of the hotels along the beach, for the use of depleted and nerve-shattered flyers who had completed their fifty missions over Europe. Two Red Cross women (working under my brother) served each commandeered hotel, organizing "singe binges" (weiner roasts) and beer busts on the beach, and getting up fishing parties. My sister, having run away from home, worked as a barmaid and elevator operator at the Roney Plaza, lived with a zapped-out flyer for a while, was married to him for four months, and never saw him again. Once, driving down to Key West on the overseas highway in a borrowed car, he had to pull over to the side and stop and let her drive the rest of the way because the whumps the tires made on the concrete joints of the roadbed sounded so like the flak explosions he remembered over Germany. Men and women everywhere—a lot of the women with husbands overseas—took what love they could get from each other on a day-to-day basis, and then moved on. A person took what fun he could find. Because no one person counted for anything anymore in the sweeping calculations and ramifications of this big war that was moving them all along.

But if the sense of displacement and increasing insignificance was befuddling and benumbing to a lot of the civilians at home, it was worse to the combat soldier overseas, as he watched the war grow in scope and depth around him.

The British Isles were filling up with U.S. troops and equipment. Training and waiting for the invasion of France was becoming a way of life. Air force units were swelling the countryside to bursting, as the mass bombing raids against Hitler's Europe got into even higher gear. The size of everything, the numbers involved, the tonnages required to supply them, the shipping required to move it all overseas in two directions and at the same time make up for the staggering prodigal losses, all were reaching such vast proportions by mid-1943 that any one single soldier became dwarfed by it all, meaningless except statistically, one faceless head in the myriads of his counterparts. In the line outfits, where there had once been divisions, now there were corps, and soon there would be armies. Eisenhower had an army *group* now. Patton had an army, the Seventh. Mark Clark had another army, the Fifth, in training in Africa for the invasion of Italy.

In the Pacific it was perhaps not so noticeable, since the buildup there must wait on Europe. But the trend was there, and in the Pacific it was the navy that was getting the buildup. The age of managerial, organizational war was in full flex, almost without having realized it had been born.

Major generals and up had become of necessity corporation executives, moved around with their staffs so swiftly and so often, on paper, that a line soldier often didn't know from week to week who his chief commander was.

By sheer weight of numbers, the weight of numbers that in fact would win the war for us, corporation war and managerial technology had come into their own. Even generals, if they were only brigadiers, could begin to worry and feel lost in the shuffle. And for the lowly, mud-sucking private up front with Mauldin—recognized, wielded and maneuvered in mass but virtually invisible in the press as an individual—it was practically hopeless. The *x* hundreds of thousands, *x* millions, the *x.y* per cent of the whole, would assuredly, mathematically, return home when it was all over and we had won. *He* might not. Probably wouldn't. Not if he stayed.

CASUALTIES

Illustrations 60–65

Something strange seems to happen when a man is hit. There is an almost alchemic change in him, and in others' relationship to him. Assuming he isn't killed outright, and is only wounded, it is as though he has passed through some veil isolating him, and has entered some realm where the others, the unwounded, cannot follow. He has become a different person, and the others treat him differently.

The dead, of course, really *have* entered a different realm, and there is a sort of superstitious mystique of dread and magic about the dead. Where do people really go when they die? Do they go anywhere? Nobody has ever gone through death and lived to tell the tale. So it can only remain a question. There is a sort of instinctive dislike of touching them, as though what has happened to them has contaminated them and might contaminate the toucher.

Perhaps part of this feeling passes over to the wounded as well. Perhaps we think some of their bad luck might rub off, too. In any case, while they are treated as tenderly as humanly possible, and everything to make them comfortable as possible is done for them that can be, they are looked at with a sort of commingled distaste, guilt and irritation, and when they are finally moved out of the area everybody heaves a sort of silent sigh of relief without looking anybody else in the eyes.

The wounded themselves seem to acquiesce in this attitude, as though they are half-ashamed for having been hurt in the first place, and feel that now they can only be a drag and a weight on their outfit. Nor do the wounded seem to be less isolated from each other. Being in the same fix does not make them closer, but even farther apart than they are from the well.

The first wounded I ever saw were the remnants, picked up by the rescue boat, of the bombed-out barge that was hit in the air raid the day we arrived at Guadalcanal. Of course we were all totally green hands at the time, so perhaps we watched with more awe than we would have done later. But only a short time before, some of us had been talking to some of these men on the ship. With practical comments as to the extent of the various injuries in our ears from nearby old-timers who had been there longer, we watched as the survivors were landed and led or carried up from the beach to where a field dressing station had been set up at dawn. A few of them could walk by themselves. But all of them were suffering from shock as well as from blast, and the consummate tenderness with which they were handled by the corpsmen was a matter of complete indifference to them. Bloodstained, staggering, their eyeballs rolling, they faltered up the slope to lie or sit, dazed and indifferent, and allow themselves to be worked on by the doctors. They had crossed this strange line and everybody realized, including themselves dimly, that now they were different. All they had done was climb into a barge and sit there as they had been told. And then this had been done to them, without warning, without explanation, perhaps damaging them irreparably; and now explanation was impossible. They had been initiated into a strange, insane, twilight fraternity where explanation would be forever impossible. Everybody understood this. It did not need to be mentioned. They understood it themselves. Everybody was sorry, and so were they themselves. But there was nothing to be done about it. Tenderness was all that could be given, and like most of our self-labeled human emotions, it meant nothing when put alongside the intensity of their experience.

With the Jap planes still in sight above the channel, the doctors began trying to patch up what they could of what the planes had done to them. Some of them would yet die, that much was obvious, and it was useless to waste time on these which might be spent on others who might live. Those who would die accepted this professional judgment of the doctors silently, as they accepted the tender pat on the shoulder the doctors gave them when passing them by, staring up mutely from liquid eyes at the doctors' guilty faces. We watched all this with rapt attention. The wounded men, both those who would die and those who would not, were as indifferent to being stared at as they were to the tenderness with which they were treated. They stared back at us with lackluster eyes, which though lackluster were made curiously limpid by the dilation of deep shock. As a result, we all felt it, too—what the others, with more experience, already knew—these men had crossed a line, and it was useless to try to reach them. The strange, wild-eyed, bearded, crazily dressed marines and soldiers who had been fighting there since August didn't even try, and stood around discussing professionally which wounds they thought might be fatal, and which might not.

Even the army itself understood this about them, the wounded, and had made special dispensations about their newly acquired honorary status. Those who did not die would be entered upon the elaborate shuttling movement back out from this furthermost point of advance, as only a short time back they had been entered upon the shuttle forward into it. Back out, further and further back, toward that amorphous point of assumed total safety: home. Depending upon the seriousness of their conditions, they would descend part way, or all way, to the bottom of the lifeline home. The lucky ones, those hurt badly enough, would go all the way to the bottom, and everybody's secret goal: discharge. . . .*

Casualties are one of war's grimmer realities. In a way perhaps its most important element. An army that cannot take casualties cannot fight. And an army that takes too many will lose. Somewhere in between there is the ultimate fact of it that whatever you do you are going to have casualties, if you fight. Like the poor, they are always with us. We got more inured to them, as time went on. But, unless you are too busy yourself to notice, there is always that sense of awe and sorrow when a man you know goes down. Or even a man you don't know. But people, civilians, really don't like to think about casualties. Even combat soldiers don't.

The two casualties I've remembered the most vividly were both of them men I didn't know and never met. I don't know why these two, instead of some others, but whenever I read or hear that word, CASUALTY, it is my mental pictures of these two which come leaping into my mind.

The first was a man who was not even in my battalion. My company had been ordered up to relieve a company from the other battalion, and my platoon took over along a hilltop from a platoon of the other company. In the confusion of making the relief, and then the excitement of having to repel a light, feeling attack of Japanese almost immediately after, we had

* I suppose I should confess here that parts of the above passage about our first air-raid wounded I have excerpted from a longer similar passage in a combat novel I wrote about Guadalcanal called *The Thin Red Line*. Realizing when I came to write about them that I could never write about them better than I had done there, I used from it.

paid little attention to our surroundings, and so hadn't noticed our dead friend lying on the downslope behind us. But then in the quiet following the attack, in the shifting, light, hill breeze, a faint waft of him got up to us for a moment. And there was no mistaking that smell.

He must have been killed the day before, and been missed by the medics. And it had rained quite a lot during the night. With that uncanny ability the dead have of seeming to fade into and become part of the terrain, in his grimy green fatigues and olive-drab helmet he was not easy to spot. But the fellows on the line, when they began to look around for him, spotted him easily enough. Then the uproar began.

"Medics! Medics! Where the fuck are those lousy lazy medics? Get this fucking stiff out of here!" They were indignant at his having been left there for them to see and smell. Soon all the rest of us joined in the chorus, and the outcry was so great that battalion headquarters down the rear slope sent somebody up to see what was the matter. It didn't take the messenger long to find out, and he hurried back down to battalion. A few of us walked over to take a look at the stiff. Far below we could see four straggling medics with a stretcher starting the long climb up.

He wasn't even swollen enough to be grotesque, only a little. Rigor mortis had obviously set in. He was lying on his side with his knees pulled up and his hands clenched and bent up beside his face. There was no blood, and no visible signs of a wound. He apparently had curled up as he died. But the clenched hands were not touching the face; they were just stuck out there in the air at the ends of the bent elbows. In that manner of all combat dead, he appeared to be faceless. He had all the parts of a physiognomy, eyes, ears, nose, lips, but there was a peculiar indistinct haziness about them when you looked. I don't know what causes this effect. I used to think it was because we did not want to look closely, and so let our eyes slide away from the face. But later I noted the same effect in photos of the dead. He seemed, instead of being a collection of limbs and bones and parts, to have become a single, solid object of the same density and texture all the way through like a loose boulder or a tree stump or the bole of a downed tree trunk. Anyhow, there he was. And he was not even a man anymore. As short a time ago as yesterday, he had been. But now he wasn't. Subdued, we walked back to the rest of the platoon. We had all seen plenty of dead men by now, but this one seemed to move us more than usual. I think his being alone like that, a single, and from a stranger outfit, all alone on a slope that was supposed to have been already cleaned up, moved us in a way that a whole slope full of our own dead and wounded might not have done. I just felt there ought to be something more significant about it all. Suddenly one of us gagged, and went off and puked in the weeds. But nobody kidded him, as they might have done normally. We all seemed to know that his puking was not from the sight and smell of a dead man so much as from a kind of animal protest at the idea itself.

When the medics got up to the dead guy, they couldn't make him stay on the stretcher, in his curled up position. He kept rolling off it as they lifted, no matter how they placed him. Finally two of them seized him by the wrists and ankles and carted him off down the hill that way, while the other two brought up the rear with the stretcher. From behind them at the crest, men from the platoon whistled their critical displeasure.

But why should that one man stick in my mind so strongly, all these years?

The other one was a boy I saw as I walked back the day I was wounded. I had had to cross a grassy little gulch, and had to climb a long steep hillside through sparse jungle trees. I was being fired at by snipers—puffs of dirt kept popping up around me from time to time—but I couldn't climb any faster. Halfway up the hill I came upon a stretcher with a dead boy in it that had been abandoned. It lay among some rocks, tilted a little, just the way it had been dropped. He had obviously been hit a second time, in the head, and left by the stretcher bearers, probably under fire themselves. He had certainly been killed by the hit in the head, but I couldn't tell if by a sniper bullet or something else. In any case, blood had run out of him from somewhere until it nearly filled the depression his hips made in the stretcher. And that has always stayed with me. It didn't seem a body could hold enough blood to do that. His hips were awash in it and it almost covered his belt and belt buckle. And somehow, though he was lying on his back, head uphill, blood had run or splashed from his head so that there were pools of it filling both his eye sockets. All the blood had thickened and almost dried, so he must have been there since early morning. Undoubtedly he belonged to our sister company, which was making the attack with us, but I had never seen him before. He looked so pathetic lying there, one hand dangling outside the stretcher, that I wanted to cry for him. But I was gasping too hard for breath, and was too angry to cry for anybody. It was possible that if he had been hit by the snipers, they might hit me also. But even if it was possible, there wasn't anything I could do about it. I couldn't move any faster, and I was so angry I didn't care. I don't even know what I was angry at. Life, I guess. I certainly wasn't angry at the Japanese for sniping wounded, we expected that. I was just angry. And that was all. I went on up the hill and left him.

I suppose every man has his own private casualties he remembers and cannot forget. Perhaps hundreds, who knows? I have plenty of others. But these two I used to dream about, back when I still had the nightmares. But why they became my private images for CASUALTY, I have no answer for. Perhaps it was simply because they both seemed so insignificant, and useless. Pointless.

Their deaths weren't pointless, of course. Not statistically. Even if they were killed at random, simply because they were moving forward though not doing anything particularly, they were part of the statistics that were gaining us the ground, and later I realized this.

By mid-1943, a lot of Mediterranean veterans and Pacific veterans were brooding over this phenomenon of statistical casualties, too, I expect.

The Forgotten Year

Illustrations 66–74

On July 10 of 1943 Patton's Seventh Army and Montgomery's Eighth invaded the south coast of Sicily. On June 4, 1944, the Allied armies entered Rome. Two days later, on June 6 (for ever after "D-Day" in history), Eisenhower launched Overlord, the long-awaited French invasion.

On June 30, 1943, U.S. infantry began their less-than-one-division assault on New Georgia (central Solomons), by invading Rendova Island. June 15, 1944, Spruance's Central Pacific Forces, based on Honolulu, with two divisions and one in reserve invaded Saipan in the Marianas, the first Japanese possession to be attacked.

In just about exactly a year the United States, however unwilling, naive and unprepared for it, had become the major world power, and for the moment, the first and only of what would soon come to be called the superpowers.

It is perhaps unfair to call this year from June, 1943, to June, 1944, the forgotten year of the Pacific war alone. There was also Italy, Still, the Pacific had perhaps a bigger claim. That great Shakespearean actor General MacArthur, as some newsmen called him, himself called it sourly, "the stony broke war." The ground troops who fought it, even more sourly among themselves, referred to it as "this fucking pore man's war." And when comparisons are made in the numbers of high-ranking commanders, troops, armaments and matériel used, there isn't any question. Given the Churchill-Roosevelt grand strategy decision to go for Hitler first, there wasn't any way the Pacific could not feel itself forgotten.

On the other hand, the Pacific war was to a great extent essentially a sea war, and the huge buildup of the U.S. Navy in that year of June to June to a large degree made up for the army's neglect. At the same time, a lot of Government Issue civilian soldiers, bogged down in the mud of Italy's bad winter of '43–'44, were feeling themselves sunk in a forgotten year of a forgotten war, too.

At home the industrial machine continued to grind out the war materials in gross ton lots, but not always smoothly. There were race riots in Detroit, riots so bad federal troops had to be called out to quell them. Coal strikes, rail strikes, steel strikes, all for higher pay and benefits, threatened to choke down the civilian "War Effort." On December 28 of 1943, the day the press reported the landings of the good old First Marine Division from Guadalcanal on Cape Gloucester in New Britain in the Bismarcks, the lead headlines were taken up by the rail strike and the fact that the army had seized the railroads on the President's orders. The ol' home folks evidently weren't putting out a hundred per cent, despite Norman Rockwell's covers for the *Saturday Evening Post.* Slowly rotting men lay in their wet holes in the snow-laced winter mud of Italy or the rain-lashed tropical mud of the Pacific and read about it in their hometown papers the Red Cross was able to deliver occasionally.

They had a year of battles, fought without any great

victories to stimulate troop morale. And they were battles that had to be fought, nevertheless, to prepare for the joyous victories of late 1944 and '45. It is a little weird to think that the Americans who died in that June-to-June year died without knowing for sure the Allies were going to win. Maybe, though, that was a better way to go. Especially in the Pacific.

In early February of 1943 the fight for Guadalcanal was over. But it had taken six months of tough, sharp, bloody fighting. The next step, New Georgia, required all of July and most of August. And it was not a major base. At this rate, moving up the Solomons to Bougainville, Rabaul in New Britain, Truk, Borneo, Sumatra, the Philippines, attacking each strong point frontally and in detail, the war could take twenty years. Thus a principle was established in the Pacific war: bypass the strong points, build your own airfields out of the jungle, and leave the strong points to wither. Using this tactic, Halsey and his South Pacific Forces attacked Choiseul and Treasury Island, entered the back door on Bougainville, hit the Green Islands further north, attacked Emirau, northwest of Kavieng, New Ireland. Short, sharp, costly fights, each of them, which got scant publicity at home compared to Eisenhower's beginning buildup in Europe, but which gnawed away continually at the Japanese expansion.

Meanwhile, using the same tactic, MacArthur's Southwest Pacific Forces were leapfrogging up the north coast of New Guinea and the islands offshore, in the same kind of short, sharp battles. Salamaua in September '43. The marine landing at Cape Gloucester in December. The First Cavalry Division into Manus of the Admiralties on February 29, 1944. Aitape and Hollandia in April. Wakde and Sarmi in May. The island of Biak in late May. Numfoor in July. Finally, Sansapor in Vogelkop on the head of the New Guinea turkey on July 30; and MacArthur was ready to think about going back into the Philippines.

A year it had taken, from Guadalcanal to Sansapor. And how many invasions? Fifteen? Almost all of them names people in the United States never heard of, and still haven't.

Pacific Chess

Illustrations 75–78

Not many people knew the strategy of the Pacific war. Not many know now. A lot of the men who fought in the Pacific probably still don't know how the strategy worked. There was a bunch of islands out there nobody had ever heard of, and almost nobody wanted. With deep and ancient interservice rivalries further confusing the issues, and bitter personal rivalries between various commanders making things even worse, plus the vast oceanic distances to be covered, it was hard even to remember the tongue-twister names and where the islands were, or understand why they were important.

Before December 7, 1941, Japan's ambitions had already won her a sizable chunk of real estate. She had garnered or annexed Korea (1910); Formosa and the Ryukyus (Okinawa) (1895); Manchuria (1931–33); a big piece of north and central coastal China, with most of the ancient capitals (1937–38); Hainan Island (1939); French Indochina (1940–41). Moving always southward, she was taking unto herself more and more of the rich natural resources of Southeast Asia that her island nation needed.

The island empire of Southeast Asia, what is mostly Indonesia today, runs in a sort of great circle from Thailand and the Peninsula of Malaya south and east to the huge island of New Guinea (shaped like a turkey gobbler) just north of Australia, with the big island of Borneo and the Philippines group sitting in the middle like two off-center bull's-eyes. Out beyond this island ring with its various smaller seas with the romantic names (South China Sea, Sulu Sea, Celebes Sea, Java Sea), extending tiny fingers into the vast reaches of the Pacific off New Guinea, are the Bismarcks and the Solomons, Bougainville, New Georgia, Guadalcanal). It was into this area—mostly British- and Dutch-owned anyway, except for the Philippines—that Japan moved after the attack on Pearl Harbor.

Out beyond all these, lying like a great barrier across thousands of miles of open ocean, stretches a long wall of small-island groups reaching far out eastward into the Pacific toward Hawaii, and running all the way from French New Caledonia and the New Hebrides off Australia northward to the Bonin Islands (Iwo Jima) off Japan: the Gilberts, the Marshalls, the Carolines, the Marianas. Japan, taking amongst them after December 7 those she didn't already control before (such as Truk in the Carolines and Eniwetok in the Marshalls), garrisoned and began to fortify them.

It was her idea, or the idea of her strategists, to seize the atolls of this huge area, and while the United States was licking its wounds, build an impregnable defensive wall along the outer islands which, served by her powerful navy and naval air arm, would make the retaking too costly for the Allies and thus allow her time to develop, or colonize, or exploit, take your choice, the rich island lands in the center. Each far-flung coral atoll was immediately turned into a bastion of tunnels, coral rock and cement.

To get her out of there, a salient had to be driven

into this outer ring somewhere, and preferably into the inner ring. At Casablanca it was decided to strike straight across the central reach of the Pacific via the Marshalls and the Marianas to Formosa and Hong Kong, thus cutting Japan's home islands off from her new island empire and its raw materials. This plan was engineered by Navy Chief of Staff Ernest J. King, and Admiral Chester Nimitz in Honolulu was given the command. Churchill and Roosevelt approved it. But they had reckoned without the powerful personality and dramatic flair of Douglas MacArthur. MacArthur was a hero and a symbol to the Filipinos. If he was not allowed to retake the Philippines, MacArthur argued, the United States would lose enormous face across all Asia. He was persuasive enough to convince the President. The objective was changed from Formosa to the Philippines. Nobody apparently has recorded what the close-mouthed Admiral King had to say about this.

Perhaps MacArthur was right in seeing himself in the role of symbol to the Orient. In any case, while he was hedgehopping up the northern New Guinea coast, and Halsey was climbing up the ladder of the Solomons, keeping Japanese ships and troops busy, Admiral Spruance in fleet command of Central Pacific Forces for Nimitz was moving westward against the coral bastions. On November 20, 1943, the Marines went in against Makin and Tarawa atolls in the Gilberts. And for the first time American corporation war and its managerial technology showed up in the Pacific.

Nimitz had been building up and training units for this operation since July 1. (When first told by the Chiefs of Staff he could expect to invade the Marshalls, Nimitz had demurred, saying he couldn't go into the Marshalls leaving his left flank open to be hit from the Gilberts, and at his request the initial objective had been changed.) Admiral Spruance, for Operation Galvanic, as the Gilberts assault was named, had under his command no fewer than 139 vessels. These included

22 troop transports carrying the Second Marine and Twenty-seventh Army Infantry Divisions. The Assault Force, in addition to 7 battleships, 8 cruisers, and 34 destroyers, carried 8 escort carriers with 218 aircraft. The Covering Force, Task Force Fifty, had 5 new battleships and 11 carriers with over 850 aircraft.

This was the first serious display of the "new" American strength in the Pacific. And air power, land-based or carrier-based, was the key. If Japan's best strategists understood this (Hitler apparently never did understand it) there still wasn't much they could do about it after mid-1943. She did not have the designers or land space, the worker force, the industrial potential to replace and expand her aircraft and her carriers on a level that could match the United States. Japan was, after all, a small nation. Her initial successes up to December 7, 1941, were due to the fact that she was developed *industrially* only in comparison to her neighbors.

And the new American might was an impressive display. All of it had come right off the homeland assembly lines. In 1943 alone the war effort at home had brought into service: 2 fast battleships; 6 fleet aircraft-carriers; 9 light aircraft-carriers; 24 escort carriers; 4 heavy cruisers; 7 light cruisers; 128 destroyers; 200 submarines. Just about all of it earmarked for the Pacific. If the Japanese naval staff could have seen the list, they would have shuddered. It was a far cry from Guadalcanal, and all I can think of is how insignificant and small a single infantry private must have felt, standing at the rail of one of those 22 transports.

On January 31 and February 17, 1944, Kwajalein and Eniwetok in the Marshalls were invaded and taken also. And that summer Spruance's Central Pacific Forces, even more strongly reinforced than at Tarawa (535 ships; 127,000 men), were ready to hit Saipan on June 15; Guam on July 21, and Tinian on July 24.

In addition, on June 19–20 in the Battle of the Philippine Sea off Saipan, Spruance's Fifth Fleet effectively ruined the Japanese naval air arm by sinking two of her great fleet carriers, *Shokaku* and *Taiho,* and shooting down or sinking all but 35 of the 473 planes of Admiral Ozawa's First Mobile Fleet.

All of these feats received but scant attention back home in the press, because of Dwight Eisenhower's June 6 Normandy landings.

In such an ironically appropriate way did the end of the "forgotten year" in the Pacific come to its close.

TARAWA, SAIPAN, PELELIU

Illustrations 79–82

Peleliu did not come until mid-September, but I include it here because it was part of the same Central Pacific thrust to set up the Philippine invasion and because these three battles came to symbolize the brutal ferocity of the later Pacific island war. In each case they were the most heavily fortified islands of a particular island group, others of which fell to American invasion much more easily, sometimes with no casualties at all. Probably nothing equaled them for prolonged intensity of fire and of fighting, and for the American casualties they exacted, which were staggering.

On our side, the marines bore the brunt of this. At Tarawa, perhaps the most intensely costly for the amount of time involved, in four days of fighting the Second Marine Division (Guadalcanal veterans) lost 1,069 killed and 2,391 wounded. Only 17 of the 4,500-man Japanese garrison survived to be captured, and they were badly wounded. The offshore shelling and pre-invasion aerial bombardment had failed to do much damage to the Japanese in the concrete bunkers.

Because of tricky tides, the landing craft hung up on the outer reef and the men had to wade in across half a mile of shallow reef in the face of heavy fire. Once ashore, marines had to flush the Japanese out of their beautifully constructed bunkers and pillboxes individually, with flame-throwers and grenades, step by step, pillbox by pillbox. To move on one bunker brought the moving men under fire from other bunkers nearby in intricately crossed lanes of fire.

If there are special battle streamers on the appropriate marine colors for these battles (and I'm sure there are), they should be in gold.

With the Japanese at last on a diminishing defensive, and the American war machine at last reaching the peak of its mass-war dehumanizing industrial production, there was a head-on confrontation between these two broad map-arrows of twentieth-century attack and seventeenth-century fanatical defense; and the men on both sides who met at the tiny area where the arrow points touched, went up in a blaze of horror.

At Tarawa by sheer weight we had it won from the beginning, with an armada of 139 ships and 18,000 marines, against 4,500 Japanese on a coral atoll, most of whom were on one islet ten feet above sea level, two and a half miles long and less than half a mile wide. But we had it won only if our men had the stomach for the kind of costly fighting they were required to do (largely because of mistakes made in planning), and certainly our men had it.

And what of the Japanese? For the first time they were committed to fighting a truly defensive war, which was a kind of war they had been taught to hate and consider demeaning, and which they had been ill-prepared to fight. They had been heavily propagandized about the torture they could expect from the American "barbarians." Their extravagant Emperor-worship, so strange to encounter in the twentieth century, so out of all reasonable proportion (after all, the Emperor was flesh and blood, only another man like themselves, could they not see that?) was a further inducement to die. Kindness to prisoners had no place in their code of manhood, and they did not expect it from others. They were urged on not only by their traditional death-in-battle national hunger, and their special Oriental fatalism. For the officer caste at least, and obviously for many of the men, surrendering or being captured was abject cowardice, as unmanning and humiliating as cuckoldry or castration. They preferred to stab themselves ceremonially with their swords, or shoot themselves in the head, or hold a hand grenade against their bellies.

Besides, they usually had specific orders to fight to the death. Especially in Saipan and Peleliu, which were considered home islands. So they did, and in droves, taking as many of our people with them as they could. The small numbers of prisoners were astonishing by Western standards. It is almost certainly a fact that the suicidal nature of Jap fighting, and their mass banzai charges, aided us and hastened the fall of many of their island bastions.

I don't want to go into some layman's speculation on Japanese psychology. Historically, at the beginning of World War II they were a still-feudal nation, yanked bodily into industrialized mid-twentieth century out of their own private latter-day Middle Ages. Only a slight knowledge of modern Japanese literature shows their ritualistic preoccupation with blood, and various blood-lettings by knife and sword, and death-honor. It is a kind of joyous national sadomasochism which borders on a sensual despair in defeat and is fascinating to get into. A fairly close reading of the works and biography of their modern novelist Yukio Mishima, who committed suicide by ritual *seppuku* (hara-kiri) in 1970, bears this obsession out. In our own way, we Americans have our own tradition of and private obsession with blood and violence and manhood, which somewhere way down deep in us ought to make us at least intuitively understand the Japanese obsession. Certainly sexuality and sexual taboos and myths are bound up with and tied into both obsessions. And although we

69.
Jungle bivouac *on Bougainville was no great place to rest.*

70.
Action in the South Pacific *shows a small mortar crew (above) and a rifle company (below) assaulting Japanese positions.*

71.
Jungle trail *in Bougainville provided rough going.*

72.
Nightwork *sees a marine crew manning a 155 mm aimed at the Japanese on Bougainville.*

73.
Jungle rot *sometimes had to be treated by a buddy when medics were unavailable.*

74.
Beachhead *at Rendova in the Solomon Islands depicts American forces now moving with more confidence against the Japanese.*

75.
Flight deck *was drawn by Robert Greenhalgh, who was fascinated with the action aboard a carrier in combat.*

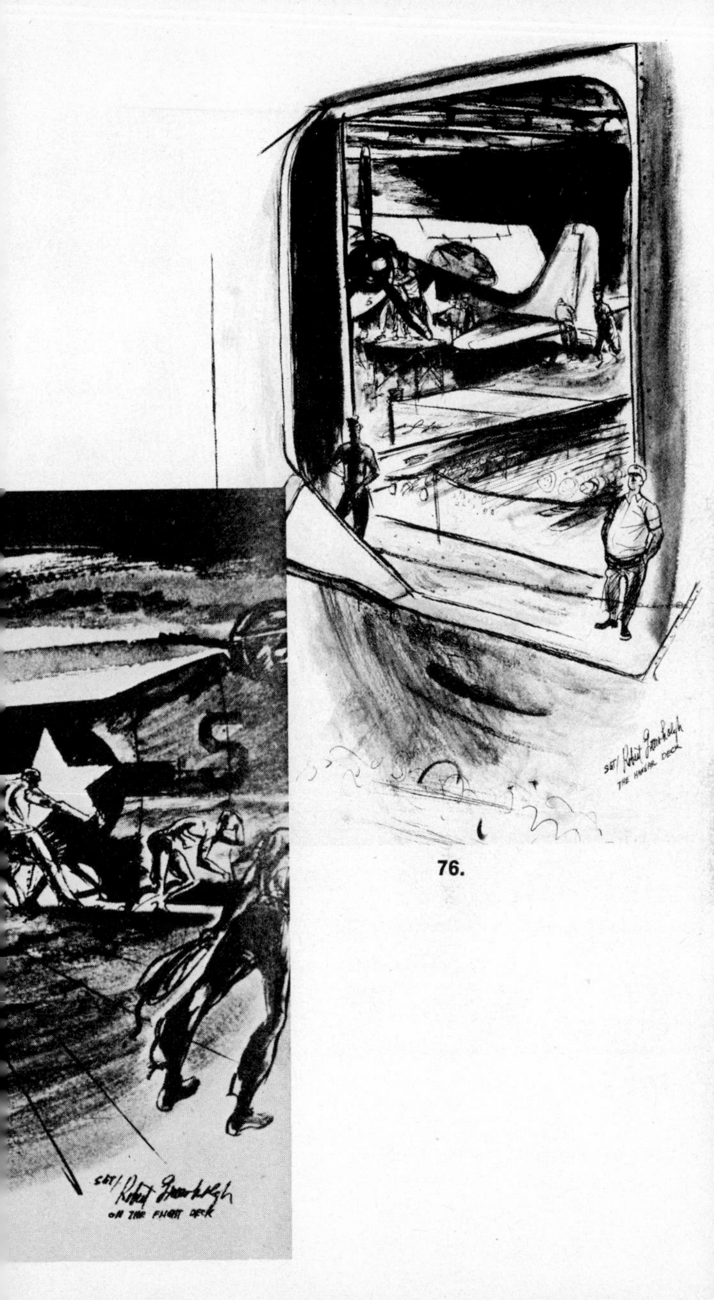

SGT/ Robert Greenhalgh
THE HANGAR DECK
SGT/ Robert Greenhalgh
ON THE FLIGHT DECK

Irkutsk
RUSSIA
Manchouli
Ulan Bator Khoto
MANCHURIA
MONGOLIA
Mukden
Sea of Japan
Peiping
Tientsin
KOREA
Pusan
Yellow Sea
CHINA
Osaka
Nanking
Shanghai
East China Sea
Hangchow
NEPAL
BHUTAN
Myitkyina
Foochow
OKINAWA
INDIA
Amoy
FORMOSA (TAIWAN)
BURMA
Canton
Hong Kong
Chittagong
Mandalay
Prome
Rangoon
South China Sea
LUZON
Philippine Sea
THAILAND
Manila
Bangkok
FR. INDOCHINA
Bengal Sea
PHILIPPINES
Phnom-Penh
Saigon
YAP
MINDANAO
PALAU IS.
N. BORNEO
MALAYA
Singapore
SARAWAK
SUMATRA
BORNEO
NETHERLANDS EAST INDIES
CELEBES
INDIAN OCEAN
Batavia
Java Sea
JAVA

77.

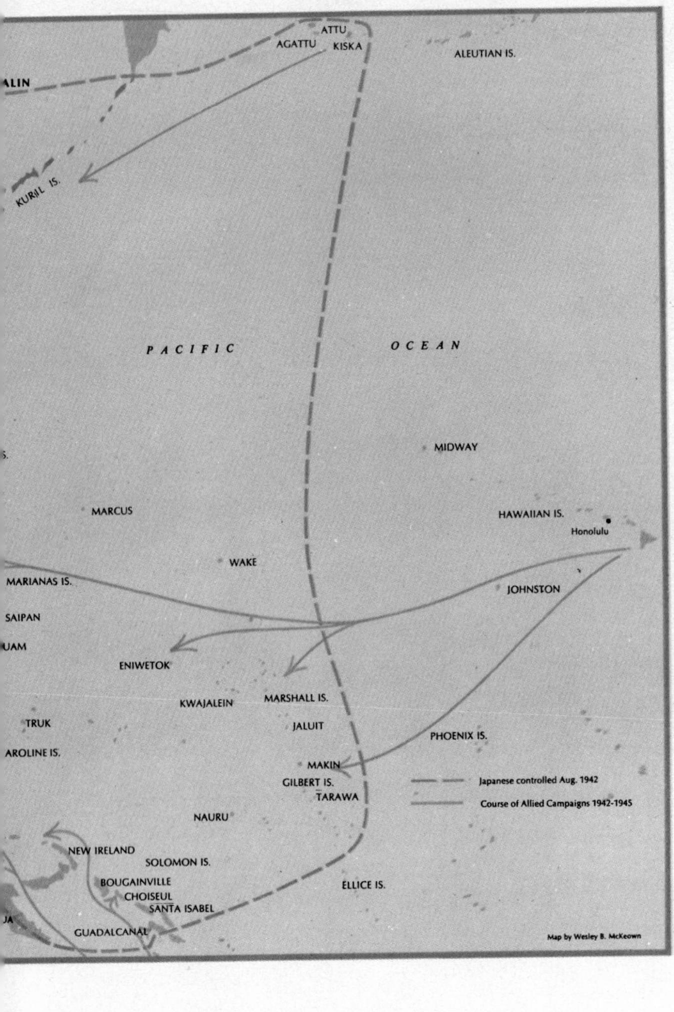
ATTU
AGATTU
KISKA
ALEUTIAN IS.
ALIN
KURIL IS.
PACIFIC
OCEAN
MIDWAY
MARCUS
HAWAIIAN IS.
Honolulu
WAKE
MARIANAS IS.
JOHNSTON
SAIPAN
UAM
ENIWETOK
KWAJALEIN
MARSHALL IS.
TRUK
JALUIT
PHOENIX IS.
AROLINE IS.
MAKIN
GILBERT IS.
TARAWA
Japanese controlled Aug. 1942
Course of Allied Campaigns 1942-1945
NAURU
NEW IRELAND
SOLOMON IS.
BOUGAINVILLE
CHOISEUL
SANTA ISABEL
ELLICE IS.
GUADALCANAL
Map by Wesley B. McKeown

78.
A kamikaze *or suicide unit of the Japanese Air Force, also known as a banda unit, attacks the U.S. fleet off the Philippines in this painting by a Japanese artist.*

79.
Right:
Fighting on Tarawa *left little room to hide for desperate men.*

80.
It was a long walk in *for later waves of men under fire.*

81.
Moving Forward *is a dramatic charcoal by Kerr Eby, showing the marines on Tarawa.*

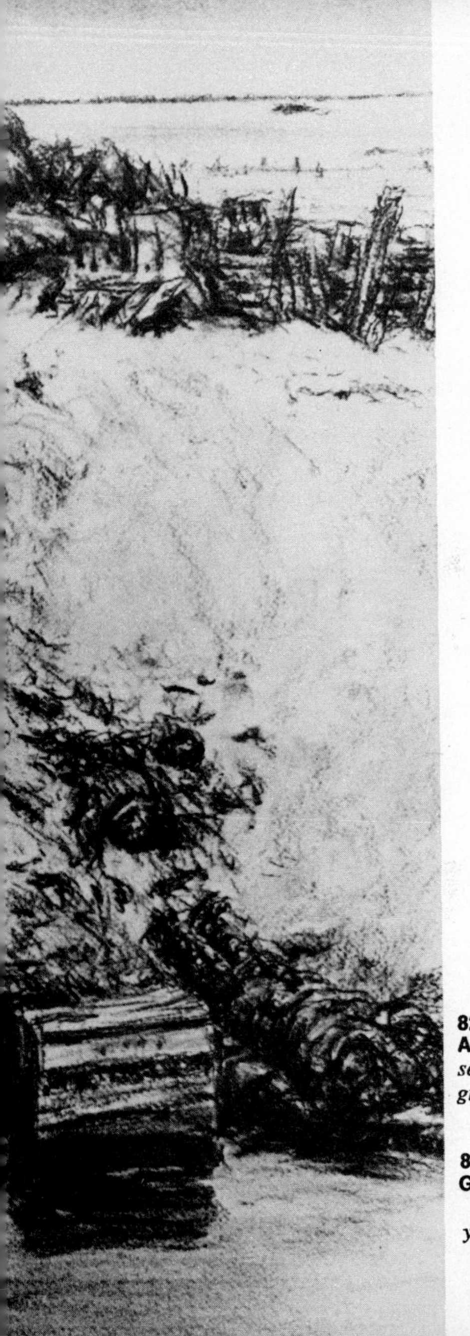

82.
After the battle *a lone sentry remains on guard.*

83. *Following page:* **Going In.** *The second time, or the third, you had evolved into a soldier.*

84.
Two-Thousand-Yard Stare *the marines called it. The look of the man who no longer cares.*

85.
The Price, *a painting of Peleliu. The action had deeply affected the work of artist Tom Lea.*

86.
In WW I *they called it shell shock. Then they called it combat fatigue. You had to grab them quickly.*

87.
Down the Net. *Even in a calm sea it was easy to slip and break your back on a barge gunnel.*

88.
Protection for the wounded *was often minimal or nonexistent.*

89.
Direct hit *wiped out the crew of this amphibious tractor hit on the beach by a mortar.*

90.
Ebb tide, *when the sea went back out over the reef, left these men at Tarawa. Kerr Eby, a veteran of two wars, said "This is the most frightful thing I have seen."*

91.
Crosses and stars *in row upon row mark the resting places of thousands of G.I.'s who fell in combat.*

92.
Purple Heart Valley *was aptly named, for it lay just beyond the Rapido River. The crossing of that river was one of the most difficult episodes of the Italian campaign.*

93.
Cassino landscape *was scarred for weeks by the fierce and unrelenting action, between Americans and Germans in Italy.*

94.
The Abbey of Monte Cassino *was one of those objectives commanders say must be taken "at all costs."*

95.
"You'll get over it, Joe. Once I wuz gonna write a book exposin' the army after th' war myself."

96.
"I feel like a fugitive from th' law of averages."

97.
"Don't startle 'im, Joe. It's almost full."

98.

Action in Italy *in views shown here as Americans and British fought their way up the boot and backed the Germans against the mountains in the north.*

99.

try to put ours in the closet and lock the door, it certainly helped us in our war with the Japanese. But this is something the Japanese never understood about us.

On the other hand, the United States has never been a nation to accept avoidable losses, as the Japanese seem to have been. The mistakes made at Tarawa were not made again. When Spruance's forces went into Kwajalein, in the Marshalls, in February of 1944, they began with heavy bombing; before any troops went ashore, the navy threw in fifteen thousand tons of shells. Sufficient amphtracks (the amphibious tracked vehicles for getting over shallow reefs) were provided for assault waves. And the American losses at Kwajalein were only a third of the losses of Tarawa, although Kwajalein was held by nearly twice as many Japanese. The Japanese dead on Kwajalein counted 7,870.

Saipan and Peleliu were a different proposition. Saipan was no coral atoll but a real island, with mountains and limestone cave formations. And it had been under Japanese domination long enough to be thought of as a home island. Every foot of ground was contested furiously. In the first day on shore alone, after suffering heavy fire crossing the reef, the two marine divisions making the assault sustained two thousand casualties. By July 9, a little more than three weeks later, when the island was finally declared secured, the American losses in army and marine killed and wounded were 16,525, of whom 12,934 were marines. On July 6 the Japanese commander General Saito issued his last order, an attack order, ate a farewell dinner and cut open his stomach with his family sword. His adjutant then shot him in the head. Vice-Admiral Nagumo, who had fought and lost at Midway and was in command of naval detachments on Saipan, shot himself. Each Japanese soldier was ordered to kill seven Americans in exchange for his own one life. And on July 7 some 2,500 Japanese troops launched a final banzai charge against the U.S.

Twenty-seventh Infantry Division. Of the 29,000 Japanese defenders, less than 1,000 were taken alive. Half the Japanese civilian population, with the remainder of the defenders, crowded onto Marpi Point, the northernmost tip of the island; urged on by the soldiers, the civilian men and women hurled their children over the two-hundred-foot cliff and then jumped themselves. The soldiers followed them or blew themselves up with hand grenades.

For the victors, the surviving marines and infantry, their prize—the prospect of invading Tinian just across the Saipan Channel, and Guam, the former United States possession, farther south—lay immediately ahead.

Peleliu in the Palaus, farther south and closer still to the Philippine objective, was hit September 15, 1944. This time it was the First Marine Division, veterans of Guadalcanal and Cape Gloucester. This brutal, difficult battle lasted into November. It was November 25 before the last pockets were cleaned out, though the island was declared secure in mid-October. The United States had absorbed more heavy losses: two thousand dead, and over eighty-five hundred wounded, when another Japanese suicide garrison holed up in caves along a massif named "Bloody Nose Ridge" by the Americans. Over eleven thousand Japanese were killed.

And now, for everybody, the big invasion of the Philippines lay ahead. The way was finally open.

I did not intend to get into a sterile, statistical casualty-counting, here. That never means anything. Unless a reader is willing to stop, and think seriously of the numbers. It is so easy to talk or write (or read) about the bravery of other men, and about their slow, halting movements across hundreds of yards of rough, waist-deep reefs under decimating fire. When you've had your own ass shot off once or twice doing a lot less, it is impossible to think of them with anything less than near-total admiration.

Painting It

Illustrations 83–90

Two artists in particular recorded the later Pacific island war and its ferocity. Tom Lea, working for the *Life* Collection, made the landings in Peleliu and did a remarkably graphic series of oils on canvas which showed what it was like there. Kerr Eby, working for the Abbott Laboratories, was present at a number of marine battles in the Pacific, and observed the invasion of Tarawa, and sketched a long series of charcoals on paper which perhaps more than any other captured what it was like to fight in the Pacific jungles and atolls.

As has been said, all war art must be by definition propaganda. But it is remarkable that these two men, working in such different styles, both seem to have at least for a while transcended the "propaganda" they were hired to paint, and taken unto themselves something of the feeling of the men who had to do the fighting.

Lea was one of the artists put in the field by *Life* after their takeover of the defunct army program.

Various of his works appeared in the magazine, and up until the time he went into Peleliu, most of them could be pretty well classified as excellently done but high-grade propaganda. There was very little American blood, very little tension, very little horror. Mostly, it was what could be called the *Bravo America!* and *This Is Your Boy* type of war art. His almost photographic style easily lent itself to that type of work, as did the styles of Rockwell and others.

But something apparently happened to Lea after going into Peleliu. The pictures painted out of his Peleliu experience show a new approach. There is the tension of terror in the bodies here, and the distorted facial expressions of the men under fire show it, too. If his propagandistic style has not changed, his subject matter certainly has.

One of the most famous, of course, is the *Two-Thousand-Yard Stare* portrait of a young marine who has had all, or more than, he can take. The staring eyes, the slack lips, the sleepwalker's stance. I've seen men with that look on their faces. I've had it on my own face. It feels stiff, and the muscles don't want to work right when you try to smile, or show expression, or talk. Mercifully, you're out of it for a while; *un*mercifully, down in the center of that numbness, though, you know you will have to come back, eventually. But until you have to you're pleased not to think much. Strangely enough, the marine in the portrait would be quick as a cat if a mortar round came shu-shu-ing in, or a fight developed there in back of him. His trained instincts by now are something he can depend on, and have been developed over a long period of combat fighting. The only thing not dependable is whether, if he has bad luck, they will still save him. And he knows that, too. I'm sure the men in Europe wore the same face.

The most moving of Lea's series, for me, is *Going In*. If you discount the propaganda elements for "middle America"—the cute cowlick, the boyish hair over the eyes, the too-handsome face—there is a quality on the face of this boy that about says it all. It's a tough face; hard, determined, knowledgeable. He is no replacement; he's been there before, back down the line: Guadalcanal, Cape Gloucester, somewhere. But (if the photographic reproduction is good enough) there is more. It is one of those paintings where the facial expression seems to change. One moment he seems to be glaring, the next moment he appears about to weep. There is genuine fear, deep in the eyes, and there is regret and reluctance in the lines around the nose and mouth. A resolute reluctance, though. The quiescent hands seem to be feeling and lightly touching the steel side as if to assure themselves of a reality, and of an awareness that soon these fingertips might not be there to touch anything.

But the capper of Lea's series is the one called *The Price*. It is a painting I have never seen reproduced anywhere except in the army files. No one else I asked had ever seen it. It is a painting at once so bitter and so unreal that it tends to turn into an abstraction, a fantasy. For example, the falling marine (or soldier) does not seem to be so wounded anywhere on his person as to cause the amount of blood which is flowing from him and which dominates the picture. The face is bleeding, but could not cause such blood flow. The shoulder and arm do not appear to be mangled, but even if they were, could not have caused the blood on the face. It is as if Lea, with one sudden unthought-out spastic gesture, recorded in one swiftly done canvas a distillation of all the death and horror he had seen and been bitterly unable to digest. Unreal or not, it is a monument to the blood and death that all of us, even those who have been there, prefer not to see or think about when we are away from it.

Kerr Eby works in a quieter way. But his drawings, with their brooding greens and ominous yellows, have an effect just as powerful. The men, powerfully built but fatigued to the very bone, do not seem to be individual men so much as faceless appendages of some greater organism which moves and manipulates them. Grimy anonymous helmets almost always hide their faces. When the faces do show, they are twisted grotesque masks, as on the wounded, or the face of the man who has flipped his lid in the drawing entitled *Shell Shock*. But for the rest, they are nameless and anonymous; truly anonymous; numb, stumbling, but determined one-man units of a fatiguing horror so powerful, so all-engulfing, that the original reason for it all seems lost somewhere in some ancient antiquity. The green gloom of the jungle looms and lingers over them with a dim cathedral-like intensity, as helmeted and faceless they slog by with hunched shoulders, past jeeploads of wounded coming out and being given transfusions—always transfusions, in the mud, in holes, on the beaches.

In the one called *Down the Net—Tarawa,* Eby's marines come flowing over the side in a stream of anonymous helmets and packs and legs, their backs always to us, so alike as to be indistinguishable. Yet the viewer never forgets each is an individual, vulnerable man. In the one called *March Macabre,* again they are anonymous as they haul a wounded buddy over the coconut-log sea wall for protection. In the one entitled *Grapes of Wrath* they are anonymous in death. Eby says of it: "I make no apology for drawings such as this. The official designation of my job was activities of the marines and dying terribly and magnificently is one of those activities. This is the inside of an amphibious tractor that was hit by a Jap mortar on the beach at Tarawa." In the one called *Ebb Tide—Tarawa* they have ceased even to be anonymous dead, and have become a pair of hands, a pair of boots, an ass, a floating thigh. Eby said of this one, "The attack was at flood tide and when the sea went out over the reef this and much besides was left. In two wars, this I think is the most frightful thing I have seen. Perhaps because of its isolation on the reef." Perhaps also it was because the sea in its inexorable flow knows no kindred and no friends. Only anonymity, the true anonymity only the sea bestows.

Eby was born in 1889, in Japan in fact, where his father was a Methodist minister. In World War I he served as a sergeant in the Fortieth Engineers in France, and his sketches made there formed the basis for his book *War,* published by Yale University Press in 1936. In 1943 he was accredited for Abbott Laboratories, and went in with the marines at Tarawa. For the next four months he followed the fighting in the Pacific, sketching the scenes for his later drawings. He returned to the United States in March, 1944. He died in 1946.

Anonymity

Illustration 91

In writing about the work of Kerr Eby, I found myself using the words anonymous and anonymity over and over, in describing his paintings. And I think that same anonymity is one of the last big obstacles the EVOLUTION OF A SOLDIER has to encounter and step over. To accept anonymity, along with all the rest he has to accept, is perhaps the toughest step of all for the combat soldier.

Anonymity has always been a problem of soldiers. It is one of the hardest things about a soldier's life. Old-time regular soldiers (like Negroes, women and other slaves through history) learn ways to cherish their servitude and ingest it and turn it into nourishment for power over the very establishment figures who administer it for the establishment which creates it. The old-timer first sergeant is analogous to the Negro mammy slave who ran the master's big plantation house and family with a hand of iron, or the modern housewife who carefully rules her lord and master's life with dexterity from behind the scenes.

But to do that the soldier, like the slave and the

housewife, must first learn duplicity. He must immerse himself in and accept wholeheartedly the camouflage position of his servitude—in his case, the unnamed, anonymous rank and file of identical uniforms stretching away into infinity, all of them sporting identical headgear (caps or helmets) to hide the individual faces, which themselves, even, must remain forever fixed and set in expressionless expressions to match all the other expressions. He must work within the mass of anonymity to find his freedom of expression, and this is probably the hardest thing of all for the wartime civilian soldiers to pick up and learn. Most never did learn it.

But to accept anonymity in death is even harder. It is hard enough to accept dying. But to accept dying unknown and unsung except in some mass accolade, with no one to know the particulars how and when except in some mass communiqué, to be buried in some foreign land like a sack of rotten evil-smelling potatoes in a tin box for possible later disinterment and shipment home, requires a kind of bravery and acceptance so unspeakable that nobody has ever given a particular name to it.

Of course the catch is always there: you may live through it. But the drain on the psyche just contemplating it is so great that forever after—or at least for a very long time—you are a different person just from having contemplated it.

I don't think I ever learned this one of the last steps in the EVOLUTION OF A SOLDIER, and I think it was just there that my EVOLUTION OF A SOLDIER stopped short of the full development. I remember lying on my belly more than once, and looking at the other sweating faces all around me and wondering which of us lying there who died that week would ever be remembered in the particulars of his death by any of the others who survived. And of course nobody else would know, or much care. I simply did not want to die and not be remembered for it. Or not be remembered at all.

I think it was then I learned that the idea of the Unknown Soldier was a con job and did not work. Not for the dead. It worked for the living. Like funerals, it was a ceremony of ritual obeisance made by the living for the living, to ease their pains, guilts and superstitious fears. But not for the dead, because the Unknown Soldier wasn't them, he was only one.

I once served on a Grave Registration detail on Guadalcanal, after the fighting was all over, to go up in the hills and dig up the bodies of the dead lost in some attack. The dead were from another regiment, so men from my outfit were picked to dig them up. That was how awful the detail was. And they did not want to make it worse by having men dig up the dead of their own. Unfortunately, a man in my outfit on the detail had a brother in the other outfit, and we dug up the man's brother that day.

It was a pretty awful scene. In any case. Even without the man's brother. The GRC lieutenant in charge had us get shovels out of the back of one of the trucks, and pointed out the area we were to cover, and explained to us how we were to take one dogtag off them before we put them in the bags. He explained that some of the bodies were pretty ripe because the fight had been two weeks before. When we began to dig, each time we opened a hole a little explosion of smell would burst up out of it, until finally the whole saddle where we were working was covered with it up to about knee deep. Above the knees it wasn't so bad, but when you had to bend down to search for the dogtag (we took turns doing this job) it was like diving down into another element, like water, or glue. We found about four bodies without dogtags that day.

"What will happen to those, sir?" I asked the lieutenant. Although he must have done this job before, he had a tight, screwed-up look of distaste on his face.

"They will remain anonymous," he said.

"What about the ones with dogtags?" I asked.

"Well," he said, "they will be recorded."

ITALY

Illustrations 92–94

It was in Italy that war art and the war artist first began to come into their own. Paintings and drawings by men like Edward Reep and Tom Craig, working for the *Life* Collection, began to appear with some regularity and were looked forward to by readers.

A lot of military writers have stated flatly that the Italian campaign of 1944–45 was a serious strategic blunder. To keep driving up the narrow mountainous peninsula where geography worked on the side of defense and hampered armored ground advance seemed folly to many, even at the time. Over and over you hear of commanders complaining because after pulverizing the German defenses with artillery, they could not advance fast enough to exploit the gain due to roads choked with rubble of their own making. As a result, inevitably, old-time foot-slogging infantry warfare came back into vogue in a way it had never done across the flat dry spaces of North Africa.

The argument was that the painful, costly Italian drive pinned down German divisions that could have been used elsewhere in Europe. A lot of modern military writers disagree. Had the Allies stopped at the "Gustav Line," and been content to hold the river line from the Garigliano across to the Sangro on the other coast (a line they reached in January, 1944), they would have retained the vital air bases in the south for attacking inner Germany, gained the port of Naples, and such a strategy would have forced the Germans to keep large troop concentrations in Italy, anyway.

But the Allies didn't. They decided to push on. How much the political expediency decision to take Rome influenced the overall decision is hard to say, but it counted. Had they held up, Anzio wouldn't have happened, the battle of Cassino might not have happened, and Mark Clark's Fifth Army (British and American) on the western coast would not have had to inch their way toward Rome in the worst winter in Italy in decades, leaving a broadening trail of dead, wounded and trench foot cases behind them, evidence of their toughness.

The Salerno landings took place on September 9, 1943. The Allies met with stiff resistance immediately, and between September 12 and 15 a devastating German counterattack very nearly threw them out again. On October 1, Naples fell, undefended. On October 13, the Fifth Army advanced across the Volturno River. Throughout November and December in the winter rain they worked their way yard by yard, hill by hill, every hilltop village a major battle almost, northward toward the objective. It was the middle of January, 1944, before they arrived in front of Cassino, and the Gustav Line. They would remain there for four months, until the middle of May, before they would break through. In the mud and rain and cold and trench foot. It was a winter of gross discontent in Italy, as well as in the Pacific. More and more, for everybody, the war was becoming a permanent way of life, a condition that would just go on and on and on, for Americans now as well as Europeans.

After Naples, the British General Sir Harold Alexander's Fifteenth Army Group contained *two* armies, Clark's Fifth in the west of Italy and Montgomery's Eighth in the east. Each army was composed of two corps of three divisions each. And during the rest of 1943 more units were brought in as reinforcements, and the staff of the U.S. II Corps arrived to begin taking over for the VI so that the U.S. VI Corps could be withdrawn to make the Anzio landings.

Before Cassino in January, Clark's Fifth Army had fifty-four battalions. And Alexander's armies included divisions of Americans, British, Canadians, French, New Zealanders, South Africans, Poles, Indians, Moroccans, Algerians, units of Senegalese, Brazilians, Greeks, a brigade of Palestinian Jews, and a handful of royalist Italians. The day of the big war, administrative, managerial, depersonalized, industrialized and mechanized, had arrived in earnest.

A more horrible place would have been hard to imagine. The mud stuck like glue in the middle of the day, and was hard as iron at night. Cold wind and snow scourged the upper mountain slopes. Dead American bodies lay and froze in the valley the Americans had named Purple Heart Valley, their throats eaten out by packs of wild dogs.

The town of Cassino was hit again and again by Allied guns and aircraft. One raid was supposed to have used more planes than had ever yet been used in any single operation. Yet when Allied patrols tried to fight their way into Cassino, they were driven back by the sturdy, still solid German First Parachute Division.

And it would not stop here, and it would not stop when finally they got to Rome—two days before Eisenhower's D-Day invasion.

About the most apt, and pathetic, comment I've seen on the Italian campaign I take verbatim from a World War II encyclopedia: "On December 24th (1943) Generals Eisenhower, Montgomery and Spaatz flew to London and the Italian theater of operations was relegated to the background."

A lot of men had died and would yet die to achieve and maintain that "background" position. And up until D-Day, Cassino and Monte Cassino behind it were about the most painted subjects of the war by artist-correspondents.

More on Humor: Mauldin

Illustrations 95–97

Any mention of the Italian theater calls to mind at once the figure of Bill Mauldin. I guess no book on World War II graphics could go out without a special place in it reserved for him.

There was a lot of jealousy about Mauldin out in the Pacific because he only drew and worked for the European soldier. We wanted a share. Out there we didn't get *Stars and Stripes* (which was strictly a European paper) except only very occasionally, as when some air force planes fresh from Europe would put down near you. But since he drew and wrote mainly about mud and infantry and about the misuse of privilege by officers and noncoms and rear echelon types, we felt he was also drawing and writing about us as well. Mud was the same everywhere. So was the abuse of privilege. Our jungle rot was the equivalent of their trench foot. But we didn't have much in the way of female civilian populations, or wine cellars.

But we did have "raisin jack," or what we guys from Honolulu called "swipe," which was a Hawaiian word for bootleg liquor. Mauldin did a lot of cartoons about booze—cognac, Chianti, schnapps, vino, and wine—and, although later he made a sort of mild apologia for it in his book, in general he endorsed it. I am glad, because at least in my outfit we got blind asshole drunk every chance we got. About the only real genuine liquor we ever got hold of was when some plane flew up with some general from Australia, and the crew might sell us an English imperial quart of scotch for fifty dollars, or an especially good souvenir. So mainly we had to make our own. We made our "swipe" by stealing a five-gallon tin of canned peaches or plums or pineapple from the nearest ration dump, and putting a double handful of sugar in it to help it ferment, and then leaving it out in the sun in the jungle with a piece of cheesecloth or mosquito netting over it to keep out the bugs.

It was the most godawful stuff to drink, sickly sweet and smelling very raunchy, but if you could get enough of it down and keep it down, it carried a wonderful wallop. The worst, most terribly awful bar-none hangover I ever had in my life before or after, I got from one of these late night "swipe" parties where I passed out, to wake up lying in the mud in full tropical sunlight in the coconut groves not far from our tents. I think it was that same night that the tough little Southerner I eventually drew Witt from in *The Thin Red Line* came staggering up drunk to the ears, and declaimed in a loud command voice that we had all heard him promise that if he ever got out of our last fight up on the line alive, he would crawl on his belly like a hound dog and bay at the moon. Well, he was goin' to keep his promise, he said. In front of all of us other "swipe" drinkers he proceeded to get down in his clean uniform in the mud and wriggle along through it like a man hunting a hole under fire, throwing back his head and stretching his neck and baying like a hound at the big full tropical moon above the cocopalms, until finally an officer in a tent nearby sent a sentry over to tell us to stop the racket.

I think that the great thing Mauldin did was to show people over and over again that it was not only the danger of war that slowly did men in. It was perhaps even more that long haul of day after day of monotony and discomfort and living in perpetual dirt in the field, on and on with no prospect of release and no amenities. Without women, without tablecloths, without a decent bathroom.

As he himself says somewhere in *Up Front:* "The endless marches that carry you on and on and yet never seem to get you anyplace—the automatic drag of one foot as it places itself in front of the other without any prompting from your dulled brain, and the unutterable relief as you sink down for a ten-minute break, spoiled by the knowledge that you'll have to get up and go again—the never-ending monotony of days and weeks and months and years of bad weather and wet clothes and no mail—all this sends as many men into the psychopathic wards as does battle fatigue."

Somehow or other down the years, I've never met Bill Mauldin. I think I talked to him once, over the phone, long distance, about some mutual project or other that never came off. I hope this time, what with all the various spadework to be done compiling this book, we'll be able to sit down, in some nice quiet dimly lit old-infantryman's dream of a bar somewhere and have a belt together.

Here are some of my Mauldin favorites.

ANZIO

Illustrations 98–103

It was Winston Churchill's baby. He had fought hard for it, and was determined to have it. History will never know whether—if it hadn't been so woefully mishandled—it would have worked.

Churchill wanted a quick-hitting invasion, and a fast breakout toward Rome by the initial shock troops, to be followed by reinforcements brought in in the succeeding waves. Unquestionably this was one of those gambles. But British Intelligence had information that the German reserves near Rome had been depleted to reinforce the Gustav Line. A swift strike taking Rome, with the Italian people already in the right mood and on the Allies' side, would force Field Marshal Kesselring, outflanked, to abandon the so-hard-to-crack Gustav Line of his own volition.

But Churchill's strategy depended upon a swift breakout and a fast attack on Rome, and that was just what he did not get. The American commanders had little faith in the "former naval person's" amateur strategy. Most British and many American writers point the finger at Mark Clark for this. Clark (who, as the custom went in America, had reached high enough status with his Fifth Army command to be spoken of familiarly by the great U.S. public) wanted to be cautious at Anzio. He still remembered his own bad experience at Salerno. He expected heavy resistance at the beachhead, and not only did he choose a cautious, worn-down commander in the person of General Lucas of VI Corps, he even went so far as to warn Lucas, "Don't stick your neck out," as he himself had done at Salerno.

Lucas didn't. He waited an entire week, spending it in meticulously consolidating and improving his beachhead defenses, before sending out anything in force to probe. Almost all that time the Rome road lay wide open before him, ready for the taking. By the time he felt he was ready to move, even Clark was getting jittery. And the Germans had amassed enough divisions around the beachhead to insure that he would not break out of it.

The result of all this chess playing and fiddling around was to place five divisions of American and British troops in one of the most untenable positions and some of the worst and most vicious fighting of the entire European war. For a period of something like three and a half months.

It was one long hellish nightmare. In a pocked, surreal, destroyed, pest-inhabited landscape. In mid-February the Germans launched a massive counterattack which almost broke through to the beach. Had they had a thousand more men to invest, or even five hundred, they might have split the British and American sectors. Instead, our artillery shook them so badly and exacted such casualties that with victory in their grasp, they broke and pulled back. After that, it settled down into what was called a "lull." Some lull. There were artillery concentration attacks by day, and at night fireworks displays. Patrol and platoon fights never ceased. Always on the high ground, the Germans were often close enough to roll grenades down into the Allies' entrenchments. At night, when the darkness fell, after that awful moment of waiting that always comes at dusk in a war, the men would watch the flares go up and the soaring Verey pistol rounds, listen to the cough of mortars and the stuttering of Bren guns and Spandaus.

In the early 1960s on a trip to Italy while living in France I drove down from Rome to look at Anzio. Today what used to be minefields is completely built over with seaside villas, restaurants and bars. But it is easy for any old soldier to see the complete hellishness of the position, with the two towns, Anzio and Nettuno, dominated by the Alban hills, and no rear area at all beyond the harbor except the expanse of the open sea.

I went around to look at the American Military Cemetery afterward, which is placed off a few miles somewhere else. For a while I walked around among the crosses that formed the headstones, on the green, well-kept grass. The magnitude of all the long lines of white crosses was truly awesome. I talked to the man in charge of the caretaking a while, a red-bearded American who lived right there. No, not many people came, he said. It was too far away, and off the main tourist routes from Rome. And of course the local Italians had no reason to come there. But he liked to make sure the place was always well-kept, anyway. Sometimes it was hard, on the budget the U.S. government allotted him. But once in a while somebody might come by who had a relative buried there; or else someone like myself, who was just interested. I thanked him, and told him his caretaking was superb, which it was. What else was there to say? I got in my little car and drove back.

Going Out

Illustration 104

In March of 1943 I left Guadalcanal by ship, evacuated to the base hospital in Efate in the New Hebrides. In Efate my right ankle was operated on and I was shipped to New Zealand and from there, I shipped out home to San Francisco aboard one of the hospital ships that plied that long voyage between the United States and Australia.

In March of '43 my division was getting ready for the move up on New Georgia, and everybody who could get out was getting out. This was not so easy, however. Restrictions were being tightened up, and unless you had something pretty serious wrong with you, you didn't stand much chance. In late March we went through the required division physical examination, before starting a newer intensive assault training, and a few malaria cases and several cases of jungle rot were singled out for evacuation to New Zealand. But most of us passed the rather perfunctory exam without much notice.

Then, a few days after the physical, I turned my

right ankle again. I had had this bad ankle quite a long time, since long before Pearl Harbor. And I was used to taping it up before going out on marches, or maneuvers, or—later—up on the line. I always carried a couple of rolls of two-inch adhesive tape with me in my pack for that purpose.

The day I turned it anew, I happened to be walking through the bivouac with our old first sergeant. Old, I say; but he must have been only about thirty-four. In any case, I went down into the mud. I had turned it on one of those thick rolls of half-drying mud turned up by one of the jeeps.

"What the hell happened to you?" the old first said, when I picked myself up and tried to brush some of the wet, gooey mud off my pants. "You're white as a sheet," he added.

It always hurt a lot when I did it. But I had learned to favor the ankle, and it didn't happen very often. I tried to explain to him about the ankle.

"You're crazy," the old first sneered. "Didn't you show that leg to them up at division?"

I only shrugged. They wouldn't pay any attention to a bad ankle, I said. They'd only think I was malingering.

"You go up there and show it to them at division medical," the first said. "If it's as bad as what I just saw, it could get you out of here. If it's as bad as what I saw, you got no business in the infantry."

I just stared at him. The funny thing about it was that if I set it down carefully and absolutely straight on the ground, even after I'd turned it, I could still walk on it. It had never occurred to me it might be bad enough to get me out of there.

"If you don't, you're crazy," the old first said, and turned and walked off to his orderly tent.

I stared after his contemptuous back. He had presented me with a serious moral problem. I talked it over with a few of my buddies, and with a few of the other noncoms in the company. (I was a corporal at the time.) All of them urged me to go up to division medical with it. They would certainly go up with it if they had it, if they were me and maybe it could get them out of there. They echoed the first: I was crazy not to try. "But what about the company?" I asked the mess sergeant, and supply sergeant, and a couple of the field sergeants. "Would you leave the company?"

"Are you kidding?" the supply sergeant said. "I'd be out of here like a shot."

I was smart enough to understand that if I did go, and did get sent out, it was not going to affect anything in any appreciable way. Some poor-ass, bad-luck replacement would replace me, and one of the guys would get my corporal's rating. I understood that numbers were what counted in this war, vast numbers, of men and machines. I was intelligent enough to see that. And I had no more romantic notions about combat. On the other hand, if everybody who wanted out got out, there wouldn't be anybody left to fight the Japs, *or* the Germans. Of course, they couldn't all get out. Even if they wanted. They had to stay. The regulations were getting tougher and tougher about that. You had to have something genuinely wrong with you. Finally, I went.

The surgeon at division pursed his mouth into a silent whistle and raised his eyebrows, after he had wiggled my ankle around and bent it in to the point of almost turning it again. Certainly, I had no business in the infantry. He did not know what they would do with me further down the line, but he was sending me out. He looked up at me and grinned. I grinned back. If he could only have known how I was hanging on his every word and expression. But perhaps he did.

The head surgeon in Efate was a young man. He said he would like to have a try at operating on it, but he couldn't guarantee he could fix it completely. He could probably tie it up sufficiently so it would not turn all the way like it used to, but it would almost certainly be partially stiff. It was an interesting problem, surgically. But of course it was up to me to make the final decision. Did I know the evacuation regulations? I nodded: I did: roughly, the evacuation rules were that if your wound or ailment was such that you would be fit for duty in three weeks, you would be kept at Efate and sent back to your old outfit. If you were going to take six weeks to be fit for duty, you would be sent on to New Zealand and reassigned to a new outfit. Longer than that, and you would be sent back home to the States and reassigned there. How long would I be in the cast? I asked. At least two months, or two and a half, he answered and grinned at me. I nodded and grinned back. "Then go ahead and operate."

The next morning they wheeled me in and put the ether to me. Ten days later I was on my way to New Zealand on another hospital ship. Three weeks later, on still another, I left for the States. I remember Major James Roosevelt, the President's son, was on the same ship. I saw him once, at a distance. But I don't remember the name of that lovely ship.

When we passed under the great misty pink apparition of the Golden Gate bridge, I stood on the upper decks on my crutches and watched grizzled tough old master sergeants and chief petty officers break down and cry. I had been away three and a half years.

OVERLORD

Illustrations 105–112

As far back as January, 1942, it was being considered and worked on. Only, back then it was divided into two attack plans, which were called "Round-up" and "Sledgehammer." Round-up would be launched April 1, 1943, Sledgehammer four and one half months later on September 15, 1943.

Round-up would involve thirty American divisions and eighteen British divisions. Six divisions (reinforced by parachute *regiments* on both flanks!) would land between Le Havre and Boulogne, and strengthened by one hundred thousand men a week, would attack along a line Deauville–Paris–Soissons, the shortest route to Germany. Sledgehammer, coming so much later, would have the limited objective of taking Cherbourg and the Cotenin peninsula. Two whole long years and two months later, put together and greatly modified to fit new existing tactical conditions, the two would become OVERLORD.

With Overlord a historical reality today—a historical reality, in fact, ever since June 6, 1944—

it is weird to read of these old plans which were its ancestors. Most of the aircraft, bomber and fighter, most of the tank designs, much of the infantry weaponry, in use in June, 1944, were not even on the designers' boards back then, in 1942. All of the landing craft designs and the mother ships that carried and served them were not even in existence. The war of June 1944, was not even the same war as the war of April 1, 1942—when General Marshall first presented the earlier plans to Roosevelt. Yet the plans in basic strategy were essentially unchanged. How many strategic planners, how many administrative staffs, how many clerical personnel groups and supply service groups, had labored over them how many man-hours since? Here was truly a managerial war.

No wonder Montgomery, Eisenhower, Bradley, Patton were pulled off their Mediterranean commands and sent to London. No wonder Italy and all its dead were suddenly and without ceremony "relegated to the background."

This was the moment half a dozen heads of major states had been waiting for and working for, since even before Pearl Harbor.

In November, 1943, at Cairo, the main outlines of Overlord were agreed on by Roosevelt and Churchill. The command structure was organized, with Eisenhower as Supreme Chief. (Roosevelt had wanted Marshall, but had been prevailed upon to keep Marshall in Washington. Marshall picked Eisenhower.) All the other great men—Leigh-Mallory and Tedder, the British Air Chief Marshals; Admirals Ramsay (British) and Kirk (American); Montgomery, Bradley and Patton, the ground commanders—were fitted to their slots. The final detailed planning, with a target date for May, began in January, 1944. In the end this target date had to be postponed a month, in order to have available for use the extra landing craft production of that month. That's how tight the squeeze was for sufficient landing craft.

By the end of May, and for some long time before,

all of southern England was one vast armed camp holding over three million five hundred thousand men of eleven nationalities. Every port and anchorage was jammed with shipping and the necessary landing craft. Every airfield and airstrip was working to full capacity. Fifty thousand men and their units had been ticked off as the spearhead forces. Two million more would follow them into France. The British Seventy-ninth Armoured Division alone had nearly one thousand vehicles to lead the assault. The month's postponement was also needed to finish work on the "Mulberries," the great artificial harbors that would be towed across, parts to be sunk, parts to be floated off the beaches.

In the whole of England civilian life had almost ceased to exist. In the spring of 1944 two million "foreign visitors" had been crowded within her shores. Close security clamps had been placed on everything. Many English girls became pregnant, but the British did not complain.

At the Teheran Conference in November, 1943, after flying off from Cairo where these momentous decisions had been made, to meet with old Joe Stalin, Ruler of All the Russias, Winston Churchill had celebrated his sixty-ninth birthday as a finale to Teheran, and with considerable honesty proudly recalled that the day was a "memorable occasion in my life. On my right sat the President of the United States, on my left the master of Russia. Together we controlled a large preponderance of the naval and three-quarters of all the air forces in the world, and could direct armies of nearly twenty millions of men."

He was so right, old Winnie. Always a man of almost boyish pride and willful enthusiasms, he does not appear to have reflected even briefly on what a frightening and obscene comment he had just made to himself.

To what a strange state had our hectic race risen in its long millennia of evolutionary process, that three such men, heroes or no, could sit together at a dining table, controlling the lives and deaths of so many of their fellow humans. And that, just across the Channel from the swarming English ports in May of 1944, a group of madmen could make an almost identical statement, if the numbers were reduced somewhat.

When I read Sir Winston's statement, I was immediately set to thinking, not so much of glory, but of the strange process by which the assault force had been chosen, and what it must have felt like. If you were a rifle private in a rifle squad.

For an old-soldier rifle private, if his division had not been chosen, what a sense of relief. But if his division had been chosen, there was still a chance. A division has three Regimental Combat Teams (as they are called now) and they could always choose one of the other two. If his RCT was chosen, still perhaps they might not choose his battalion. If his battalion was chosen, still there were three companies to pick from. His company chosen, still there were three platoons. And in his platoon, four squads. In the squad the Squad Leader would have the right (aided by the company commander, of course) to choose his point man out of the twelve. (Or was it fifteen men to a squad, by then?)

All that way, down the chain of command. All the way from Winston and FDR and Joe. All those chances not to be chosen. But *somebody* would be chosen—sure as hell. Somebody was. I wonder what he would have thought of Churchill's understandably proud, understandably vain statement? Probably he would have agreed with it. At least in public.

And in the ports of all southern England, the whole huge massive operation of the plan called Overlord was already in irreversible movement.

Hospital

Illustrations 113 and 114

In the Army General Hospital in Memphis, where I was sent from San Francisco, we had two full wards of foot and lower-leg amputations from frozen feet in the invasion of Attu in the Aleutians, where some forgetful planner had sent the troops in in leather boots. This was in full accord with the general grim air and iron-cold mood the hospital had. Men there did not laugh and smile about their wounds, as they always seemed to do in the pictures in *Yank* and the civilian magazines.

Of course, not everybody there came from overseas. The others, broken legs, broken heads, service-connected Stateside illnesses, were still in the majority. We overseas returnees comprised about one quarter of the patients in mid-1943. The percentages would rise later as the war broadened abroad. We were among the first big influx.

There was a noticeable difference between the overseas combat men and the others. The combat men were clannish, and stayed pretty much by themselves, and there was this grim sort of iron-cold silence about them, except when they were in town and had a bottle in their hand. They made everybody else uncomfortable, and did not seem to care if they did or not. Almost without exception, they were uncheerful about their wounds. Alongside them, the others seemed much younger, and very much more cheerful about everything.

I myself was somewhere in the middle of all this. I wasn't there because of a wound—but I had been wounded, and had been overseas, and so was automatically a member of the clan, and I tended to associate mentally with the overseas men, and could understand what they were feeling, because I was feeling it myself. I suppose the best way to describe it —or the kindest way to describe it—is that they felt a certain well-controlled angry irascibility because everyone but themselves took everything so much for granted.

Whenever I looked at them I was reminded of a little scene I'd witnessed the day I was hit. I had arrived at the regimental aid station with my face all covered in blood from what turned out to be a minor head wound, no doubt looking very dramatic, and the first person I saw was our old regimental surgeon with a cigar butt in his teeth, cutting strips of skin and flesh out of a wound in the back of a boy sitting on the table. I had known old Doc, at least to speak to, for at least two years and when he quit working on the other boy and examined me, he said, "Hello, Jonesie. Getting more material for that book of yours you're gonna write?"

I laughed, a little hysterically probably. "More than I want, Doc." Though he was a light colonel, we always called him Doc. When he found I had no hole in my head, only an unseparated crack, he went back to working on the boy. The wound in his back was inside and down from the shoulderblade and about the size of three silver dollars laid edge to edge, and was just a hole, a red angry wet hole, from which blood kept welling up and spilling in a red rill down his back, which Doc had to keep wiping up. That little rill of blood that wouldn't quit kept fascinating me. "How bad is he?" I asked. "He going to be all right?"

"I think so. Too soon to tell for sure. Doesn't seem to have internal bleeding," Doc said, and picked out another shred with his tweezers and cut it off with his scalpel. "But there may be some small pieces down in there." I nodded, not knowing what else to say. The boy, whom I didn't know, turned his head, favoring his bad side, and gave us both such a silent cold unforgiving look that I have never forgotten it. "There you are, son," old Doc said around his cigar butt, and patted his good shoulder. "No, don't get up. Lie down here and they'll come get you."

That look the wounded boy gave Doc and me was the same cold silent unforgiving stare the overseas men at the hospital gave to everybody who was not one of them. It was not so much that they were specifically blaming anyone for anything, as that everybody remained unforgiven. I felt the same way myself.

They had other peculiarities. For some reason I could never find the source of, none of the combat men at the hospital would ever wear their decoration ribbons or campaign ribbons when they went into town in uniform on pass. The only decoration they would allow themselves to wear, at least for the infantrymen, was the blue and silver Combat Infantryman's Badge, with the silver wreath around it. There was an awards ceremony at the hospital about every two or three weeks, and after I had been there about a month I was awarded my Purple Heart and my mysterious Bronze Star. But I never wore either of the ribbons. I knew without being told by anyone that we just didn't wear them. So instead I bought myself a Combat Infantryman's Badge (which I had not been officially awarded yet) and wore that.

Nobody ever mentioned aloud that you shouldn't wear your decorations. It was not some kind of private conspiracy. But everybody got the message just the same. As far as I know, no one ever asked if they were *not* supposed to wear their ribbons. Once a couple of men I knew, as a sort of ironic joke, started wearing the Good Conduct ribbon—a decoration which just about every man in the army received who had not been convicted of murder. Nobody ever said to them that they should not wear it, but at the same time nobody laughed, either. After a few days they stopped.

Our hangout in Memphis was a hotel called the Peabody in downtown Memphis on Union Street. It was just about everybody else's hangout, too. In addition to flocks of ground troops and administrative troops in the area, there was a Naval Air Training Station in Memphis, as well as an Army Air Force field. It was a regular stop and center for the Air Transport Command also. Apparently before the war the Peabody had been the chic place in Memphis, and it sported a Starlight Roof with dancing music and dinner. But the great influx of servicemen had taken it over from the local gentry, and at just about any time of day or night there were always between half a dozen and a dozen wide-open drinking parties going in the rooms and suites, where it was easy to get invited simply by walking down the corridors on the various floors until you heard the noise.

Money was not much of a problem. Nor were women. There was always plenty of booze from somebody, and there were also unattached women at the hotel floor parties. You could always go up to the Starlight Roof and find yourself a nice girl and dance with her a while and bring her down. Everybody screwed. Sometimes, it did not even matter if there were other people in the room or not, at the swirling kaleidoscopic parties. Couples would ensconce themselves in the bathrooms of the suites and lock the door.

Most of the overseas men received pretty substantial payments in back pay. I received, in one lovely lump sum, eleven months' back pay at a corporal's rate, when I finally got paid. This plus an allotment I'd been sending home to a bank for years to go to college on when I got out, gave me something over four thousand dollars. Two other overseas men and I kept a living room, two-bedroom suite, paying daily rates, for something like just under two months. If none of us happened to be going to town from the hospital on any given day, we would loan one of the keys to someone else. Our suite became one of the chief centers of what passed for gaiety at the Peabody Hotel in 1943. And we liked that.

No nation in history ever laid out such enormous sums and went to such great lengths to patch up, repair and take care of its wounded and its injured as the United States did in World War II. Other nations watched and wondered at the United States's richness and largesse to its damaged. It was only in the functioning and in the administration of it that there was slippage, and graft. But the government couldn't be blamed for that. Any more than the government could be blamed for the grafting congressmen and senators the people chose to elect to office. Most of us overseas men knew that we would probably be returned to duty in some limited form or other, and that would probably mean heading out for General Eisenhower's Europe.

Except for a lucky few who were too crippled up to be of even partial use, we were essentially in the same boat as the others who had never been over and were finishing up their training and heading out every few days. Except for the sole fact that we had already been there, and knew what to expect. It was a pretty big sole fact.

There is a regulation in army hospitals that no man can be sent back into duty until he is physically fully ready for Full Duty, or physically fully ready for Limited Duty. There are only the two categories. And it could be no other way, since in the army there is no convalescent period at home. All told, I spent the last seven months of 1943 in the Memphis hospital.

I was in love at least six times. I learned a lot about living on the home front. When I was shipped back out marked fit for Limited Duty, my four thousand dollars was gone and all I had to show for it were two tailored tropical worsted officer's uniforms with shoulder straps that I couldn't wear on the post. That, and a lot of memories. Memories I didn't want, particularly. It was during a period when nobody wanted to remember things.

I was shipped to what was then Camp Campbell (now Fort Campbell), Kentucky, in late December, 1943, a Limited Duty soldier.

The Home Front

The *New York Times* on Christmas Day, 1943, a Saturday, carried headlines that Gen. Dwight D. Eisenhower had been named as Commander for the European invasion, and from that time on, every American began to wait for it to start.

We Americans had always known we were going to win the war for the Europeans. Now there wasn't any question. If there had ever been any doubts (and no one believed now that there ever had been) these were dispelled by the news that the invasion was on the way. American production was winning—had already won—the war. (Encased in its gold wreath, the coveted army-navy "E" for Efficiency proved that, didn't it?) Hadn't old Joe Stalin himself toasted American production at Teheran as the winner?

To the overseas men who returned—the wounded, injured, sick—perhaps nothing was quite the slap in the face as the vast and sanguine confidence of the home "front" after mid-1943. It was a little like the battered dogface, who, hearing "Blood & Guts"

Georgie Patton being extolled muttered into his beer: "Yeah, his guts and our blood." It was a little like that with the "E" award: "Yeah. Their 'E' and our 'B.'" It did not give him any great charge to see large color photos of pretty but unfuckable-looking young ladies sewing up huge flags and recruitment posters at the Quartermaster Depot in Philadelphia.

Another thing that shocked, and even rankled, was the richness of everybody. True, we overseas men had read all about it in the home papers that got up to us, but even the hyperbole of newsprint had not done it justice. True that the thirties had been lean years, and that everybody was happy to be back at work full swing, and that everybody was belaboring it for all they were worth. Who could blame anybody for making everything he could out of such a good thing? (After all, who knew how long it would last?) But the sheer magnitude of it shocked. And there were moments when it seemed they were truly making it off our red meat and bone. Rankled or not, the old crippled veteran was not above taking advantage of it every chance he got. But in the end, about all he could do was to cadge free drinks by telling gory made-up war stories to businessmen and their mistresses in bars, and that soon palled.

We retreads upset everybody. Retread was one of those words and phrases like Kilroy which swept like wildfire across the globe into every theater. It was a term originally coined by some soldier in World War II, when retread auto tires came into usage, to designate the used-up combat soldier who was sent back through the mill again. Later, in the Korean war, it came to mean reservists called back to service. But we had it first. And at home, the retread was like a man who has survived some epidemic, and been shipped out of the disaster area to a care center. People treated him nicely, and cared for him tenderly, and then hurried to wash their hands after touching him. They did not want what he had caught to rub off, and they did not like it that he made them think of disaster.

Another thing that irritated the retread was the movies. They didn't understand anything about the war. And they didn't try to understand. Instead of trying to show the distressing complexity and puzzling diffusion of war, they pulled everything down to the level of good guy against bad guy. Instead of showing the terrifying impersonality of modern war, they invariably pulled it down to a one-on-one situation, a man-against-man, like a tennis match. At best they made it like a football game. But modern war was not a football game. And modern war was not man against man—if it ever had been. It was machine against machine. It was industry against industry. And we had the best machine. Our industry was better than their industry. But men had to die or be maimed to prove it. Men had to die at the wheels or triggers of the machines.

It could even be worked out mathematically: *n* number of men had to be invested, and *x* number had to die, in order for objective *y* to be reached, and finale *z* achieved. That was the horrible, true meaning of anonymity to the soldier.

But the movies never showed this, except only very occasionally, and probably the movie-makers never did understand the tragedy or even the problem. And by extension, the great home public apparently never understood it either. They went religiously to see the man-against-man war movies, and thought they were seeing the real war, and then went back to the factory to make more machines.

Take hand grenades. In the movies young sailors (caught on shore in Bataan) or old soldiers everywhere were perpetually wearing hand grenades dangling by the rings from their pocket flaps, pulling the pins with their teeth, tossing grenades on the other side of a coconut log three feet away, or letting the spoons fly off and counting three before tossing the grenade. Now, grenades were one of the most fearfully respected and accident-prone tricky instruments an infantryman had to deal with. They were as often likely to hurt your own people or yourself as the enemy. Usually we spread the cotter pins so wide it took a strong arm to pull the pin at all; teeth wouldn't do it. And if we wore them hanging by their rings under our pocket flaps, we made damn sure the spoon levers were taped to the grenade body with the tape from the cylinders the grenades came in. You didn't let the spoon fly off and ignite the fuse in your hand, because many grenades, though they were supposed to have three-second fuses, had fuses of two seconds, one second, and a lethal few had half-second fuses. A lady fuse-cutter at the grenade factory defense plant with a hangover could wreak real havoc with a box of grenades.

But none of the movie-makers took any of those "industrial" problems into account, and neither did the folks back home who went to see the films. The retread coming back soon realized the home front didn't understand the war, and probably never would understand it. True, they were winning the war with their industrial production, but on the other hand, they got very well paid for it. A lot better than the combat soldier who had to maneuver their machines and pull their triggers.

Love Among the Riveters

Illustration 115

They weren't all of them easy lays, by any means. Not half easy enough, by most of the retreads. Yet it was clear enough to any eye that had been away abroad that the mores and morals of the nation's middle class were swiftly undergoing a sea change. The wild gaiety and rollicking despair that characterized the towns and cities near the camps certainly helped this. At least half of the girls who used to visit the drinking parties of our Peabody suite were defense plant workers or in some defense-connected industry. Many of them were country girls or small town girls who had come into Memphis to help the nation's war effort by working and, incidentally, get at the same time some excitement into their lives. I often shuddered to think what their trembling fingers might do next day to some piece of armament destined for some poor dogface in the mud of Italy or the Pacific. But in a mass war as mass as our war was mass, one man couldn't take account of everything. Besides, if they were cautioned to go home and sober up and get some sleep before going to work at the plant, they would only leave us and go down the hall to the next suite's party on the floor below. And we would be out a girl, and the poor Government Issue in Italy would be no better off.

We had a lieutenant in my outfit who had his hand blown nearly off by a half-second grenade. The thing hardly left his hand before it exploded in mid-air above his head. Fortunately he was not up on the line when it happened, but was using the grenade to go fishing in the Matanikau River. So they were able to get him and what was left of his hand back to the hospital quickly. The principle, of course, of grenade fishing was that the concussion of the grenade going off underwater would kill all the fish nearby, where they would float belly up with their air bladders ruptured to be picked up by the fisherman.

I ran into him later in the hospital, where he had his various fingers stretched out and pinned to a big wire frame the size of a large baseball glove. When they finally let him out on pass, I went out with him drinking a couple of times. He certainly had a way with women. He was a cheerful, rapacious, malevolent type of a guy, and claimed that because of what the bad grenade had done to his hand, it was his project to screw every riveter, welder, lathe-operator and fuse-cutter that he could get his one good hand on for the rest of the war. That was to be his revenge. The little I saw of him, it appeared he might realize his ambition, if they would only transfer him around to enough different hospitals in different cities.

For a while I went with a little girl who worked in a defense plant and lived at home in Memphis. This little girl's parents and two older sisters worked in defense plants, too. This family's morals had changed sufficiently that nobody in the household cared if I came home and slept with her there in her little thin-walled room, as long as I did not keep her from getting to her plant in time for work on whatever shift it was she happened to be working at the time.

But of course we lost out on all that sport when we were returned to Limited Duty at Camp Campbell, Kentucky.

D-Day

Illustrations 116–123

Volumes and volumes have been written about it. Probably more than has ever been written about any other single military operation. Certainly more paintings were painted of it, and the few days following, then of any other part of the war. Every artist-correspondent and writer-correspondent who could possibly get permission to be there, was there. It must have been one of the big highs of the war, to be in London and hit the pubs during the last two months before D-Day.

War buffs have argued its pros and cons and various details since about June 7, 1944—and are still arguing them. Concerning argument, suffice it to say that, once started, no matter how terrible the cost, it was successful. The lodgement was made. And more important, it served to funnel inward all the huge mass of men and matériel, waiting, like a ton-weight albatross around the neck of England, to pour ashore in France.

General Eisenhower issued on SHAEF (Supreme

Headquarters, Allied Expeditionary Force) stationery over his signature a confident hortatory message which was distributed to every man just before the great armada got under way, and which today reads honestly and truthfully, but which, having seen a facsimile of it, I must in all honesty say, would not have exhorted me unduly had I been a private in the First Infantry Division's first wave forward element.

Just the same, Ike's terrible sincerity, and terrible responsibility, came through it. He had no way of addressing his assault troops personally.

Five divisions (2 American, 2 British, 1 Canadian) were attacking abreast, over 5 different beachheads. One hundred thirty-eight major warships with 221 smaller combat vessels would support them in the assault. Four thousand landing ships or craft would carry them in. Eleven thousand aircraft would bomb preparation and give them air cover. Over 1,000 minesweepers and auxiliary vessels, 805 merchant ships, 59 blockships, several hundred miscellaneous small craft would be involved. It would have been pretty hard for Ike to shake hands with everybody.

It is interesting to note that at the same time he issued his statement to the troops, old Ike also wrote out another statement, to cover a different contingency, a statement he devoutly hoped never to release. It announced a withdrawal from the French shore due to invincible enemy resistance. When one thinks of that, and the responsibility it entailed, it makes the hairs on the back of the neck move.

The whole project seemed doomed to uncertainty and near-unbearable tension from the start, and particularly from the day it was postponed from May to June. In June only the three days were available, because of tide and moon: the fifth, the sixth, and the seventh. And bad weather was predicted. Everyone knows the story of how, with the huge fleet already at sea in the Channel on June 4, the operation was postponed one day because of the weather, and how Ike agonized most of June 5 over whether to go on the sixth. Most of his senior commanders had advised him Go. But in the army it is the commander who makes the final decision, and takes the final full responsibility. It was probably Eisenhower's finest moment. And the thousands of vessels cruising the rough night Channel began to form up in their groups and head for their landing designations.

The sheer weight of the attack almost assured a landing. But that was not the problem. The assault divisions must move inland, consolidate their positions, hook up right and left with units from the other landings, so as to present a united front that could hold and leave sufficient room in its rear for the vital all-important buildup behind it that was to follow. The plans called for four additional divisions to be landed by D + 3, and a further eleven by D + 14. The total force envisioned for this stage was therefore twenty-three divisions, including the three airborne which had jumped in before dawn on June 6.

Hundreds of thousands of men and thousands of tanks and other vehicles waited at the staging areas to be shuttled over as soon as time and space permitted. Without them to extend and solidify a front and base from which armor could attack overland northeast toward Soissons and Germany, the successful landings themselves were meaningless. The first day's objectives therefore called for an Allied line from Quineville in the west around the corner of the Contentin peninsula, all the way to Cabourg in the east beyond the Orne River. In the fact of it, none of the five assault forces reached their objectives on the first day.

The German resistance encountered varied greatly. In the west at Utah Beach the U.S. Fourth Infantry Division encountered almost none, lost 12 men killed in the first 24 hours. The pre-invasion aerial bombardment and naval shellings were marvelously successful, and the losses of the Fourth Division for the first day were only 197 in killed, wounded and missing. It was incredible luck. Yet they had not taken their objective, had not linked up with the Eighty-second and 101st Airborne, who had jumped into the Cotentin corner the night before. British commanders then, and British writers later, would maintain they had moved too cautiously. Omaha around the corner, 10 or 12 miles farther east, was different—a veritable blood-bath. Still farther east on the three British beaches, Gold, Juno, and Sword, the British and Canadian divisions, like the excellent professionals they were, moved briskly and rather stylishly ashore and inland against marked resistance, picked up most of their airborne, but failed to meet their objectives also, taking somewhat under 3,000 casualties in killed, wounded and missing in the process. At Omaha, Gerow's V Corps alone sustained 3,881 in KIW, WIA and missing.

Omaha had had bad luck all around. It was known beforehand that the Omaha terrain was perhaps the roughest of the five, a crescent-shaped dish with a bluff on top and only two exit roads, which could be a devastating defensive position. It was not known that a fresh, crack division, the 352nd, had been moved into the area a few days before. In addition the air bombardment had missed its target, the majority of the Duplex Drive tanks (semi-amphibious tanks that were to lead off) had sunk in the heavy seas before they reached the beach, and the beach and underwater obstructions were much tougher than expected. As late as 1030 hours the good-as-gold old First Division lay pinned down behind the seawall while the enemy swept the beaches with small-arms fire. German artillery chased the landing craft where they milled offshore. By 1300 hours the crisis was pretty much over. Much credit for that goes to Admiral Kirk, the U.S. naval commander, who bunched his destroyers off the coast and delivered maximum fire on the German strong points. At the same time, the German 352nd Division was running out of shells, as the excellent U.S. aerial bombardment on the roads behind them kept them from getting resupplied and reinforced.

But at midnight the deepest penetration on Omaha was barely more than a mile. For almost 3,900 casualties.

In 1961 I worked as a scriptwriter on the Zanuck film about D-Day, *The Longest Day*, and I had occasion to tramp all over the D-Day beaches and the disputed terrain inland, and even over the U.S. Rangers' assault area at Pointe du Hoe (which, when the Rangers finally scaled it, at great cost, was found to have no siege guns at all)—until I got to know them very well.

Utah was a long, lonely windswept beach that stretched for miles and miles, with one tiny little monument on it to mark the landings. The English beaches were relatively flat country, much of it through towns and built-up areas, with the large town of Ouistreham and its famous casino and the Orne estuary on the left flank. At Arromanches about half-way between the Orne and Omaha—where the remains of the huge British false port "Mulberry" could still be seen—there is a war museum with the uniforms and equipment of the time and an animated, colorful diorama of the action. But at Omaha I climbed up and sat a while on the edge of the bluff, and looked down into the cup-shaped area with the sea at its back. It too had been built back up, and the six or eight tall spindly French summer homes have been rebuilt. It was easy to see what a murderous converging fire could be brought to bear on the beaches from the curving bluff. Especially to an old infantryman. And it was easy to half-close your eyes and imagine what it must have been like. The terror and total confusion, men screaming or sinking silently under the water, tanks sinking as their crews drowned inside, landing craft going up as a direct hit took them, or grating ashore to discharge their live cargo into the already scrambled mess, officers trying to get their men together, medics trying to find shelter for the wounded, until finally out of the welter a "certain desperate order began to emerge," and men began to move toward the two bottleneck exits. I sat there until my friends began to yell at me from down below, and I fervently thanked God or Whomever that I had not been there.

Bloodbath at Omaha

Illustrations 124–127

Along with all the others, an Anglo-American controversy (still unresolved today) grew up out of this matter of Omaha. British Intelligence (which had had men on shore at Omaha occasionally, beforehand) claimed it had observed the bringing in of the German 352nd, and had passed this piece of information on to the U.S. First Army Command, but that the First Army had found the information suspect, and had not informed the assault troops. The British found it "inconceivable that they [the U.S. troops] had been briefed to expect less than the worst the enemy could be expected to perform," in attacking "this superb defensive position." Also, they claimed, General Bradley had rejected the British General Hobart's "magnificent array of special assault armour," and had accepted the Duplex Drive tanks only with reluctance.

Now, General Hobart's "special assault armour" requires a bit of explanation. British troops called them the "Funnies." Hobart had been a tank advocate as far back as 1934. He had, in fact, raised and trained

100.

101.

102.
Anzio Harbor, *once taken back from the Germans, became a major Allied staging base.*

103.
Orderly room *at Anzio was wherever the sign could be posted.*

104.
Return to the Golden Gate *was in store for some of the wounded, who crowd the rail for a first glimpse of home.*

105.
Crap games *were a favorite form of tension breaking.*

106.
Mail call *was often the only welcome call of the day.*

107.
Negro engineers *prepare to set things up.*

108.
Tank group *gets ready to move out.*

109.
Queen Elizabeth, *the largest liner ever built, converted to carry thousands of troops.*

110.
Mulberry *was a huge operation preparing for the invasion, in which complete harbors and installations were built in England and Scotland to be towed across the Channel. Royal Engineers and American Seabees helped assemble the massive structures.*

111.

112.
Getting ready *to go, every unit assigned to participate in the invasion practiced and practiced, knowing the time was soon coming when it would not be practice anymore.*

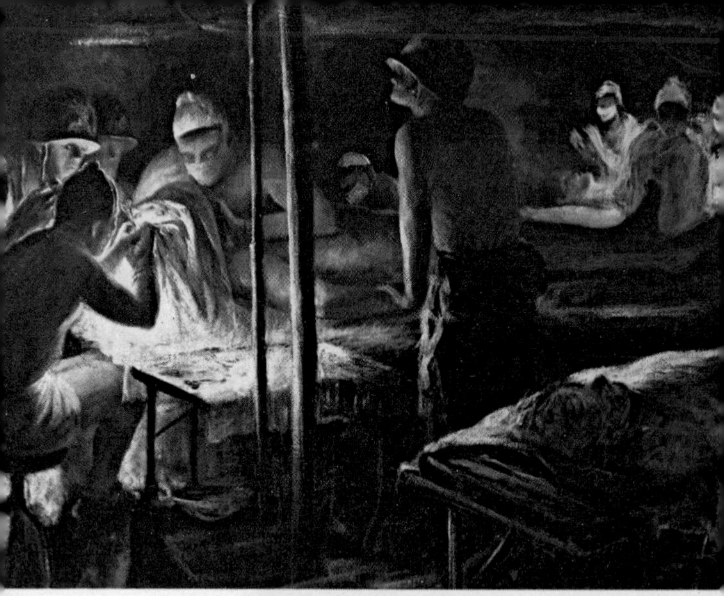

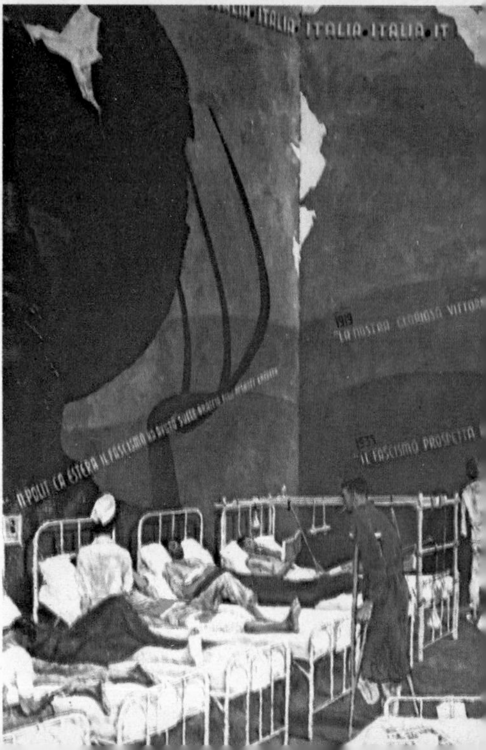

ITALIA · ITALIA · ITALIA · IT
1919
LA NOSTRA GLORIOSA VITTORIA
IL FASCISMO PROSPETTA
IN POLITICA ESTERA IL FASCISMO

113.
Left:
Surgery by flashlight *was not uncommon in the field. Doctors and corpsmen found their resourcefulness tested time and again as combat grew fiercer.*

114.
Hospital scene *in Italy shows a bizarre contrast. An American hospital was set up on the site of a former "Fascist Fair" and the wounded soldiers were able to gaze wanly at enemy propaganda as they recovered.*

115.
Rosie the Riveter *became the symbol of the home front.*

116. *Right:*
Dawn, *June 6, 1944, D-Day.*

117.
German sentries *patrol the coast of France, watching and waiting for the invasion.*

118.
The Battle for Fox Green Beach *was on at about H-hour plus 6. This painting by Dwight Shepler shows the vast plane on which the action took place. The largest amphibious assault ever mounted moved forward hesitantly but relentlessly.*

119.
D-Day Normandy.

120.
Demo unit *places a charge on a "Belgian Gate," an obstacle with a steel framework. These finely-trained demolition crews often preceded the first wave of assault troops.*

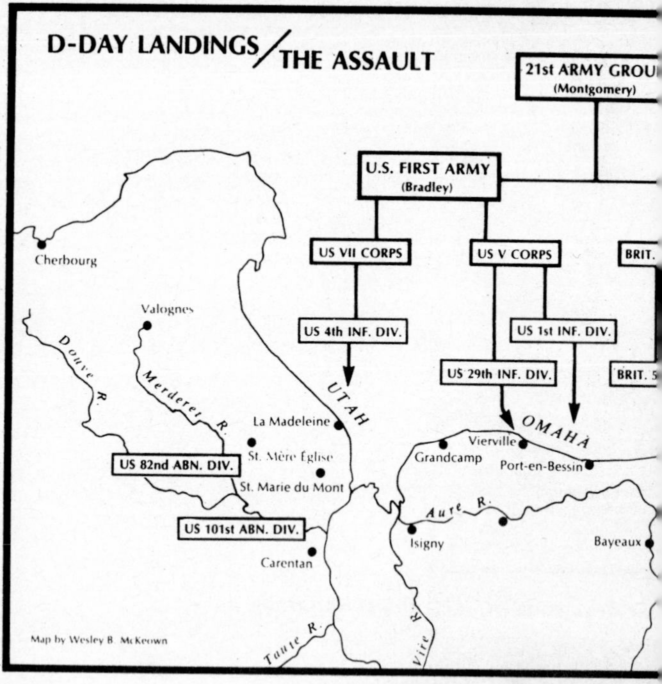

D-DAY LANDINGS / THE ASSAULT

21st ARMY GROU
(Montgomery)

U.S. FIRST ARMY
(Bradley)

US VII CORPS

US V CORPS

BRIT.

US 4th INF. DIV.

US 1st INF. DIV.

US 29th INF. DIV.

BRIT. 5

UTAH

OMAHA

Cherbourg

Valognes

Douve R.

Merderet R.

La Madeleine

St. Mère Église

St. Marie du Mont

US 82nd ABN. DIV.

US 101st ABN. DIV.

Carentan

Grandcamp

Vierville

Port-en-Bessin

Aure R.

Isigny

Bayeaux

Taute R.

Vire R.

Map by Wesley B. McKeown

121.

122.
Utah Beach *was one of the main landing points for the Allied army on D-Day.*

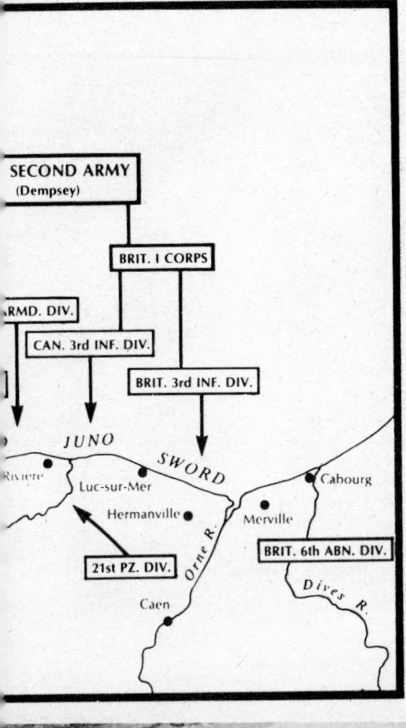

SECOND ARMY
(Dempsey)
BRIT. I CORPS
RMD. DIV.
CAN. 3rd INF. DIV.
BRIT. 3rd INF. DIV.
JUNO
SWORD
Riviere
Luc-sur-Mer
Hermanville
Merville
Cabourg
21st PZ. DIV.
BRIT. 6th ABN. DIV.
Orne R.
Dives R.
Caen

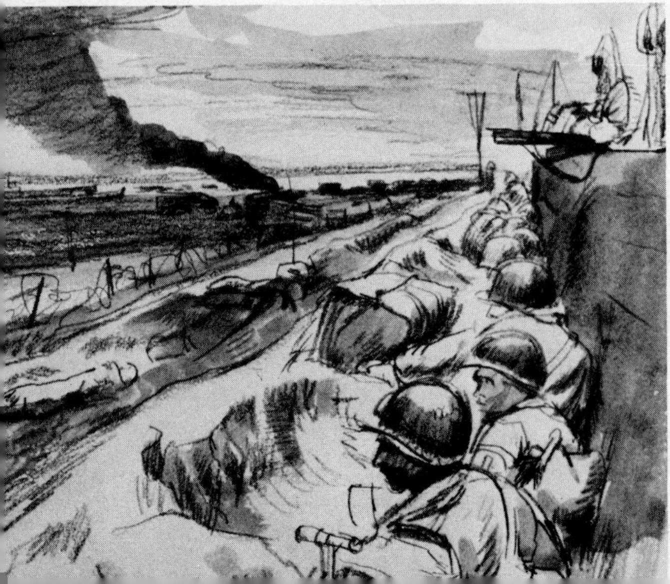

123.
First aid station, *set up right on the beach, took care of the first casualties as the beachhead battle moved slowly inland.*

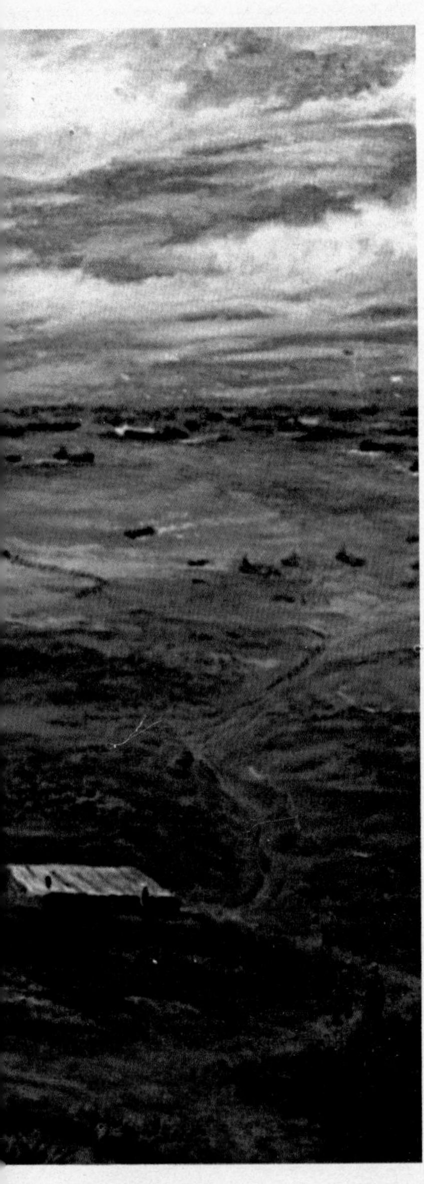

124.
Omaha Beach *turned out to be a bloodbath on the morning of June 6, 1944. This painting, based on sketches made from the top of a German gun emplacement, shows the area covered by the day's carnage.*

125.
Tough coastal defense *by Germans at Omaha Beach had tricky multiple obstacles.*

126.
Normandy: Low Tide *shows the same scene by Mitchell Jamieson as the one done by Kerr Eby at Tarawa. (See illustration number 90.) The artists differ in approach and technique, but they felt the same sense of horror, and were able to convey it.*

127.
The storm destroys *what the enemy could not. A few weeks after D-Day the Omaha pontoon barges and Mulberries are seriously damaged. The weather has pounded and ground them into uselessness and the scene of wreckage seems complete. Supply will be hampered for weeks to come.*

129.

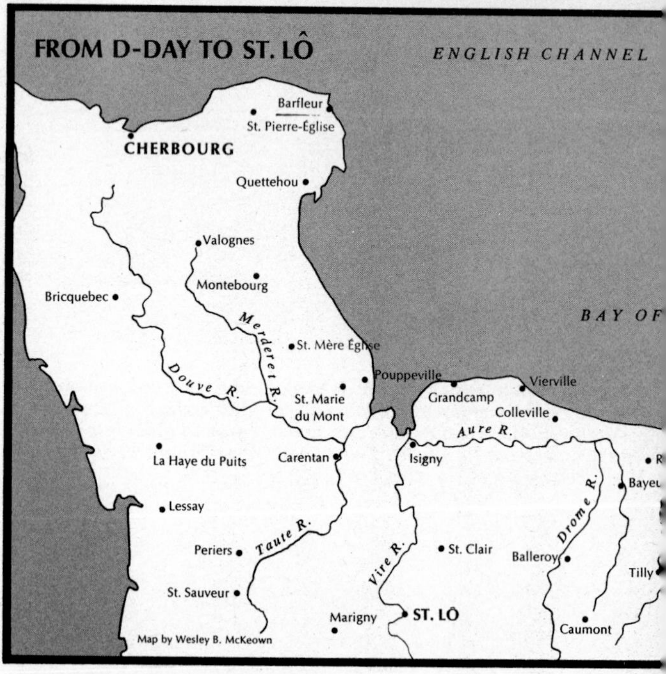

FROM D-DAY TO ST. LÔ

ENGLISH CHANNEL

BAY OF

Barfleur
St. Pierre-Église
CHERBOURG
Quettehou
Valognes
Montebourg
Bricquebec
Merderet R.
St. Mère Église
Douve R.
Pouppeville
St. Marie du Mont
Grandcamp
Vierville
Colleville
Aure R.
La Haye du Puits
Carentan
Isigny
R
Bayeu
Drome R.
Lessay
Taute R.
Periers
Vire R.
St. Clair
Balleroy
Tilly
St. Sauveur
Marigny
ST. LÔ
Caumont

Map by Wesley B. McKeown

128.

The St. Giles Strong Point *was a particular obstacle in the path of the 137th infantry regiment attack in July of 1944. The German defense used machine guns firing through holes in the walls of the church. The Americans had to bypass the Strong Point and isolate it before capture was possible.*

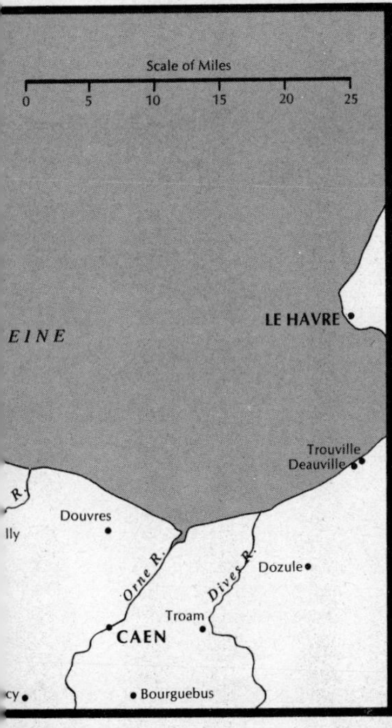

130.
Advance on St. Lô *was stalled when American troops came to this savagely defended "draw." Nearly an entire platoon was lost trying to advance. Some time and many purple hearts later, a flanking maneuver forced the Germans to abandon the position.*

131.
Time out *on the road to St. Lô.*

the first British armored division in Egypt (the outfit which became the famed Seventh Armoured "Desert Rats"), but had been removed by Wavell because Wavell could not accept his concept of the use of armor (which later became standard practice). Prematurely retired in early 1940, Hobart was brought back at the personal insistence of Churchill. (Hobart was also the brother-in-law of Montgomery.) And he raised and trained the Seventy-ninth Armoured, which in 1943 was charged with the development and training of the special armored devices and personnel to be used to lead the assault across the invasion beaches.

Hobart apparently threw his British heart and soul into his task. The "Funnies" were a weird assortment of odd-looking beasts. The *Duplex Drive* (called DD) was one: an amphibious conversion which could be fitted to a normal Sherman tank. A collapsible canvas screen around the tank gave it buoyancy (up to a point) and it was driven by two propellers which worked off the main drive. With its screen raised, it looked more than anything else like a mechanized bathtub. The *Bobbin* was a "road" layer, with a huge drum forward built on a regular Churchill chassis, designed to lay a ten-foot carpet of matting across soft sand for the tanks that followed. The well-known flail-tank (called the *Crab* by the British) was another Hobart invention, and carried a whirling drum fitted with chain flails for exploding mines and opening a ten-foot path through minefields. Then there was the *Churchill AVRE* (Armoured Vehicle, Royal Engineers) with *SBG* (Small Box Girder) *Bridge:* a Churchill tank chassis adapted to carry a bridge which could be dropped in 30 seconds over a 30-foot gap, or surmount a 15-foot wall while supporting 40 tons. The now commonplace *Armoured Bulldozer* was another of Hobart's. Lastly there were the *Churchill Crocodile,* a flame-thrower conversion of the Mark VII, which carried the flame-gun fuel behind it in its own little armored trailer, and the *Petard* tank, designed to fire a heavy "dustbin" charge straight into gun emplacement openings.

Weird as they sound, and look, the British gave these monsters much of the credit for the comparative ease with which they broke through the defenses of their beaches to move inland. And Montgomery offered this array of "special armour" to General Bradley, who refused them, and chose to stick with his own flesh-and-blood engineer demolition teams.

I assume Bradley saw demonstrations of the "Funnies" before rejecting them. And they must have worked. Perhaps it was simply the weird look of them that put him off, and the "chin-up, stiff-upper-lip" British games-playing attitude to the war and its death and destruction may have angered him. In any case, that the American demo teams failed at Omaha because of heavy casualties is a fact. And that "much of the [Omaha Beach] difficulty had been caused by the underwater obstructions," was admitted by the U.S. First Army chief of staff. The British credited Bradley's refusal of Hobart's monsters for the Dantesque horrors, as they termed it, of Omaha. They still do today.

One British writer went so far as to say: "No one may ever know what General Bradley thought about it [the comparative failure of Omaha]. Why had he refused the flails, the petards, and all the rest of Hobart's armour? Chester Wilmot believed that it was Bradley's contempt for British 'under confidence and over-insurance.' Captain Sir Basil Liddell Hart summed up: 'Analysis makes it clear that the American troops paid dearly for their higher commander's hesitation to accept Montgomery's earlier offer to give them a share of Hobart's specialized armour.' "

But there were other factors at Omaha. The very DD tanks Bradley did accept sank (all but a very few) in the high seas without ever reaching shore; sank, most of them, with their crews. (The same British writer claims that this was due to an irresponsible commander who launched the DDs six thousand yards out, much too far out for the heavy seas.) But the bad weather and heavy seas could not be blamed on Bradley. Other factors were the fact that the pre-invasion aerial bombardment missed its targets, and that fresh, crack German troops had been moved in a few days before.

The fact remains, the British did get through their beach obstacles, the "hard crust" of beach defenses, in considerably better shape than the Americans. Their DDs did not sink, or not many of them, and their "special assault armour" did work for them, and spring their boys through inland with relatively fewer casualties.

It may well be that there is (or was) a fundamentally different psychological outlook between the British soldier and the American soldier. Bradley was a man who worried deeply and brooded over the lives lost among his commands. He did not commit them lightly. Generally, most high American general officers felt the same (with the notable exception of Patton and a couple of others), and usually preferred to act on the side of caution. Probably this is a peculiarly American attitude, growing out of the basic fact that the American army was essentially a civilian, and a reluctant, army. An American general who "wasted" troops was looked on very unkindly by the civilian population and by the troops themselves. Whereas the British officer had more the general European attitude, that the men were there to be used, and the strategist and tactician were there to use them. We have seen over and over that the American commanders chose the line of caution, when there was a choice, and as often as not it cost them more men in the end than if they had gambled. The American cautious, slow-moving attitude at Anzio is a classic example, when compared to Churchill's swashbuckling wish for a swift over-extended drive on Rome. We still do not know if Churchill's way would have worked at Anzio. We know the American cautionary way did not. Omaha was perhaps similar.

As one British writer put it so succinctly: "The cost of the day in killed was not more than 2,500 men, 1,000 of them on Omaha Beach. At Towton Field, on 29th March, 1461, 33,000 men perished by the sword and were buried there. Nearly 20,000 British troops were killed on the first day of the Battle of the Somme in 1916." So it wasn't so bad, in his view.

On the other hand, General Bradley wrote somewhere, about the whole European campaign of 1944: "The rifleman trudges into battle knowing that statistics are stacked against his survival. He fights without promise of either reward or relief. Behind every river, there's another hill—and behind that hill, another river. After weeks or months in the line only a wound can offer him the comfort of safety, shelter, and a bed. Those who are left to fight, fight on, evading death but knowing that with each day of evasion they have exhausted one more chance for survival. Sooner or later, unless victory comes, the chase must end on the litter or in the grave."

A basically American point of view, perhaps. For a general. Certainly not European.

CONSOLIDATION

Illustrations 128–137

To "link up the beachheads and peg out claims well inland" was necessarily the first aim of Overlord. Only thus could the Allies hope to bring ashore the troops and the armor to fight their way out of what at any moment might become their death trap. By evening of June 10, despite the slow start at Omaha, this first objective (expected to be won by midnight of D-Day itself) had been achieved and a single front stretched from near Quineville on the Cotentin peninsula to beyond Ouistreham and the Orne estuary. The major exception was the city of Caen in the British zone, ten miles inland, which was to become a painful boil in the British flank for the next six weeks, and the basis for another unending controversy between British and American military historians yet unborn.

In the American zone, by night of June 8 the U.S. Twenty-ninth Division of Gerow's V Corps of Bradley's First Army had taken the town of Isigny in one corner of the Cotentin. By the tenth, on Eisenhower's express orders, they had joined up with the 101st

Airborne near Carentan to complete the beachhead line.

Strategically, this turning of the Cotentin corner was very important. From this position Maj. Gen. J. Lawton "Lightning Joe" Collins (who won his nickname and his reputation off my division, the Twenty-fifth, on Guadalcanal—not in Europe) and his VII Corps could drive westward across the thumblike Cotentin peninsula, cutting off the port of Cherbourg and all the German troops in the peninsula, and giving the Allies their first much-needed major port. This Collins proceeded to do, reaching the west coast at Carteret on June 17, though Cherbourg itself (twenty miles away) did not fall till June 27. Collins was hampered by the rains, swampy terrain and hedgerow country that were going to be such troubles to Bradley in reaching St. Lô. When it did fall, Cherbourg and its port were so thoroughly destroyed that it was useless for the three vital weeks it took to clear it, and would require several months before the Americans could discharge cargoes in any important quantity.

Meanwhile the rest of Bradley's sector had to pretty much rest in place and mark time while the available reinforcements went to VII Corps and its attack. This gave the Germans time to stabilize and dig in on the "hedgerow front" before St. Lô. In addition, the "Great Storm" of June 19 blew up, as if some malign fate wished to test the Allies to their fullest, and in three days of seas and high winds completely ruined the American "Mulberry" port at Omaha, so badly it had to be abandoned, and seriously damaged the British one at Arromanches.

In the meantime, General Sir Bernard Law Montgomery, still in front of Caen on July 1, kept poking attacks that failed into the increasing ruins and house-to-house work of that miserable city. The last of the Germans would not be out of it until July 19. And thus the Great Anglo-American Caen Controversy was launched.

Poor Caen. I spent several days there two or three

times in 1961, when the Zanuck *Longest Day* film was being shot. Caen, being so central, was the headquarters for the Zanuck production people. And I guess the people of Caen hadn't had so much excitement or attention since June of '44. John Wayne, Robert Ryan, Peter Lawford. And "a host of other stars," as they say.

But poor Caen itself was pretty hopeless. From reports it must once have been a lovely old city with stone houses and a medieval quarter. Some of the old landmarks remain, but today it is mostly rebuilt in the boxlike architecture of cracking concrete and loosening glass laughingly labeled "French Modern."

The Great Caen Controversy proceeds from two apparently diametrically opposed statements of fact. One school, mostly British, claims that Monty's strategy from the very beginning (even before the actual invasion) was to keep the Germans and the bulk of the German armor occupied around Caen, so that Bradley's U.S. First Army would be freed to make the final breakout and wheel east to trap the German Seventh and Fifteenth Armies in what came to be known as the "Falaise Pocket." This school states unequivocally that this strategy was included in the final Overlord plans. Thus they lay at Monty's feet the full credit for the victory Bradley and the Americans effected—with some forty-four thousand casualties.

The second school, mostly American, claims equally unequivocally that no such strategy was written into the Overlord plans. That in fact the Overlord strategy was directly opposite. According to the pre-invasion plans. Bradley's army was to cover the right flank of the British army, which was to head left for the Seine. This would seem reasonable, since in that direction lay the only territory open enough for swift attack by armor. Why would Monty and Ike, knowing the kind of difficult *bocage* hedgerow terrain in front of Bradley, lending itself so to defense, decide on their major offensive precisely through such bad ground? They wouldn't, this second school says; and adds that only after Montgomery failed to take Caen and move out onto the open Falaise plain, did the Allies reverse their pre-invasion concept, and in desperation to expand the beachhead, begin to push Bradley through the hedgerow country for the breakout. The drawback was that the terrain in front of Bradley made success very costly.

Probably any terrain would have been costly, at this point. The Germans were fighting desperately to hold in France. And probably the truth lies somewhere in between the two theories. Certainly Monty, by ordering Dempsey (the almost forgotten commander of British Second Army) to make small probing attacks at Caen to keep the Germans off balance, did prevent the Germans from launching their crushing counterblow against the early beachheads. (He had as a helpful ally in this Adolf Hitler, who kept refusing to believe the Normandy landings were the main landings.) And certainly Monty's strategy worked beautifully, when Bradley did break out and make his sweeping end run. Probably, like the field genius that he was, Montgomery was improvising his strategy as he went along, according to the situation as it developed. The pro-Monty school, however, say they have letters and memos from Monty to General Sir Alan Brooke, the British chief of staff, stating his hold-Caen push-Bradley strategy from before June 6. The anti-Monty school say they do not have them, or are interpreting them with hindsight. Either way, Montgomery can be accused of ordering the Canadian II Corps to a major offensive which he either did not intend for them to win, or knew beforehand that they could not win.

In any case, here they all were, both British and American, on July 24, poised for the breakout, with a line running all the way from Ouistreham and the Orne to Lessay on the Brittany coast, with Cherbourg and the Cotentin peninsula in their hands, with both St. Lô and the infamous Caen finally inside the perimeters. There were now five British corps in the

British sector, and five American corps in the American sector. It was now almost impossible to speak of individual divisions in relation to these actions, but only of corps. And soon it would be armies instead of corps: Patton's U.S. Third, Bradley's First, Canadian First, British Second, French First, U.S. Seventh, U.S. Ninth. That was how the U.S. war was growing.

On the American flank, to get out of the hedgerows and take St. Lô, twelve divisions had incurred a total of forty thousand casualties in seventeen days and had advanced the U.S. First Army front less than seven miles. (Add the fighting before that, and the American casualties came to over sixty-two thousand.)

AIR WAR

Illustrations 138–146

So much for the poor infantry. That kind of casualty count seems staggering, when placed beside the short period of time and the short amount of gain. But even that number of casualties would have been low, had it not been for the near total air superiority the Allies had achieved.

During the invasion and the months immediately following, the enormous numbers of new Allied fighters and bombers controlled French airspace to an almost total and hitherto unbelievable degree. The famed Luftwaffe, terror of the 1940 Blitz and the Battle of Britain in 1941, flew almost no tactical combat missions and very few strategic ones. And the story of how this came about is essentially the real story of the air war in Europe.

I have dwelt very little on the air war in detail in this book. Partly it is because, for those of us who fought on the ground, the battles and missions in the air seemed to exist in another world, in another dimension even—as, in fact, they did. The men who flew them seemed like special beings, with all their specialized mysterious gear and equipment and delicate specialized training, insubstantial beings who when their task was done (if they survived it) flew off home somewhere back behind the lines, where there was booze and decent food, a bed, and even occasionally a night off and the company of women.

In spite of all that, there is no question but that all of the great sea battles and land battles of World War II were decided, finally, by air power. All the great amphibious invasions of the Europe war from North Africa to Sicily, Salerno, Anzio, Normandy, to the south of France, could not have been won without tactical air, and tactical air superiority. And in the Pacific, almost all of the great sea battles across the thousands of miles of uninhabited ocean were, in the end, air battles. It was the carrier task forces that decided the issue, attacking with dive-bombers and torpedo-bombers across great distances, while the battleships and cruisers, formerly the power factor, were relegated to steaming back and forth to protect the precious carriers and their precious planes, their big guns useless at such distances.

Another aspect of the Pacific war, which received scant attention then and gets even less today, is that of the use of land-based fighters and bombers by the air force. In April, 1942, Lt. Gen. (later General) George C. Kenney arrived in Australia to take command of MacArthur's nearly defunct, debilitated air forces, and served as air commander there till the end of the war. A stubby, prickly, pugnacious little man, it was Kenney who with his few land-based P-38s, B-17s and B-25s, aided by some Australian Beaufighters, won the Battle of the Bismarck Sea which stopped the Japanese advance in New Guinea, and which eventually helped force the Japanese to retreat from New Guinea. Kenney's uses of weaponry were innovations in the South Pacific (such as his techniques of surface skip-bombing, for example) and his planes sank all eight Japanese transports and four Japanese destroyers, a total of twelve of the sixteen ships which had left Rabaul to invade Port Moresby. The Japanese never again placed so many men and ships within range of land-based aircraft. It was also Kenney's Fifth Air Force which essayed to "take out" the Jap air bastion of Rabaul, to take pressure off the Allied invasion and offensive in Bougainville. While he never did take out Rabaul completely, his attacks on it with land-based air force planes aided the American push in Bougainville and helped force the withdrawal of the tactical air units by January of 1944, and materially aided in allowing Rabaul to be bypassed—an invasion which, had it been tried, would have created a situation in which "Tarawa, Iwo Jima and Okinawa would have faded to pale pink in comparison with the blood that would have flowed," in the opinion of naval historian Samuel Eliot Morison. It was General MacArthur himself who nicknamed Kenney's flyers "Kenney's Kids," partly because they were all so young, but also partly because of the way Kenney mothered and clucked and fretted over them. These "kids" included such "youngsters" as Richard Bong, America's ace of aces (41 planes); Neel Kearby, Medal of Honor winner (22 planes); Thomas Lynch (19 planes); Thomas McGuire (34 planes). None of these men survived the war—although Bong might be said to have died peaceably, since he crashed at the controls of a jet plane he was testing for Lockheed, in California, on the same day the atom bomb was dropped on Hiroshima.

But the mounting and carrying out of the main mission of the Combined Strategic Air Command in Europe was perhaps the main air war story of World War II. It had all the drama, irony and insanity of a *Catch 22*—the novel which was drawn out of the deep-down guts and heart of its prime effort. Like so many other things, it came into being at the Casablanca Conference of Roosevelt and Churchill. One of the basic goals agreed upon there was a cross-Channel invasion during 1944. Among the objectives to be won before the larger strategies could be achieved was control of the German submarine pack; another was control of the Luftwaffe, which prevented strategic bombing and, unless dealt with, would preclude any mainland invasion in 1944. Both of these objectives, it was felt, could be handled by the use of air power. Out of this came the Casablanca Directive, outlining the future combined operations by the British and American Bomber Commands.

And almost immediately the arguing began. The British believed in night bombing; the Americans believed in day bombing. Seems simple enough. Right? But no. Nothing in war is ever simple. The British wanted the Americans to do it their way. They had found out by experience that day bombing was deadly: too costly in aircrews, too costly in planes. They themselves had defeated the Germans in just such costly daytime bombing in 1941 in the Battle of Britain, when the Luftwaffe had tried to bomb England into submission, and failed. The British had resorted therefore to what they called night "area" bombing. At night, which was admittedly safer for attacking planes, it was nevertheless impossible to bomb with any real precision, so they developed a technique of sending advance planes over to drop flares and an advance wave to drop incendiaries which marked the area; succeeding waves would then try to drop into this marked area. This was perhaps hard on German civilians who happened to live in the general area of a chosen target. But German cities which contained war industry plants were considered fair game for British Bomber Command's Lancasters. This was not, even at the time, considered a "civilized means of making war"—an ironic sophism if humanity ever coined one. But then, the Germans had never been too "civilized" in their earlier attacks upon London, either.

The Americans, on the other hand, insisted on clinging to their concept of "pinpoint" precision daylight bombing. They believed that a heavy bomber with its protective armor and heavy firepower (the B-17 Flying Fortress carried twelve .50-caliber MGs and the B-24 Liberator ten) could withstand attack by fighters. And the Americans did not believe you could cause the necessary industry disruption and factory destruction by "area" bombing, no matter how much you "saturated" the area. In this they were proved right. All of this was not just American cussedness and bullheadedness. Perhaps the best argument in favor of American daylight precision bombing was simply that the planes were designed for it and the American crews trained for it. To change their operational technique would have meant prolonged retraining of crews, modifications in the aircraft, and long-term delays. Just assembling the men and the equipment and getting them on a working schedule was a complex matter, and time consuming.

The British had a tough, hardheaded spokesman in Sir Arthur "Bomber" Harris, head of Bomber Command. But the Americans had a couple of tough ones too, in "Hap" Arnold and "Tooey" Spaatz. In the end it was left a stalemate, with the British to continue their night bombing and the Americans to augment it with daylight bombing.

But then there was the question—and argument—of target priorities. "Bomber" Harris had long been a staunch advocate of the "strategic bombardment" concept—or in plainer words: an attack upon Germany's industrial cities. All through 1942 he had pursued singlemindedly this objective with whatever means he had (which wasn't much), and in fact had just about singlehandedly saved Bomber Command from being disbanded in early 1942 by his successes. But Harris had two fanaticisms. He hated what he called "panacea" targets: single item targets such as Schweinfurt (ball bearings) or Ploesti (oil), which, supposedly, if hit once properly would cripple German industry. (He was wrong in thinking them unimportant, but quite right in saying one raid would not do them in.) And secondly, he remained firmly convinced that only by breaking the morale of the German people by mass at-night saturation area bombing would Germany be brought to its knees. (Why he persisted in this belief, since he knew well the failure of the Luftwaffe in 1941 in trying to do the same thing to London, no one seems to have found out; but persist he did.) Fortunately, he could go along his single-minded way, since the targets he wanted to attack for "morale" reasons were the same big cities of the Ruhr which the Casablanca Directive ordered him to attack for "industrial" reasons.

The Americans meanwhile took the Casablanca Directive at full and face value. Thus during the summer and fall of 1943 they initiated the great, famous (infamous, in the air force) bloodbath raids of second Ploesti, first Schweinfurt, second Schweinfurt, Regensburg. On the first Schweinfurt-Regensburg double mission a total of 60 Flying Fortresses were lost, and 600 trained men, killed, wounded or missing. Colonel Curtis LeMay noted, "I lost twenty-four out of my hundred twenty-seven planes which attacked the target of Regensburg," or just about one-fifth of his command. Second Ploesti cost 55 of 164 B-24 Liberators, or just over one-third. (This meant too the loss of 550 trained men.) And of the 109 planes that returned to Benghazi, barely 30 were still flyable. Second Schweinfurt started out with 291 Flying Fortresses taking off. Only 228 actually succeeded in reaching the target to place their bombs. On the way home, too, Luftwaffe fighter attacks were relentlessly pressed. Sixty B-17s were lost over the Continent and 5 others were abandoned over England. One hundred forty other planes returned in varying stages of disrepair, 17 beyond possibility of saving. Again around 600 men were missing, many whose fate would never be known. Many disappeared in exploding B-17s, or were trapped in their gyrating planes as they fell to earth.

And these raids were only the peaks of the bloodbath. On October 4, 360 heavy bombers took off for a variety of targets in industrial Germany. The second week in October proved a peak period. On the eighth, 350 bombed Bremen and Vegasack, with a loss of 30. Next day, the ninth, 352 planes bombed various targets, including the Focke-Wulf factories at Marienburg, with damage so severe no attempt was made to repair the factory. Losses for the day: 28 bombers. On the tenth bombers attacked rail and waterway targets at Munster. Of the 236 planes engaged, 30 went down.

No force in the world could continue to take such losses in trained men and planes. And when one looked at the Luftwaffe, they did not seem to be suffering: every day they swarmed up, the fighters, exacting their toll of every raid. It is no wonder a lot of the officers and men of the Eighth and Ninth U.S. Air Forces began reporting sick.

But, in fact, there was consternation inside Germany —unknown to the Allies. This bombing had taken on a serious pattern. This was no longer the swashbuckling knocking out of a dam or two, or a single low-level attack on a factory. This bombing had become "businesslike," the Luftwaffe people were saying. Bombing like this was swiftly putting Germany at the end of its rope. And the German losses that were dishearteningly unapparent to Allied airmen now, would begin to show in early 1944, when the preparations for D-Day went ahead.

But for the moment the Luftwaffe retained air superiority over the European continent.

Combined Strategic Air Command was hoist on the twin petards of its own dilemma. Serious consideration could not be given to a heavy strategic bombardment of Germany until the Luftwaffe had been eliminated. The Luftwaffe could be eliminated only by the heavy strategic bombardment of the fighter plane factories and fuel sources in Germany.

But then, suddenly, the big switch, the big change, occurred. The simple fact was: the U.S. daylight raids themselves, costly as they were (and augmented and helped along by the nighttime RAF raids), unwittingly, and in a way unintentionally, had done in the German Luftwaffe. So great was the loss in German fighters, simply from combatting the U.S. raids day after day, that the Luftwaffe never recovered from it.

The raids had done their mission, too. Despite the dispersal tactics of Hitler's evil industrial genius Speer, the replacement abilities of Germany's aircraft industries had been halved, just about, by June of 1944. Rot at the top had taken its toll also; Goring, as the war went sour, was spending more and more of his time in the comforting medieval setting of Karinhall, his hunting-lodge country estate. But the destruction of German fighters which rose in clouds to meet the great flights of American bombers, essentially a secondary result of the raids themselves, was a major factor.

By February of 1944 the P-51 Mustang was in action over Europe. With drop-tanks (also a recent development) the Mustang fighter could escort the big bombers all the way to Berlin. The "little friend," as the bomber pilots called their fighter escorts, and the "big friend" as the fighters called the bombers, could take on the Luftwaffe together. And the German air force became a specific target, with the May or June date of D-Day specifically in mind.

So all the carnage and destruction which the bomber boys witnessed within their ranks of planes, and were scarred by, were not without their particular purpose, which showed up as a long-range success in the skies over Europe after D-Day: Allied air superiority.

But the scars remained, nonetheless. Many flyers never forgave commanders like Generals Brereton and Frederick Anderson for repeatedly extending their numbers of missions, and for ordering the suicidal raids. So also remained the haunting picture of what it was like above Germany's industrial cities in the last half of 1943 and all of '44, the picture which has been described hundreds and hundreds of times. The great bombers rearing up and falling off as they were hit. Single bombers, then in twos and threes, cartwheeling down the sky with an illusory dreamlike slowness, a wing gone, or a tail section sheered off. The sudden blossoming of great flame flowers from a hit engine or a stricken midsection. Debris floating past your plane from a friend's midair explosion. A fighter trailing smoke trails down the winter sky. Black flak bursts dotting the sky as far as the eye could see with a series of punctuation points. Live bodies diving out of planes with parachutes afire, and a five-mile fall to think it over, before crashing into the earth.

Scars, yes; and only time would heal all those. The other day I was talking to a friend of mine who was a Liberator pilot with the Fifteenth Air Force, flying out of Foggia, where he completed something like sixty missions over Europe. He is a still-trim man of about fifty-five now, with hair white all over, a successful optometrist who spends all his weekends off alone in the Everglades in a canoe. He looked at me with clear, honest eyes and smiled, a little shyly. He had seen more than one friend's plane waver and fall off beside him, to go drifting down, cartwheeling and crumpling, or explode in flames. "Well, you know," he said hesitantly, "that war was one of the big experiences of my life, you know? Maybe *the* major one. Bigger than my marriage. Bigger than the birth of my kids." Then, a little embarrassed, but knowing exactly what he was saying, he said the greatest cliché of them all, "I hated it. But I wouldn't have missed it for anything. I'm just glad I didn't miss it." Over the years he has built up a very large, comprehensive library on it, most of it devoted to the air war.

Nose Art

Illustration 147

In the very beginning, when this book was still in the talking stage, one of the things I suggested and insisted would be a positive asset was a representative collection of airplane nose art. Amongst all the other art to come out of World War II, I felt plane nose art should have its special place of honor. Nobody has ever done a serious study of it, and I think one should be done. Perhaps it is too repetitious for a study. Like so many things Americans did (and do), there is a lot of imitativeness in it. But there are various themes and variations on themes which grew up as the war progressed.

One of the clearly evident themes, of course, was the bird theme. Planes fly, and are therefore like birds. A direct offshoot of this is the egg theme. Birds lay eggs, bombers drop bombs. Bombs equal eggs. Two variations of this are the B-29 called "Special Delivery," and the B-24 Liberator named "Wongo Wongo."

The theme of the female nude, in some context or other, was another highly popular trend. Sometimes the bare-assed lady would be dragged into a plane name for just about no other reason than that she was a lady and was nude, or near nude, as in the planes named "Super-Chief," "Mad Russian," "Photo Fanny," and "Lucky Strike." The Super-Chief was a fast-moving luxury train from California to Chicago, back in those far-off days. Still is. Mad Russian probably refers to the name of the pilot, but the painter brought a good-looking woman into it anyway. Photo Fanny was probably an air photo plane of some sort. Lucky Strike is tied in with the cigarettes of the same name by the circle, and of course the pun on Lucky Strike is that the plane is lucky and as a bomber made some good, or lucky, strikes. The only reason to drag a near-nude girl into it is the further pun that if you could get laid by one like her, it would be a lucky strike.

But men thought about women. In fact, women were probably always in their thoughts when they weren't actually in combat or immersed in work, getting ready for combat. When the presence of death and extinction are always just around the corner or the next cloud, the comfort of women takes on a great importance. Woman is the antithesis of war. Soft, pliable, decent, clean, sensitive, understanding, and great to fuck. One might live with a woman day after day and this opinion might wither, but living without them at all in the midst of the hairy angularities of other men enhanced it. Just how warlike, aggressive and bellicose women might be faded as their proximity faded.

"Madame Pele" here of course is the Hawaiian goddess of fire who resides in the volcano. (Hawaiians were perhaps a little more realistic about their women.) The plane was bought with the contributions of school children in Honolulu, and perhaps because of this the nose-art artist who painted her turned her away just a little so he would not be required to show a nipple, and thoughtfully blanked out the inner part of the armpit.

Another theme used frequently was caricature, as

in the plane called "Waddy's Wagon." Here, as in so many, alliteration serves as a fillip to the wit. The painter has let his imagination go with the use of a wagon, which suggests children. The pilot and co-pilot are hauling it of course, the bombadier is dropping bricks and peering through a reading glass, the gunners are using pea-shooters and slingshots, the navigator is scratching his head. There is no doubt that the men's faces were carefully done caricatures that are fully recognizable.

Most of these nose-art jobs were done fairly late in the war, when the idea of nose art had caught on and become a fad, and aircrews went to great lengths and pains to have their nose art and names be funny and original.

One can't help wondering if all of them got back home.

BREAKOUT—AND THE LONG HAUL

Illustration 148–152

It was touched off by the massive "saturation" air bombardment of German ground defensive positions, the first such of the war. General Bradley had requested it, always mindful of saving American casualties when he could.

In fact, the great tactical air bombardment (using B-17s and B-24s against troops tactically for perhaps the very first time) was highly successful in places along Bradley's front, and woefully ineffective in others. In the first place it was ordered for July 24, and actually started, and was then called off by Air Marshal Leigh-Mallory because of weather. Some of these deliveries, falling a day early, killed 25 Americans and wounded 130 by falling on the wrong side of the demarcation line (the Périers-St. Lô highway). But, as had happened before in the Normandy fighting, the Allies' mistake worked in their favor. The Germans thought a serious attack had been launched, and that they had repulsed it. When the main attack was delivered next day, on the twenty-fifth, in four to five times the force, the Germans were unprepared for it.

This time, too, Americans were bombed by their own. One hundred eleven killed, 490 wounded. And the famous accidental killing of U.S. Lieutenant General Lesley J. McNair, visiting to inspect the American troops in action, happened. But even this did not stop the troops. They had changed, and toughened, since the Normandy landings. Outfits which had been bombed into a frightened daze nevertheless moved out forward and attacked when ordered. At first the going was rough. Rugged—a word much in use in those days. The massive air bombing appeared not to have sprung the infantry loose and through the German line as hoped. For a day the issue hung undecided. Then "Lightning Joe" Collins, still commanding the attacking VII Corps, came to the fore. He decided to gamble and ordered tanks in.

It was not known whether the Germans had pulled back their main forces to escape the second bombardment. If they had, they would be in perfect position to spring a large-scale ambush. In fact, such was not the case. In the rear of the German lines there was nothing but a large gaping hole. Most of the Americans were totally unaware of this. Only a few seem to have suspected that the Germans lacked depth and reserves. But the truth was that the hard fighting of the Normandy invasion and the Battle for the Hedgerows had depleted the German Seventh Army's men, matériel, fuel and supplies to an enormous degree.

In all this, Adolf Hitler had once again been remarkably helpful to the Allies. Still convinced that the Normandy invasion was only a feint to cover a main invasion to the Pas de Calais, he refused to withdraw reserves from there to send to Normandy. The result was the huge hollow emptiness behind the German line which the American VII Corps on the right of St. Lô now broke out into.

At first Bradley's rather modest objective had been Coutances, a road and rail center twenty miles south and west and near the western coast of the Cotentin peninsula. But by July 28, with nothing much in front of him to stop him, he decided to move on to Avranches. If he could take Avranches, he would have the whole of the Cotentin, and perhaps could turn the corner into the much greater peninsula of Brittany. Squeezing Middleton's VIII Corps into the line on the right flank along the coast, and turning Collins' VII Corps off a little to the left, he ordered both to keep advancing. By now the armored units had leapfrogged the infantry which had broken the way open for them, and mechanized columns were racing ahead down all the important roads with only sporadic resistance meeting them. One of Collins' columns had cut off a large German force below Coutances, near Roncey.

At daybreak of July 30, all the wreckage of defeat and retreat lay scattered over the countryside—vehicles, wagons, dead horses, abandoned guns. A single armored division had captured over four thousand Germans in three days. By nightfall of July 30, Americans were in Avranches, and found no Germans had yet arrived in the town. Bridges over the two rivers were still intact. Taking them, the Americans were free to move west into Brittany, and more important, free to swing south and east toward Paris. What had begun as a modest breakthrough was turning into a true breakout. Farther north and east Montgomery and Dempsey were attacking the now thinly held German defenses and moving inland toward Falaise. The entire German left flank in the north of France had been turned at Avranches.

The Great End Run was on, and it would not stop until Bradley's First and Patton's Third Armies reached the Seine above and below Paris, and hardly pausing, drove on to the Meuse where shortages of all supplies, but mainly fuel, caused them slowly to grind to a halt, at least temporarily.

During the course of this wild, confused, headlong rush, there occurred the latest in the Sir Bernard Law Montgomery Saturday-afternoon Perils-of-Pauline controversy series. (There would be at least two or three others.) This latest installment was called the Great Falaise Pocket (or Falaise Gap) Controversy.

Good old Sir Bernard Law. He was always great copy for the newsmen. His men adored him (newsmen said) because he had once whipped Rommel at El Alamein, he was the needed popular British hero, and he could be depended on to grab for more than his fair share of the notoriety. But this time he had really fucked up seriously.

Asking for, and getting, an advanced meeting line with Bradley and more territory than he could in fact take and hold, Montgomery called for encirclement of the German Seventh and Fifth Panzer Armies at Argentan, fifteen miles beyond Falaise. When Bradley's First Army arrived at Argentan, Monty's forces still had not taken Falaise. Waiting twenty-four hours at Argentan for an invitation from Montgomery to cross over the Army Group boundary and drive north to close the gap, an invitation which never came, Bradley sent half of his XV Corps troops on east to try and cross the Seine. Montgomery still insisted his troops could reach the Army Group line. Later, the British would as usual blame Bradley for Monty's failure—why hadn't Bradley crossed the Army Group line anyway, without Monty's invitation? In the meantime, between August 14 and August 20 when the Gap was finally closed, some forty thousand Germans escaped through the narrow fifteen-mile opening.

It would seem that the honest and simple truth about good old Sir Bernard Law was that never after El Alamein did he fight his troops with the dash and élan that would give him the major victory he hungered for.

The carnage of the Falaise Pocket, observers said, was the greatest of the European war. And this time it was the Germans doing the dying. The roads and fields were strewn with thousands of enemy dead and wounded, wrecked and burning vehicles, smashed artillery pieces, carts laden with loot overturned and smoking, left behind, dead horses and cattle swelling in the summer heat. In spite of the mistakes, the Allies took fifty thousand prisoners and counted ten thousand German dead.

With Allied artillery pouring down on them from all sides as they moved, never once did the German troops falter or panic. In its way the German withdrawal from Falaise was one of the great feats of the war. Nor did they collapse and panic on the long retreat back to the German frontier. They were hardened, dedicated soldiers, the seasoned old-timers of years of battles, and never did they show it better than in their escape from Falaise. They and the British units across from them had fought each other for years. The sporting Britishers were forever paying them these fantastic compliments on their soldiering.

Now they had facing them massed armies of equally hardened, dedicated Americans, growing steadily in numbers and matériel and sagacity. Being a reluctant draftee army, they were perhaps not so sporting. Still, the fighting since D-Day had made veterans out of the ones who survived, and they justified Bradley's confidence in them. Combat-wise now, they were less likely to make the mistakes of the inexperienced, as Bradley enumerated them: "reliance on rumor and exaggerated reports, failure to support maneuvering elements by fire, and a tendency to withdraw under high explosive fire rather than to advance out of it."

And this fighting from Avranches to the Meuse was an exhilarating if fatiguing kind of fighting. In general it was a scrambling pursuit, a mechanized advance with everybody riding somewhere or other—on tanks, on trucks, on jeeps, on weapons carriers. When the Germans stopped to make a stand somewhere, there would be a sharp, short fight in which men died as painfully and unwillingly as in the hedgerows. The countryside passed in a monotonous unrolling canvas full of dust and windburn. At night there was little rest; too much had to be cleaned and serviced for tomorrow's push on. A victorious army in pursuit could even be called happy. A kind of sadistic happiness of sorts, anyway. Especially when it liberated a village that had wine, or captured a train of luxury supplies complete with cognac.

On August 15 the Mediterranean invasion had begun, and Hitler ordered the retreat of his armies in the south, to cover for the turned flank and match up with his splintered northern armies, in order to make a line in eastern France. The weary British, Canadian and U.S. Armies pushed on a little farther, but then were forced to stop again. And this time it was a complete halt. Supplies, especially the precious fuel for tanks and carriers, simply could not keep up. To stop now to re-outfit and reorganize was to give the Germans equal time to beef up their defenses and revamp the doughty Siegfried Line. But there simply wasn't any choice. There was not enough gasoline to go on. There were no reserves to form a backup. The Allies' Great End Run was finished and done, and the war was still not won. And the long haul from the Normandy hedgerows almost to the German border was over.

But the long haul of my title is not the long haul of the Allies' Great End Run. Nor is it the long haul of the Red Ball Expresses, trying desperately over systems of one-way highways to reoutfit the supply-impoverished advancing armies. The long haul I refer to was to be the long haul of the succeeding, additional nine long months of further combat, until Germany was finally brought to surrender: whole series of major engagements; a bitterly cold and bitterly fought winter campaign; an insane, doomed, costly counteroffensive that came to be called the Battle of the Bulge; and after, a months-long campaign inside Germany itself and across the Rhine.

The green American outfits who had landed on the Normandy beaches had in three months' time passed through all the many and subtle EVOLUTIONS OF A SOLDIER and become (just as were their cousins in the Pacific) a conglomeration of hardy, mean, cynical, tough, canny, knowledgeable troopers and professionals. And before them all lay the one final EVOLUTION OF A SOLDIER that was perhaps the worst, or best, of all.

The Final Evolution

Illustrations 153–157

I suppose the best way to describe it would be to say it was the miserable reawakening of hope. This was the worst despair of all, and somehow it had to be handled. Probably the best way to handle it was to become like the British soldier and the German soldier: a "professional." We already had nuclei of these in some of the older outfits like the First Division. And we were getting more nuclei of them in the greener units since D-Day. Probably the man in question had to already be three-quarters of a "professional," before he could go ahead that last half-step and become wholly one. So it took the new men a while longer.

I put the term professional into quote marks above because I did not intend it to mean the true professional of the officer corps or the permanent party NCO corps, whose sole career was the army. Rather, just the reverse. I meant the draftee or volunteer soldier who by dint of having served his apprenticeship and survived, came gradually to be an expert in his work and to love it and to take great pride in his performance of it.

The problem itself—this miserable, shitty reawakening of a hope long since laid to rest—stemmed from the realization that he was now fighting in a war which was already won. A won war, but a won war whose fighting was going to continue for a while, and in which he might still be killed just the same: one of the last KIAs of a waning war. Not an enviable position. Perhaps the *only* recourse was to take refuge in his professionalism.

Up to now, he has already accepted the correctness and rightness of his own death, and has even gone so far as to write himself off the rolls. He has gone the subtle step further and faced and accepted the anonymity of his death, and its lack of recognition—except in the grossest numbers. Accepted that he will be more unknown, and therefore deader, than the Unknown Soldier. He has gone through all that, all these successive abandonments of hope; and has come out on the other side into that other bath-to-bath, bottle-to-bottle hope that is the only hope the combat men can have. (Woman-to-woman, that third element in his litany, was too far above his restricted possibilities except very occasionally.) He had done all that, and here suddenly the old-fashioned human kind of hope had pushed itself back up into his thoughts because the war was won. Any fool could see that, in the closing days of 1944. And if the war was a won war, then there must be some point in time in the foreseeable future when it would cease. There was suddenly a possibility he might survive its end. Such thoughts awakened all the pain he had learned so laboriously over the months, in many cases years, to amputate at the root.

It was the last metamorphosis that would be asked of him. And if he could weather that one, he would be about as fully a soldier as a non-professional could be, a "professional" among the Professionals.

He had a lot of things to help him with it. He had

his professionalism, first of all. The craft he had mastered from a raw apprentice and had come to love. That could give him pleasure now. The doing of a job—from its projection and inception on through to its completion—even if it meant shooting and killing a lot of other people who perhaps felt about the whole thing the same as he. Then there was his *esprit de corps,* that fine French phrase which the French are so fond of using loosely, and which Webster defines as "The common spirit pervading the members of a body or association of persons. It implies sympathy, enthusiasm, devotion, and jealous regard for the honor of the body as a whole." *Esprit* can be overvalued by sentimental civilians, since the key word there is the *jealousy,* as many a replacement found out to his dismay, and his demise. But in its best function, it kept the members of a platoon, a company, a regiment, a division going when there was little else to cling to. Victory, and being victorious, was still another big shot of adrenaline in the veins. And then there was a thing which, for lack of a better term, I have labeled "the combat numbness." This seemed to be composed of equal parts of sheer physical fatigue, insupportable fear, and a sort of massive, strained disbelief at what was happening. It seemed to wax in a man in direct ratio to the number and length of the times he had felt it before, and afterwards it waned in him in the same predictably divisible ratio. The oftener and longer he felt it, the quicker it came over him next time and the longer it took to leave him after. So that, if handled properly and if the man's outfit stayed up on the line often enough and long enough, it could even become a mercifully blissful permanent state.

Also, his canny, healthy (or unhealthy) cynicism served to aid him, which was why volunteering for the dirty jobs was on the decrease, and why so many replacements were blown away on war's wind, in both the fields and woods of Europe and the jungles and sands of the Pacific.

But even with all these to help him, many men would not metamorphose through this last transition. In the later phases of the war in Europe, that is to say after Bradley's Great End Run, the number of cases of AWOL, desertion, sickness and combat fatigue were on the increase at an alarming rate. When elements of the First and Third Armies crossed the Seine above and below Paris, and bypassed it in the chase after the Germans, ten thousand men went over the hill and descended on the newly liberated, playtime city. Most of them showed up back at their outfits in a week or two. But the number was so alarming that Eisenhower declared Paris off-limits to American troops. While First Army was fighting in Belgium, the number of desertions reached such a high that Eisenhower signed, and did not rescind, the order for the execution of Pvt. Eddie Slovik for desertion in the face of the enemy—the first American soldier to die for desertion since the Civil War. Slovik was a replacement, badly trained, badly educated, one piece of the walking meat to help beef up the strength of the shrinking divisions. It seemed an open and shut case. But the main point was that an example was needed.

The old-timers, of course, were too canny, too battle-wise, to get caught for anything like desertion under fire. They took their vacations between battles, or let themselves get trench foot. But the restrictions laid down by the army in Washington and London were getting tougher and tougher, and they found that only back in their home outfits were they understood and appreciated. If they could get back to their outfit under their own power, the Old Man would likely let them off with an ass-eating; but everywhere else they were considered criminals and potential jailbirds. An MP provost marshal cared little for and paid no attention to the years of former service in Africa, Sicily and Italy.

Back in the outfits, the same old grind went on. Fight and run, run and fight. Walk. Walk, walk, walk. A friend of mine had as his jeep driver an infantryman

132.
Taking a breather *on a hill overlooking the marshlands near St. Lô. Rest was like gold.*

133.
Field bath *was a rare and unusual treat, particularly in a liberated tub.*

134.
Destroyed town *of Vire had the hapless luck to be in the path of the Axis retreat and the Allied advance.*

135.
Night fire *of the dreaded German 88 mm guns as portrayed by a German artist.*

136.
Sabbath in combat *rarely coincided with a day of rest.*

137.
Left:
Liberating Cherbourg *and rebuilding it was a critical effort in supporting the sweep across France. It was sorely needed to supply the advancing Allied ground forces.*

138.
Allied raids *on Hamburg and endless raids on dozens of other cities helped to soften the Germans and limit their ability to supply their weakened war machine.*

139.
German defense *of Hamburg was stubborn and Allied air crews paid dearly. This painting was made by a German artist portraying his country's antiaircraft.*

140. *Right:*
Total destruction *was faced by many of Germany's cities, being overwhelmed from the air and the ground.*

141.
Hell's Angels *was a name for a group of B-17s, here being led on a last raid by one of their number called "Old Thunderbird," about to be retired.*

142.
Sweating it out. *Ground crews in the Aleutians wait for the return of planes.*

143.
Wounded crewmen *are taken off a crippled bomber which managed to limp home.*

144.
More bombs *are being loaded by marines in a clearing.*

145.
Working by floodlight, *a crew repairs a damaged plane during the Battle of Cape Gloucester, New Britain.*

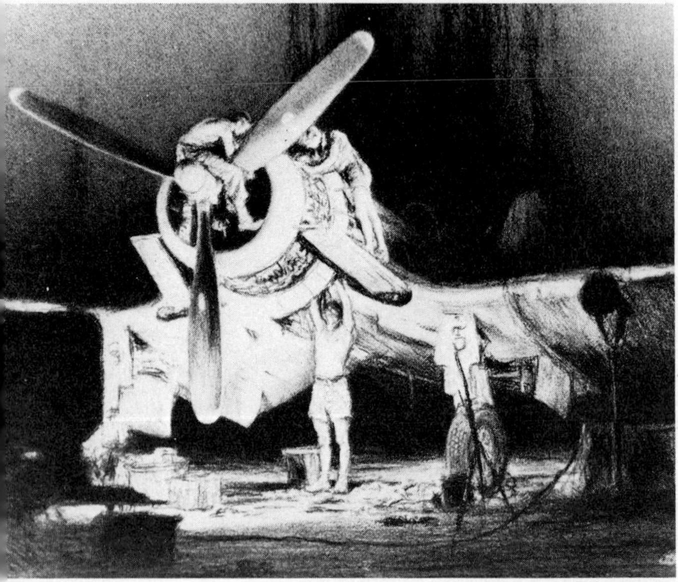

146.
Night landing *is being carried out aboard the U.S.S.* Hornet. *The landing-signal officer brings the fighter in, his fluorescent clothing lit by ultraviolet light.*

Photo Fanny

The
JUMPIN STUD

Madame
PELE

Special Delivery

MAD
RUSSIAN

The Super-chief

WADDY'S WAGON

WONGO WONGO!!

'Lucky Strike'

BREAKOUT
Brest
18 Sep.
Lorien
Scale of Miles
0
25
50
Map by Wesley B. McKeown
USA

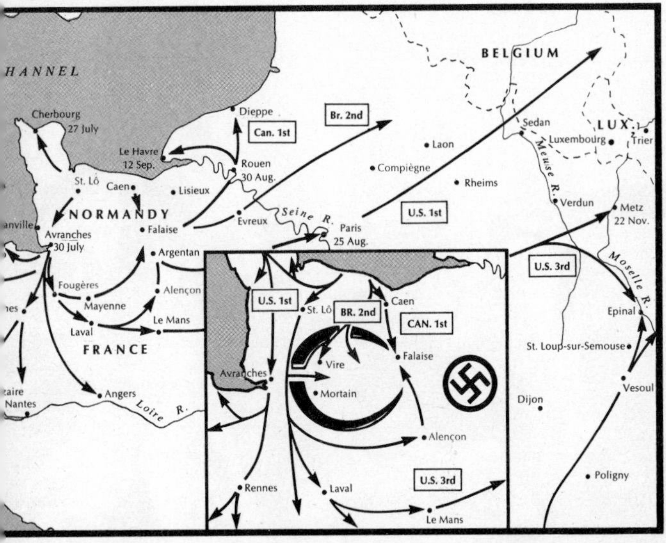

149.

148.
Left:
A sharp lookout *is maintained by a tank crewman.*

150.
Truck ride *gives these soldiers a chance for a needed nap before going on to a new attack.*

151.
German surrender *has become a more common sight than before.*

152. *Right:*
Relaying instructions *from the top of a tank.*

153.
Moving Up *by Howard Brodie.*

154.
Going down for cover, *a G.I. does the only thing possible during a German 88 mm barrage.*

155.
Caught in a flare, *these two men were on night patrol when suddenly an enemy flare lit the landscape. They froze and avoided detection.*

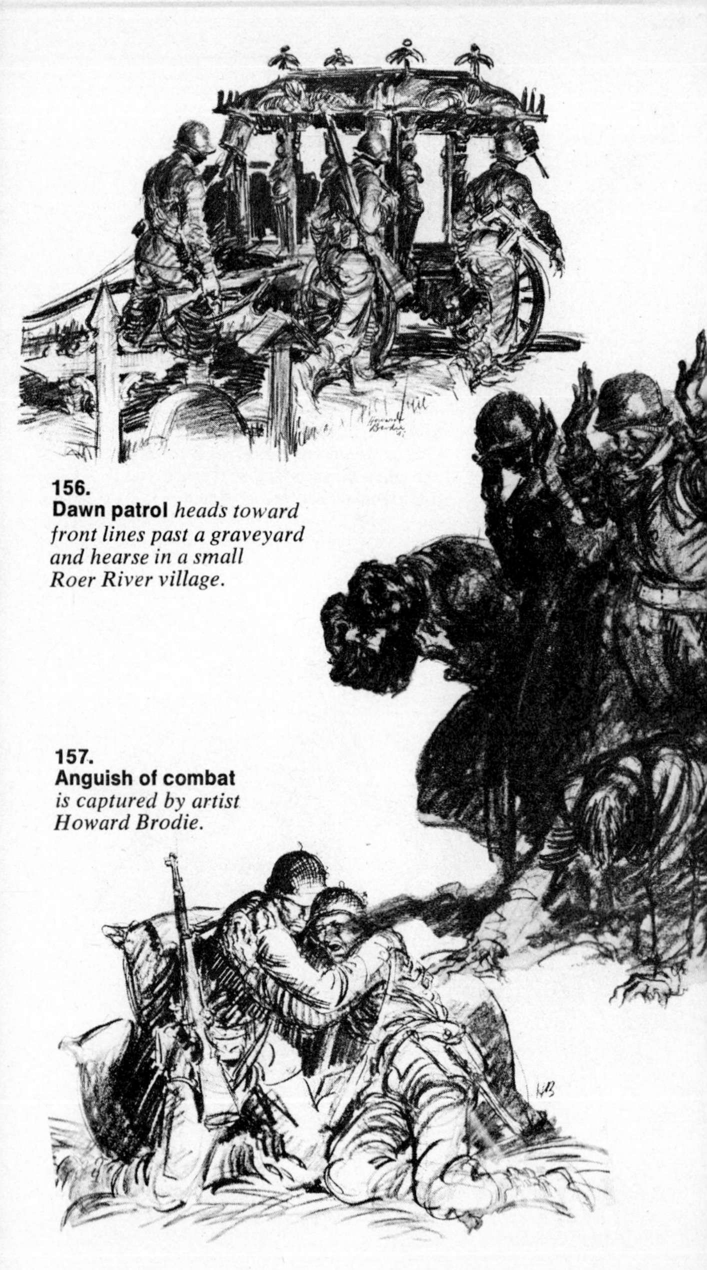

156.
Dawn patrol *heads toward front lines past a graveyard and hearse in a small Roer River village.*

157.
Anguish of combat *is captured by artist Howard Brodie.*

158.
Massacre at Malmédy.

159.
Numbing cold *and winter took out G.I.'s not reached by German guns.*

160.
Battlefield execution *was the fate of this German infiltrator who dressed in G.I. clothing.*

161.
Left:
Three years later *to the day, December 7, 1944, the United States Navy landed the Seventy-seventh Division at Ormoc, surprising the Japanese defending Leyte. It was the beginning of the final phase of the land fighting on Leyte.*

162.
Return to Luzon *and the Philippines came on January 9, 1945, just three years after the Japanese had landed there. In this painting, the Seventh Amphibious Force closes in on the beaches after a furious bombardment by the Seventh Fleet.*

163.
Landing at Lingayen Gulf *brought the island-hopping U.S. forces one step closer to Japan.*

164.
Liberation day *finally came for P.O.W.'s at Santo Tomas University in Manila.*

165.
Camouflaged guns *wait for calls.*

166.
Filipino craftsman *fashioning a barong knife.*

167.
A Moro warrior.

168.
Japanese pillbox *has been silenced and life resumes at Dagopan, Luzon.*

169.
P.O.W.'s: *Americans on the day they were freed from Japanese captors at Bilibid prison, Manila.*

170.
Kamikaze attacks *intensified as Japan fought with increasing desperation against advancing U.S. forces.*

171.
Preparing to die, *Japanese pilots are cheered on their graduation.*

172.
Souvenir scarf *was called the "Scarf of a Thousand Stitches." Made by Japanese women and worn around the waist by their soldiers, they were highly prized as war booty. One saying had it that they were stripped off "before the enemy hit the ground."*

who finally had refused to walk anymore. He had been courtmartialed for this, given a month in a stockade, and when he came out, had been put to driving my friend's jeep. This much was okay, drive he would do; walk he wouldn't. He would not even walk to the latrine. When he had to go, he would come out of his shelter, drive the jeep fifty yards to the latrine and hop out. When he had finished his crap, he would drive the jeep back to the CP. He had made his separate peace.

Others found other ways for themselves. The anguish of a suddenly reborn imagination was almost too much to bear. For those who made the final step over in their EVOLUTION OF A SOLDIER, and became the hardened, dedicated professionals the army had always hoped from the beginning to make of them, the slow agonizing reawakening of hope was like a case of frozen feet. As long as you left them alone, frozen feet didn't hurt and didn't bother you. It was only when your buddy started rubbing the deadened members with snow, to restart the flowing of the blood, that the hot burning excruciating pain began to come. Men have actually been known to strap their boots back on and walk on until they fell over, to avoid the cure. That was what the reawakening of hope was like. Get numb, stay numb, and do the thing they knew best how to do, now; that was the password. In the Pacific, as MacArthur began his moves back into the Philippines, marines and infantry were teaching themselves the same thing.

Few knew then, or cared, that the coming of pain would always be the first symptom—the beginning of the DE-EVOLUTION OF A SOLDIER. For them, as fully evolved professionals, they could fight on forever and victory or defeat meant practically nil. It was better than having to go home and get to know their wives and kids again.

Up against these men would come Hitler's last insane *Götterdämmerung* of a counteroffensive.

THE BULGE

Illustrations 158–160

It began before dawn on December 16. There were five things the Germans had to do if they wanted to reach their final objective, Antwerp. First and second, they had to set up "hard shoulders" at both edges of the salient where it penetrated the Allied line. These corners were the most vulnerable points and were absolutely vital. Third, the Panzer SS spearhead must quickly overrun the American center and race to capture the bridges across the Meuse before they could be blown or defended. Fourth, von Manteuffel's Fifth Army moving on the Sixth SS Panzer Army's left, must with its right wing capture St. Vith, the key road and rail center in the north; and fifth, with its left wing capture Bastogne, key likewise to the road and rail traffic in the south.

In fact, none of the assigned objectives was reached within the allotted time on the strict schedule. And four of them were never reached at all. St. Vith was finally taken (abandoned by the Allies, actually), seven days behind schedule, too late to be of great help, and

Bastogne was never taken. No Panzer units ever reached the Meuse. More important, the German troops trying to secure the "hard shoulders" at the corners of the salient were repulsed repeatedly and never did break down the corners of the American line. The effect was to choke the counteroffensive between these two angled points. So, tactically, the much-vaunted, Hitler-inspired counteroffensive was a lost cause from the start.

Almost certainly it was doomed from the start strategically, also. It was much too ambitious a plan for the resources available to the Germans at that point of the war, both in men and fuel, and in guns and armor. All of Hitler's field marshals and chiefs of staff had counseled him against it. In fact, its very lack of feasibility helped gain for it the high element of surprise it enjoyed at its beginning. Eisenhower, Bradley, Montgomery and their staffs could not believe the Germans would try such a grand attack, with no more resources than they had. Eisenhower himself, when he called a meeting of his commanders on December 19, called the situation "one of opportunity for us and not disaster." The German Field Marshal Model, who commanded the entire operation, called it a failure as early as December 18 (two days after it started on the sixteenth) when he learned how far behind schedule his Panzers had fallen.

All of this could not be known, of course, to the small bands of Americans scattered through the area, cut off from each other, stubbornly defending in the snow and fog and low-hanging weather the lonely little road junctions and bridges they had been assigned. To them it must have seemed like the end of the world. Here, with the war practically won, and the Germans falling back slowly in exhaustion and defeat, out of nowhere came this whirlwind counterpenetration squandering men and tanks and gasoline at a prodigal rate even the United States could not afford. Did they have unlimited resources, these Germans? Stories passed up and down the line and the outposts, of

Skorzeny's commandos dressed in American uniforms and speaking English, penetrating far to the rear and seizing ahead of time bridges for the Panzer units to cross. One story said thousands of paratroopers had been dropped in the rear expressly to assassinate Eisenhower and any other high-ranking officers they could grab. The chilling tale of the Malmédy massacre passed from lonely junction to lonely junction in the equally chilling fog: one hundred fifty American prisoners cut down by Panzer SS troops where they stood lined up in a field, after being captured. Now, if ever, was the time to heed Bradley's wise dictum about not placing "reliance on rumor and exaggerated reports." Things always look different from the other side of the line. And nobody knew fully just how far the Germans had already overextended themselves.

No one of these little road junction stands could have had a profound effect on the German drive. But hundreds of them, impromptu little battles at nameless bridges and unknown road crossings, had an effect of slowing enormously the German impetus—particularly in the restricting terrain of the Ardennes where there were few roads and narrow valleys and no open country. These little die-hard "one-man-stands," alone in the snow and fog without communications, would prove enormously effective out of all proportion to their size, in slowing down the German advance in the compartmentalized Ardennes terrain. They would also prove just how far the U.S. soldier had come in his professionalism since the early days in North Africa.

But they could not be expected to hold back some two hundred thousand men and a thousand tanks. The first major defensive moves and actions, makeshift though they were, were vitally important and set the form of the battle for the weeks to come. Since World War I, American staff schools had taught that the way to contain and finally reduce the salient of a major offensive was first to hold the shoulders of the penetration. U.S. commanders acted on this teaching automatically. Holding these shoulders would constrict the enemy in the number of major forces he would be able to commit. Without sufficient width to the salient, the Panzer columns would run into and block each other. In the north Hodges' First Army held at a ridge outside the town of Elsenborn that came to be known as "Elsenborn Ridge" or "The Elsenborn Shoulder," and in so doing kept the great bulk of the Sixth SS Panzer Army occupied and out of the advance entirely. In the south at Echternach the Fourth Division of Patton's Third Army wavered, gave up some ground, but managed to hold. And in the center, blocking the two main road centers, St. Vith and Bastogne held.

In his December 19 commanders' conference, Eisenhower took these factors into account in his dispositions. The only reserves left to him, because of offensives already begun north and south of the Ardennes, were the two American Airborne divisions, the Eighty-second and 101st, recuperating from Montgomery's fiasco at Arnhem where they had been badly mauled. The Eighty-second was dispatched to strengthen and extend westward Hodges' line from the Elsenborn Shoulder. The 101st was sent on a wild one-hundred-mile ride through the sleeting night to reinforce Bastogne. Units of Simpson's Ninth Army were to extend south to free First Army units north of the salient. In the south Devers' Sixth Army Group was to extend north to free Patton's Third Army for a counterattack north. But because Hodges was in such straits containing the Sixth SS Panzer Army, the two U.S. armies, Ike said, would not attempt to strike at the base of the German penetration, the classic and most desirable maneuver. Instead, Patton would strike north farther west, straight toward the relief of Bastogne. Patton astonished his confreres by offering to begin his attack in seventy-two hours, or early on December 22. This meant he must swing his entire Third Army—six divisions and one hundred thirty-three thousand vehicles —in a ninety-degree turn from east to north, in three days. Any who secretly disbelieved him were proved wrong when on the twenty-second his attack began as promised. On this sanguine note the conference broke up.

And now it was time for Monty, the Mighty Mite, to enter the scene again. Eisenhower's chief intelligence officer, a Britisher, pointed out that soon the German advance would totally split Bradley's Twelfth Army Group, and that therefore all forces north of the German thrust should be transferred to Montgomery's command. It was an upsetting suggestion, and would become the basis for bad blood between Montgomery and Bradley that would remain forever unhealed. Eisenhower had always resisted putting large bodies of American troops under British command, and had specifically and repeatedly rejected Montgomery's request to be made overall ground commander. Just the same, the proposal made sense. Bradley's communications with Hodges' First Army were becoming increasingly difficult, but even more important, putting Montgomery in command north of the Bulge would insure the use of British reserves (of which, unlike the Americans, Monty had a great store) if they were needed. Using his head and thinking it out as he almost always did, Ike gave the order. Later when the Bulge was all but over Montgomery would use the change of command, in a press conference on January 7, to claim for himself and the British armies the entire credit for saving the Allies and winning the victory. In fact, only a very few British troops were used at all in the entire battle. This pompous claim would cause Bradley, usually the calmest and most considerate of men, to threaten resignation if he had to serve under Montgomery, and Patton added that if Bradley went, so would he.

All this, however, was in the future. At nightfall on December 21 the battle still appeared to be going badly for the Americans. St. Vith was to be evacuated next day by the Americans and so was now open to the German advance. The situation on the southern shoulder of the German salient was still unstabilized.

The U.S. forces in front of Bastogne were all but destroyed, leaving the 101st Airborne to fight alone surrounded in Bastogne. One German Panzer division was across the Ourthe River twenty-three miles from the Meuse. Another was at the town of Houffalize with nothing in front of it, preparing to move on west. And perhaps most important, the fog and low snow clouds which ever since the beginning had denied the Americans their vital aerial superiority, still showed no signs of lifting.

On December 22 the Germans were launching their last attempt to reach the Meuse. On the twenty-second also the U.S. troops defending St. Vith began their strategic withdrawal, to go into the American line beside the Eighty-second Airborne and Third Armored Divisions. But by nightfall that night a cold wind began to blow. It had snowed heavily all day, but now a front was moving in from the east that not only would freeze the ground allowing tanks to maneuver freely, but would also bring clear air for the use of Allied air power. In spite of that, so devastating were the attacks by the two German columns near the towns of Marche and Boissonville that divisions arriving from the northern First Army front had to be thrown in piecemeal to keep the Second Panzer and 116th Panzer Divisions from breaking loose. By midday of the twenty-third the U.S. Second Armored began arriving, the last of the units Montgomery had hoped to assemble as a reserve for counterattack. By Christmas morning Hodges, and Collins of VII Corps, had committed it to begin the wiping out of Second Panzer Division at a town called Celles, just three miles from Dinant and the Meuse. It was the high point of the German advance, not quite sixty miles from starting point. Second Panzer Division literally had run out of gasoline.

It was not the end by any means. On the next day, the day after Christmas, some twenty-five miles away Patton's Fourth U.S. Armored Division relieved Bastogne. On the same day Hitler was finally informed that Antwerp could not be reached, under any circumstances. Allied air continued to wreak havoc on the retreating German columns for another day. But lots of deadly and costly fighting still remained. Enough to satisfy the taste of the bloodthirstiest. On December 30, Manteuffel delivered a numbing attack against Patton's corridor into Bastogne. The fighting was worse than what the defenders of Bastogne had known even in their most critical days. But the U.S. troops held, threw the Germans back, and the corridor was not cut. Not until January 16 did the U.S. First and Third Armies link up, in Houffalize. Not until January 22 did the weather clear definitively, unleashing the U.S. pilots against the German convoys. Not until January 28 did the last vestige of the Bulge disappear.

In the end, some 600,000 U.S. troops fought in the Ardennes campaign and counteroffensive. Of these 81,000 were casualties: KIA, WIA, or captured. The British incurred 1,400 casualties. The attacking Germans lost around 100,000 men in killed, wounded and prisoners.

The dead were everywhere, in and around the heavily fought areas. More bodies than could easily be handled by the available troops, although the cold weather helped. The POWs got the unenviable dirty job of digging makeshift mass graves for the stiffened dead. Many of the POWs seemed glad to get such work.

Both sides had lost heavily in matériel. Estimates calculated as many as 800 tanks on each side, and for the Germans, 1,000 planes. The cool-headed Germans lost very little equipment by capture, and took back out with them everything that had not been destroyed by American fire.

But there was no question of who was the victor in the Ardennes. The victor was the American soldier, and he had come a long way since the days of Kasserine Pass, two years before. Accused of being pampered by his nation and his commanders, overpaid, overfed, overequipped, accused of lacking motivation (which he definitely did), he had met the hard occasion and had stood and fought with his new professionalism, and had given his commanders the time to collect and use their mobility and superior reserve power. The British had not helped him much, and the French had been too far away. The Ardennes was his own.

Many estimates have stated that the Ardennes campaign shortened the war by as much as a year. Certainly, it accelerated its end.

The American soldier, as he kicked his blankets up into a pile in the snow, and made up his pack with stiff hands, and prepared to move out forward again, wouldn't have known about that and at the moment wouldn't have cared. Weary to the bone, frozen, cold-eyed now, cold-footed, and cold-hearted to the core, he was sure only that up ahead lay another river and beyond that another hill, and that surely beyond that hill was still another river to cross, on pontoons or by wading. He had passed through and beyond his final EVOLUTION OF A SOLDIER.

German prisoners, asked to assess their various enemies, have said that the British attacked singing, and the French attacked shouting, but that the American attacked in silence. They liked better the men who attacked singing or shouting, than the grimly silent men who kept coming on stubbornly without a sound. Any old GI (for Government Issue: that term he so hated to be called) would have told them with a sour smile that he kept his mouth shut because he did not want anyone to see how badly his teeth were chattering. The German almost assuredly would not have smiled.

First Leyte, and Then Luzon

Illustrations 161–172

The great Pacific debate over the Philippines had begun as early as the Cairo and Teheran Conferences in late 1943. If the Central Pacific line of advance (as propounded by Admiral King) had been accepted at Casablanca, the actual detailed plans of operation in both Central Pacific and Southwest Pacific had deliberately been left open. However, unexpected acceleration of the advances in both theaters brought the argument to a head much sooner than even the most optimistic strategists could have imagined. The central issue became Formosa as preached by King versus Luzon as preached by MacArthur.

The truth was that, as the Japanese bastions began to be hit, though costly in casualties, they fell much more quickly than had been expected. And as the first half of 1944 worked its way down the calendar sheets, the invasion schedules kept updating themselves. Nimitz, for example, carried out his assault on Eniwetok on February 17, two months ahead of schedule. And MacArthur in his climb up New Guinea and the offshore islands was making an equal acceleration. With attrition working against her and production ballooning for the United States, Japan was collapsing far faster than ever anticipated; and after the naval battle of the Philippine Sea in June—"The Great Marianas Turkey Shoot," during the invasion of Saipan—she began to collapse even faster still.

MacArthur had always included in his series of suggested plans the idea that he would have to invade and secure Mindanao first. Mindanao, a large, very savage island and the southernmost of the Philippines, always presented a stumbling-block. It was feared the taking of it would be a long and costly jungle campaign. And up until as late as July, 1944, the Joint Chiefs' strategists in Washington had leaned toward King's Formosa invasion plan.

But on June 15 the Southwest Pacific commander had forwarded a new plan to Washington which switched his first main objective in the Philippines from Mindanao to Leyte, a smaller island in the center of the archipelago which not only would be easier to conquer but which also contained several important airstrips. He would still have to put a force ashore on Mindanao, but wanted as his principal objective the reduction of Leyte. The Leyte airfields would be needed to support an invasion of Formosa, MacArthur argued shrewdly. But then in late August he presented another plan, for a full-scale invasion of the Philippine archipelago, culminating in a seven-division assault in Lingayen Gulf on Luzon, scheduled for February 20, 1945.

Nimitz, on the other hand, following the idea of Admiral King but much less hot for assaulting Formosa than his superior, was having trouble presenting a plan of equal feasibility. He was hampered mainly by a shortage of sufficient ground forces for a full-scale invasion of anything as large as Formosa. His four or five marine divisions were not enough, while MacArthur had received six whole new infantry divisions to add to his other forces.

As late as the September 1 meeting of the Joint

Chiefs, General Marshall still did not want to commit himself to either Formosa or Luzon, and suggested giving MacArthur the go-ahead only to invade Leyte. And here luck took a hand in the game. Halsey, conducting carrier strikes on the Philippines in mid-September, reported enemy resistance astonishingly weak, and suggested other operations under planning be dropped to make a direct landing in Leyte Gulf immediately, two months ahead of schedule. Nimitz in Honolulu fell into line, offering MacArthur the force earmarked for the Yap Island invasion. The Joint Chiefs quickly issued a directive for the Leyte invasion on October 20. This decision gave the arguments for going on to Luzon a new and almost irresistible power. Especially when MacArthur reported Luzon could be attacked December 20. No such acceleration of the attack on Formosa was possible. By now even Admiral King had to go along.

To "draw the Japanese fleet into a decisive engagement and destroy it" had been a tenet of American Pacific strategy since the beginning of the Central Pacific thrust. This had nearly been accomplished in the Philippine Sea battle, the Marianas Turkey Shoot, but the Jap fleet had squeaked through and escaped, although the battle resulted in the near destruction of the Japanese naval air arm. Now again it was to be a principal aim of the Leyte invasion. And this time the Japanese obliged.

The Battle of Leyte Gulf has been called the greatest sea battle of all time. Some 70 Jap warships and 716 planes, split into 3 separate commands, came up against 160 U.S. warships and 1,280 planes. At the end of it, after three days of sea-fighting, the Japanese fleet to all intents and purposes for the rest of the war was virtually annihilated.

In the meantime, the Americans landed on October 20, and the land battle for Leyte ground on hampered by bad weather and torrential monsoon rains until December 25, Christmas Day, when MacArthur announced the end of organized resistance.

Whole volumes have been written on the naval battle of Leyte Gulf. Expecting a major American invasion assault somewhere and soon, the Japanese had drawn up a plan called Operation *Sho* (*sho* translates "victory"), intended to bring about just such a final confrontation as the Americans had been wishing for—with the sole difference of course that the Japanese plan called for the Japanese to win it. Since they did not know where the blow would fall, the Japanese had drawn up contingency plans for a number of places. Leyte in the Philippines was one of them. Like most of the Japanese great plans, it was inclined to be too complex, and to depend on a too-difficult-to-obtain precision timing. Basic to it was the fact that Japan's carrier forces, already so badly weakened as to be of little help, were to be used as a decoy to draw off the U.S. carrier forces to chase them. This was supposed to expose the remaining U.S. task forces and fleet to Japanese land-based aircraft and naval gunfire, which were expected to destroy all of the American fleet while its carriers were gone. It was undoubtedly a plan of desperation. In any case, when the Japanese learned that Leyte was the objective, Operation *Sho* was ordered into effect by the Japanese General Staff.

While Admiral Ozawa's nearly empty carriers were drawing Halsey's carriers northward, a second force under Admiral Kurita was to come into Leyte Gulf from the north, attacking the American Admiral Kinkaid's Seventh Fleet as it lay protecting the beachhead transports. At the same time, a southern force under Admiral Nishimura was to come up into Leyte Gulf from the south through the Surigao Strait, and catch Kinkaid in a naval pincer. Caught between the two, both the Seventh Fleet and the beachhead armada would be wiped out. When Halsey returned, both forces would fall on him and finish him off, too.

Due to a number of factors, it didn't work. Probably it never could have worked. Halsey did in fact finally fall for the decoy trick and ran off north, chasing Ozawa. Doing so, his Third Fleet sank four carriers, a cruiser, and two destroyers. Nishimura's southern force, coming through Surigao Strait, was anticipated by Kinkaid; and in a night battle on the night of October 24-25, the U.S. Seventh Fleet under tactical command of Rear Admiral Jesse Oldendorf destroyed Nishimura's force by the classic old sea maneuver of "crossing the T": as each Japanese ship came up, traveling in a line, the heavy guns of the whole Seventh Fleet from their "Top of the T" position could concentrate their fire on it. The entire force, except for one destroyer, was wiped out. Kurita's central force, coming up the other way through San Bernardino Strait, mistook the remaining U.S. vessels (mostly small escort carriers) for a much larger force, and broke off contact when it might have inflicted enormous damage. Having already lost *Musashi* (one of Japan's two greatest battleships), two cruisers sunk and one damaged to air attacks and submarines before coming in, Kurita retired, taking more air attacks as he fled.

The great Japanese Pacific fleet was broken, almost dead, ruined as any kind of an offensive weapon, and Luzon would not be long in coming.

The Leyte campaign in all its phases, air, sea and land, cost the United States about five thousand dead and fourteen thousand wounded—a light toll as things were going elsewhere. The toll in planes and ships was likewise relatively light. Whatever else could be said about the vainglorious old general, MacArthur, he could never be accused of "wasting" his men carelessly or thoughtlessly.

A new development had occurred in the campaign for Leyte which was to make itself increasingly felt at Luzon and later. This was the Japanese *kamikaze* air attack. The term meant "divine wind," and referred to a typhoon which supposedly blew away a great enemy invasion armada that attempted to attack Japan in the thirteenth century. Although it did nothing at all to alter the course of the war, it was able to inflict a grievous number of casualties and shipping losses from Leyte to the end of the war, and philosophically it said a great deal about the Japanese national character at the time of World War II. It was supposed to be a great privilege (at least, according to the propaganda) for young Japanese flyers to volunteer for the kamikaze suicide missions. Certainly it received a gratifying amount of international publicity. Apparently the concept was created by a certain Admiral Ohnishi who, just before the Leyte invasion, with so few planes at his disposal, ordered his flyers in the Philippines to carry only enough fuel for a one-way trip and to crash-land their bomb-armed fighters and fighter-bombers into the American ships, preferably aircraft carriers. Apparently the young Japanese flyers believed in it implicitly, because they fought and flew valiantly and with great resolve, in order to be able to crash-land on the deck of a U.S. carrier or in the superstructure of a cruiser. But just before the final surrender, when Ohnishi committed hara-kiri, as one of his last acts he wrote an apology to the souls of the kamikaze and to their parents, for his part in Japan's failure to achieve the victory the pilots had died for.

In fact, it was a desperation tactic. Most of Japan's carriers were gone, and so were most of her best airplanes. Under increasing pressure caused by the American advances, neither could be replaced. But what also could never be replaced were the lost pilots. Almost none of Japan's expert combat pilots were left alive to teach the young soldiers; nor was there reason to make expert pilots of the green youngsters. There was not the time, and without the carriers and the expert planes what could an expert pilot do? So, reasoned the government, better to use obsolete aircraft or to build cheap, poor airplanes (simple flying bombs, most of the later ones were) and teach the youngsters just enough to fly these simple planes into some American ships. Because of the ages-old-warrior's suicide code, almost nobody took exception. Many of the kamikaze spent almost no time practicing landings, since they were not going to need to know them anyway.

By the time the Leyte fighting ended, the Japanese had lost some 56,200 dead. Only 389 Japanese had surrendered. In actual fact, although MacArthur declared the island secured on Christmas Day, the grim and dangerous work of mopping up was not ended for several months after and the Jap General Suzuki, the Leyte commander, did not leave the island until March 15 with a remnant of his staff. Long before that, the attack elements of Kreuger's U.S. Sixth Army, some 68,000 men, had landed at Lingayen Gulf on Luzon.

Luzon was the biggest battle of the Pacific war. To study it is to see the fine hand of the old master-tactician MacArthur stamped on it as clearly as a signature on a piece of paper. Only on Luzon, an island the size of Britain, could units of division strength fight battles on the scale of those that were fought in Europe and Africa. More Japanese fought—and died—on Luzon than on any other Pacific island, and more American troops were committed there than in any other American campaign save the post-D-Day drive through northern France.

Luzon was a one-of-a-kind battle in other ways too. For perhaps the first time in the whole Pacific war, there was never any question about who was going to win it. The only question was how much was it going to cost? In lives, in time, and in equipment. For the Japanese, Luzon was a defensive battle from the start, and both sides knew it.

General Tomoyuki Yamashita, the "Tiger of Malaya," had been given the Philippine command in October, before Leyte. To meet the Luzon attack, he had more than 250,000 men, a sizable force, and including a large number of recently arrived reinforcements. But Yamashita's troops were in poor condition, badly led, badly organized, poorly deployed. Most units were under strength and short of food, ammo, vehicles and fuel. There was no longer a Japanese fleet to help them, and Yamashita had only around 150 combat aircraft still operational on Luzon. For the first time there would be no Japanese on the beaches to oppose the landings. Nor did Yamashita make plans to hold the central plains and the city of Manila. Instead, he would be concentrating his forces on the securing and holding of three mountain strongholds. The first and biggest was the wilderness of northern Luzon, with the bulk of his army. The second would defend the rough heights east of Manila. His third and smallest force would defend the mountainous region west of the central plains, protecting the Clark Field complex and threatening the American right flank as the U.S. troops moved south. Yamashita had been ordered to hold down and occupy as many U.S. troops as possible, for as long as possible. With his plan he hoped, and believed, he might hold up the Americans for months and even years.

Against this very un-Japanese defensive situation and position was arrayed the largest, strongest, best-equipped American army and naval armada the Pacific had ever yet seen. Walter Kreuger's Sixth Army had some 200,000 effectives, with tens of thousands more available for reinforcements. Before they were done, divisions from U.S. Eighth Army Sector to the south of Luzon would be called in, too. Kinkaid's Seventh Fleet once again, with some 850 ships, transports, and support vessels, was to put them ashore and keep them supplied. George Kenney's swiftly burgeoning Far East Air Forces were to protect and cover them.

It didn't even look like the same army. Compared to the thinly armed soldiers with their soup-plate helmets and wrap leggings who had fought here and lost in 1942, this army seemed like aliens from Mars. Even compared to their immediate ancestors, like us on Guadalcanal, they were a different army. New fatigue uniforms had been designed for them, new and better boots served their feet, new and better packs rode their backs. All sorts of new technologically improved arms and small arms accompanied them or were carried in their hands. Food and fuel and supplies followed them in such richness that it was unbelievable. Here were truly totally "new" Americans, come to reestablish and reconfirm their old association with these islands. And, after the terrors of the Japanese occupation, the Filipinos were truly glad to see them. Maybe twenty years later they might not be, but for now they truly were.

It was a long campaign, and grueling; and exceedingly bitterly fought in parts. Two entire corps of Sixth Army went in abreast on January 9, 1945—held up from their December 20 schedule by the bad-weather fighting on Leyte. Fighting their way down the central plain they arrived before Manila in less than a month. But Manila, held by 16,000 naval troops under Rear Admiral Iwabuchi, required a full month to take—and lay in ruins at the end of it, the first and only urban battle of the Pacific war. Nor did Corregidor, the old "Rock" of MacArthur's former headquarters, fall easily. From February 16 to 27, 5,000 Japanese troops held out underground in the tunnels. Nineteen survived. Not until the end of June was MacArthur able to declare the battle for Luzon over. And then, some 50,000 troops under Yamashita were still holed up in the mountains of northern Luzon. Here many held out until after the end of the war, foreign alien guerrillas living in the forests. But in the meantime, the U.S. forces were turning southern Luzon and the rest of the Philippines into a great base for the final assault against the Japanese homeland.

For the entire campaign, American losses were astonishingly light: only 7,933 killed and 32,732 wounded. In the hands of the old master tactician, who had the power and weight to smother the Japanese with casualty-laden hammer blows, finesse and superb ground tactics saved literally thousands of American lives. The Japanese lost some 192,000 killed.

One thing emerged definitively. That was the fanatical character of the Japanese defense. In at least three major instances (and in probably hundreds of minor ones) the Japanese categorically accepted suicide in order to inflict damage simply for the sake of inflicting damage—damage which could have no overall effect on the outcome. The first instance, and probably the most reasonable in any serious military way, was the kamikazes. In the approach and actual assault their attacks reached a height never before seen. These began on the fourth and continued through the seventh of January against Oldendorf's bombardment force. On the fourth, a twin-engine kamikaze crashed into the escort carrier *Ommaney Bay,* damaging her so badly she had to be sunk. On the fifth, sixteen kamikazes broke through the screen inflicting serious damage on nearly a dozen ships including two escort carriers, two heavy cruisers and two destroyers. On the sixth, as Oldendorf's ships entered Lingayen Gulf, aided by a low dense overcast that protected them from Halsey's fighter screen, the attacks reached crescendo. By nightfall of the seventh two battleships (*New Mexico* and *California*), three cruisers, three destroyers and several other vessels had been more or less badly damaged and three fast minesweepers (*Palmer, Long* and *Hovey*) sunk. Fortunately, on the seventh Halsey's planes so badly battered the Luzon airfields that the last operational Japanese planes were withdrawn.

Perhaps the kamikazes could be said to have some reason to their suicide. But the month-long battle for Manila from February 3 to March 4 had no reason to it at all. In 1942 MacArthur had turned Manila into an open city rather than have it destroyed by a battle, and apparently Yamashita had no intention of fighting there in 1945. But Admiral Iwabuchi's 17,000 naval troops determined to fight to the end there. Nor would they allow civilians to be evacuated, and 100,000 Filipino civilians died in the fighting, too. American losses were put at over 1,000 killed and 5,500 wounded. As for the Japanese, they had upheld the traditions of the Imperial Japanese Navy by dying almost to a man.

There was little sense to this, and there was little to the bloody and desperate stand made by Yamashita's *Shimbu* Group, in the southern end of the Sierra

Madre range, under the command of Lieutenant General Shizuo Yokoyama. Separated from Yamashita's larger group to their north, hopelessly cut off from any supplies, they continued to fight on in cave defense complexes for almost three full months until the end of May (by which time the German remnants had surrendered unconditionally in Europe)—for no apparent reason other than they found it embarrassing to surrender.

A lesser instance occurred in the town of Bayombong on Luzon. When the American Thirty-seventh Division entered the town, they found a Japanese hospital with all of the patients dead. Before evacuating Bayombong, rather than let their wounded and sick fall into American hands, the Japanese had gone through the wards shooting to death their own wounded, to save them the humiliation of being captured.

Evidences of Japanese killings, executions and torture deaths were coming to light as American troops moved through the valleys of Luzon. At least one atrocity was discovered by the unearthing of the remains of three to four hundred Filipino men and women who, with their hands tied behind their backs, had been bayoneted.

The Japanese had always been cruel victors. Now, in defeat, it appeared they were turning their cruelty equally upon themselves. It had always been a fate worse than physical death to be captured alive by the enemy, according to the Japanese military code of honor. It has been put forward as a hypothesis that perhaps the Japanese contempt and cruelty toward their conquered peoples grew out of their belief in this medieval code. Now, it appeared, they were more than willing to punish themselves equally severely for losing.

Most of the Americans they met were more than willing to oblige them. At least two of the American divisions fighting on Luzon—the Twenty-fifth and the Americal—had fought them at Guadalcanal; at least two—the Thirty-second and Twenty-fourth—had fought them all the way up from Lae and Hollandia. They had become at least as hardened and as toughened, as thoroughly professional now, as their European counterparts, and had been for at least as long. They no longer gave a damn how many Japanese they killed, in carload lots.

But the way the Japanese were taking to their growing defeat with a sort of insane crazy self-destructive valor boded no good for the inevitable coming invasion of the homeland.

What was it going to cost? 300,000 men? 500,000? A million?

Twilight of Some Old Gods

Illustrations 173 and 174

Military men always like it better, and feel more comfortable, if they can talk or write about a war on a purely professional level, without taking up in detail all the social, religious, political, ethical, and psychological factors which also go into giving a particular war its particular peculiar character. Military men always find it cleaner not to go into all that other stuff very deeply. But somebody always does have to go into it if a war—all war—is to be understood at all.

In Europe, as in the Pacific when the Japanese bastions began to fall, as Allied combat troops began to fight their way into Germany's heartland dark and unholy things began to be opened up and exposed. Unholy, Victorian as it sounds, is the only word that fits what the Americans and British began to find in the concentration camps and death camps they liberated on their way east to meet the Russians. Vicious, merciless, totally cynical, battle-hardened U.S. and British troopers were unnerved by what they came upon in camps like Belsen, Buchenwald, and Dachau. The bony, nude bodies with sunken faces and shaven heads, stacked in open trailers to be hauled to the incinerators like cords of wood. The still living few with little more than skin drawn taut over their bones and unable to stand or move. The bales of human hair saved, piles of gold teeth and old dentures saved, heaps and stacks of used spectacles and clothing counted and separated for recycling. And the worst of the extermination camps were still farther east, in Poland. Auschwitz (3,000,000 dead). Maidanek (1,380,000 dead). Treblinka (731,000 dead). Chelmno (600,000). Belsec (600,000). In Buchenwald only 63,500 died, in Dachau only 70,000, in Belsen only 50,000.

There still exists a much reproduced U.S. Army photo of a group of solid-looking, ordinary German townspeople, forced to parade past a line of corpses of Jewish women who died of starvation during a three-hundred-mile march. Old men in staid suits and vests and honest workmen's shoes. Schoolboys with their stockings dangling. A pretty young woman carrying a portfolio. The German civilians look half-angry and half-embarrassed as they file past with lowered eyes. The U.S. Third Army troops escorting them look coldly angry. In death the faces of the corpses themselves, mouths hanging open and battered and smudged and starved, hardly look human at all. On some, the faces have all but disappeared. In the last wavering moments of consciousness there seemed to be some instinct to warm themselves, because many of the fully clothed bodies had the arms crossed across the chest as if trying to hug themselves against the chill.

Hitler, with his implementation of his plan for the extermination of all Europe's Jews, had brought back to the West the barbarian concept of chattelized soul slavery, as surely as any Mongol emperor had ever brought it from the east across the Himalayan steppes. By May of 1945 the Germans had worked to death or otherwise destroyed some six million Jews and political dissidents. Stalin, farther east, and an old-fashioned Oriental potentate if there ever was one, had already carried out the same execution and labor-camp extermination upon some nine million political and social undesirables. Both campaigns were carried out under the perfectly legal authority of the state. Both concentration camp systems had as their basic function the carrying to its conclusion the state's legally adopted policy of political and social violence.

Instead of the Mongol emperor declaring himself divine the state itself had become divine, and being divine, could do with its chattel citizens anything it concluded was to its own perpetuation and betterment. Over and over, Britons and Americans who fell upon these examples of the state's domination would say, searching helplessly for a metaphor, "It was like stepping back into the Dark Ages."

Now, not all of these things were unknown to the Allies. Despite serious attempts at secrecy by the Germans, news of massacres and of the political camps and the Jewish extermination had all leaked out to the West. After all, Dachau was founded in 1934, as a political camp. As early as 1940 there was an international council at Evian in France, where Germany offered to give away its Jews to any nation who would take them; all refused, including Britain, France and the United States. So most men had heard of the "concentration camps" in some form or other. But to see it in the actual process and to realize the magnitude and extent of it, was a deep, frightening, psychic shock to the soldiering men of the Western democracies.

For the first time in two centuries the struggle of Western man toward some measure of security and dignity and sanctity of the individual had taken a massive leap backward toward the days of cruelty and torture and raw power of the medieval warlord, to whom no life was precious except his own. For the first time in modern history, human evolution was in danger of a very real (not just an imagined) retrogression into organized barbarism; and the door had been opened on all the dark side of human nature and duplicity which the warlord had always represented.

The result was to make men of good will and sound conscience everywhere begin to wonder whether, after all, humanity had evolved at all.

And in Europe, the war was drawing to a close not with happiness and gratitude and relief, but with a horrified and horrifying sense of destruction, starvation and terror, and an acute awareness of the shadows in us, the bestiality and vicious cruelty of which our race under its thin veneers of civilization was still capable.

Over and over again, when confronted with the horrors of the camps, German soldiers and civilians would say, "We did not know," and go on to add that if they had known, what was there that they could have done about it? It was a good question. No one seemed able to come up with a satisfactory answer for them. When the I. G. Farben corporation could invest two hundred fifty million dollars in factories in the Auschwitz area so as to use the camps' labor force, when Krupp Industries used and ran similar labor concentration camps at Essen, what could a single German civilian or a German soldier fighting in Africa or Russia do?

All this posed a serious ethical crisis for the "sportsman" type of professional soldier in both Allied armies. Just how far was a citizen or soldier to be held responsible for the political policies of his government? The truth was, and every soldier knew it, a soldier fought for his commanders. If he had good commanders, he fought well and was proud. If he had bad commanders, he fought badly and bitched and malingered. If the country that his commander was fighting for was reasonably moral politically, well and good; that was fine, that was gravy. But if the country his commander fought for was not, what then? Was he simply to retire himself from combat and refuse to fight more? Any professional soldier knew how that ludicrous idea would end. And as the war had worn on, more and more men, formerly civilian draftee soldiers, were beginning to become and to think and believe like professionals, if only in a private self-defense of sanity.

In Japan, where the Pacific fighting was still going on, and which for the first time was being reached by the war thanks to mass raids by U.S. B-29 Superforts, this problem did not occur in quite the same way. The Pacific war had always been a crueler, more vicious war. Few Allied soldiers were willing or would allow themselves to be taken prisoner by the Japanese. The news of the Bataan March and the POW labor camps in Burma had spread long before. The Japanese treatment of the conquered peoples in China had been common knowledge even before the war. And as the Philippines were liberated, the evidence of executions, torture, cruelty and starvation of both POWs and the subject civilian populations accumulated. In Japan, the Emperor, though not a Mongol, actually *was* "divine," and had been forever. In Japan, just emerging from what we in the West would call a very late case of the Middle Ages, the Emperor was the state. And the mistreatment of prisoners and conquered peoples was not only considered quite correct and manly, but was also great sport and good fun, just as it had been in the Middle Ages in the West. But in Japan too, as it had in the gloomy forested mountain fastnesses of Germany, despair was growing over the prospect of defeat.

It was not only within the Axis nations that old gods were dying. As surely as a firing squad officer pointing a pistol for a *coup de grace,* World War II was putting the quietus to the British Empire. To the Empire, and to all it had once so proudly stood for. It was no longer a proud term to be an empire-builder. In fact, the word "empire" would never again be used anywhere (not, at least, in public) without a look of apology. And when henceforth the three superpowers—America, the USSR, and China—pulled strings or nations, and rattled Saberjets or MIGs or pure manpower, they would take great caution to use some other word than "empire."

Nor was America immune. In America, the old world of "Free Enterprise" suffered such a resounding shock that it would never recover, either. Or, if it recovered somewhat, it would be to a form of free enterprise such as no American had ever yet envisioned. It would be a free enterprise and competition among a few giant corporations, fighting each other for control of the taxpayer's dollars. I said earlier that in 1943 the U.S. living standard was one-sixth higher than in 1939. Business prospered, and especially big business, which got bigger and bigger as it wove complex new ties to the military and to government. By 1945, 82 per cent of all the military and naval dollar debts were held by a top one hundred corporations. Thirty-one giant companies operated half of the government-owned eighteen billion dollars worth of new factories, and after the war these companies would acquire the factories for little or nothing. Industrial technology had won the war for us, and technology was here to stay. It would stay because the new managerial administration and technology were a more efficient way of doing things. And by staying, they would make of Americans wage slaves in a stricter, tighter way than they had ever been during the nineteenth century Industrial Revolution.

In the end, still another old god went down also. This was the concept of international clemency. For a couple of hundred years at least, the losers of wars and the leaders of losing states and commanders of losing armies had not been summarily executed by the winners. As they so often were back in the days of the warlords. Even Napoleon, that greatest of all enemies, had not been executed, neither the first time he lost nor the second, and had only been exiled to an island under guard. Now, in 1945, that year of great civilization, the Allied victors chose to try as war criminals and execute many of the political leaders and military leaders of both Germany and Japan. Trial processes were set up both in Nuremberg and Tokyo and ground on for ten full months. A great deal of legal maneuvering and haggling and legal publications of trial records were undertaken to give the proceedings the dignity and respectability of jurisprudence. Yet the fact was, no real precedent existed in international law for the kind of trials and executions that took place at Nuremberg and Tokyo. No matter how the Allies dressed it up, there remained the sneaking suspicion that it was the old blight, the same old story of the victors killing off the losers. The Allies could not put that ghost to rest.

Strangely enough, as far back as the famous dinner party at the Teheran Conference in November 1943, Stalin had jokingly suggested it would be convenient to have fifty thousand German officers and technicians shot, to insure the peace of the world. And thereby hangs an odd tale. Coming after the disclosure earlier in the year of the Katyn massacre of 4,143 Polish army officers near Smolensk (the Soviets had claimed the Germans did the killing; but it was pretty well established that the Soviets were responsible), Stalin's remark enraged Winston Churchill, who retorted angrily that the British people would never consent to mass executions. And when Stalin again pressed the idea, jokingly it is said, teasingly, Churchill became so inflamed he said, "I would rather be taken out into the garden here and be shot myself than sully my own and my country's honor by such infamy." Oddly, Roosevelt is supposed to have tried to cool the air by saying jokingly in that case they should shoot only forty-nine thousand. But the joke didn't take, and when Elliott Roosevelt, a colonel, proposed a toast which put the U.S. Army behind Stalin's (joking?) request, Churchill left the room. Stalin and Molotov had to go out after him, mollify him and bring him back. The incident was passed over, but Roosevelt's reaction seems peculiar, to say the least. But of course, once again, the Western politicians were no more able to cope with the magnitude of the German and Russian mass killings than were the Western soldiers, when they discovered and liberated the death camps.

Perhaps therein lies part of the reason for the trials themselves. God knows the executed deserved to die. And something had to be done about this—about the death camps; public opinion demanded it. In any case, the Western victors were never able to lay the phantom of simple victor's vengeance, after the trials and their executions were finished. And certainly, the Western leaders had established a precedent whereby now any winners of any war could try to execute the losers, simply by calling them war criminals.

But all of this, as the rear-rank infantry private was wont to say, was still a long way down the road. There was still the end of the war with Japan to accomplish.

The Last Mile

Illustrations 175–180

The final decisions to invade both Iwo Jima and Okinawa were taken on October 3, 1944, at the same time MacArthur was given the go-ahead to invade Luzon. And as time passed and the Philippine campaign moved ahead, both appeared more and more to be the right decisions. At the back of everything, of course, was the reluctant decision to invade the main Japanese islands.

Preliminary planning for the invasion of Iwo had begun as far back as September, 1943. Strategically, Iwo Jima was a main bastion of Japanese air defense. That Iwo needed to be neutralized and taken out was recognized early. Its position directly athwart the bomber route from the Marianas to Tokyo and Japan's other industrial cities made it a thorn that must be pulled out of the side of air war strategy. And by October of '44 the big B-29 Superfortresses had moved from China and India to bases on Saipan, Tinian, and Guam in the Marianas. They began their raids on Tokyo in November, and immediately felt the sting of

Jap interceptors based on Iwo Jima in the Bonins eight hundred miles to the north.

There were other considerations. It was a twenty-eight-hundred-mile round trip from Saipan to the Japanese home islands and back. Fighter escort was out of the question, but heavy B-29 losses over Japan emphasized the need for fighter escort. P-51 Mustangs based on Iwo could escort as far as Tokyo. Also, with its already existing airfields (plus a third under construction), Iwo Jima would be an excellent bomber base in itself. Finally, it was a necessary step in the air war advances if Japan was ever going to be invaded. It simply could not be bypassed, as, say, Truk and Rabaul had been. So, marines would have to go in and secure it.

Okinawa, planned for two months later, was more of the same; and even more important, in other ways. Only three hundred fifty sea miles from Japan proper and Kyushu, it lay at the southern end of the Ryukyu Islands chain and was a major fortress of Japan's inner island defenses. With its four airfields in American hands there would be no more outlying interceptor posts from which to attack the increasing American B-29 raids. Much more important, it had good harbor facilities and was the natural staging area and jumping-off place for the final, ultimate, costly invasion of Japan which had to come next. It was the perfect place to mount such an invasion. General Simon Buckner's U.S. Tenth Army would make the assault.

Both invasions and their subsequent land battles sound like oft-repeated tunes. So familiar by now that the reader can just about chant them in unison with me. So, also, could the veterans of the marine and infantry divisions who went in to carry out the by-now familiar blood rituals. The sequence of landing, moves inland, fierce resistance, head-on attacks, final splitting of the defenders into isolated pockets—they were like the choreographed movements of some classic military ballet. Iwo happened to have an especially refined, diabolical hardship, in that most of its surface was covered with a choking fine volcanic sand and ash. Okinawa's extra hardship lay in its comparatively large size (60 miles long by 2 to 18 wide) and the fact that it was well populated with Japanese civilians; it was true homeland. The Ryugyu chain had been Japanese since 1895. Iwo Jima was invaded February 19 and was not finished until March 26. Okinawa was assaulted April 1, on Easter Sunday, and was not fully secured until June 21, after almost three months of desperate fighting.

Iwo's commander was Lieutenant General Tadamichi Kuribayashi, cavalry officer, sometime poet who had written two famous songs (one about loving horses, one about loving his nation), whose order to Iwo Jima's defenders was, "Each man will make it his duty to kill ten of the enemy before dying." Accounts of the last hours differ, but Kuribayashi himself appears to have died leading a last banzai charge of some 200 men; at any rate, his body was reported found among the 223 Japanese corpses counted at dawn of March 26. Okinawa's commander was Lieutenant General Mitsuru Ushijima. Ushijima fought a diabolical, almost demonic defense for two and a half months. On June 10 General Buckner sent a personal appeal to him by asking him to see reason and stop the killing by surrendering. Ushijima is reported to have received the message with "vast amusement" several days later. He radioed his last message to Tokyo and he and his chief of staff, a General Ota, cut open their bellies in ritual hara-kiri on June 22. General Buckner had died under Japanese fire a few days earlier, on the eighteenth. Mopping up continued till July 2.

Iwo Jima was the most costly fight in U.S. Marine history. General H. M. Smith, the marine commander, stated flatly that the "fighting was the toughest the marines ran across in 168 years." Although it had the longest pre-invasion bombardment in Pacific war history, so powerfully and deeply entrenched were the Japs in a vast complex of rabbit-warren caves and tunnels that the bombardment had little effect and the

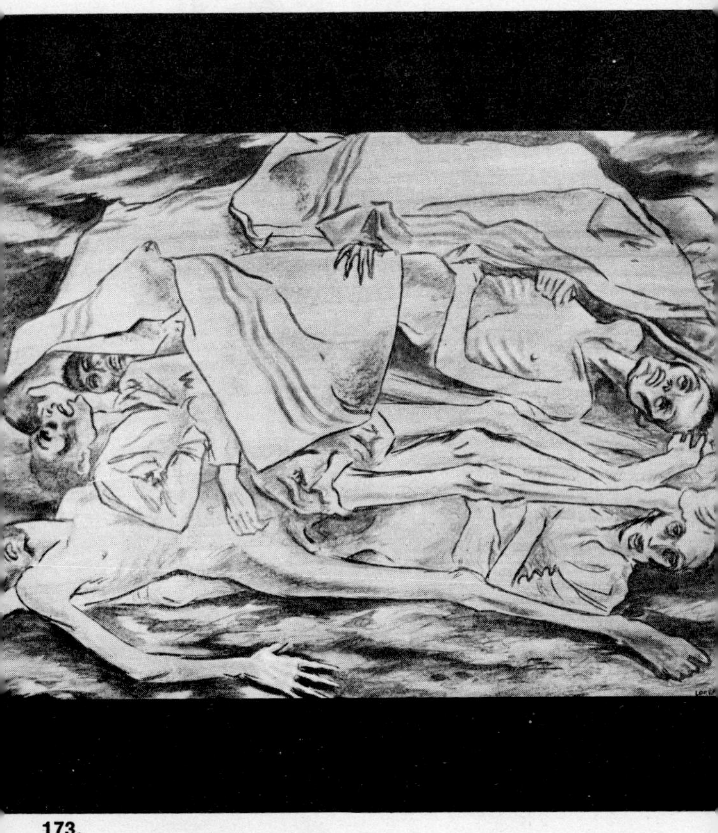

173.
Death camp at Buchenwald *was one of the many camps in which the Nazis systematically tortured, starved and murdered millions of people.*

174.
Nuremberg Trials *were covered for* Stars and Stripes *by artist Ed Vebell who, with the aid of binoculars, sketched the German prisoners in the dock.*

Field Marshal Goering - Velell '45
Hess looked very hollow cheeked and thin necked. He seemed to ignore the proceedings and kept his head down absorbed in a book
Doenitz & Raeder
Hess
Keitel tried to retain a rigid military bearing and strike haughty poses.
Keitel

175.
Attack on Iwo Jima *was painted by coast guard artist William Lawrence.*

176.
Left:
Battlewagon gun turret *of U.S.S.* Tennessee *during the attack on Iwo Jima.*

177.
Shrapnel wound *is sustained by a deckhand of the U.S.S.* Tennessee.

178.
Mount Suribachi *was the scene of some of the fiercest shoot-outs of the war against Japan.*

179.
Chow time *comes during rainstorm on Okinawa.*

OKINAWA
MAY 26-1945

180.
Standing guard *are the U.S. Marines near Naha on Okinawa.*

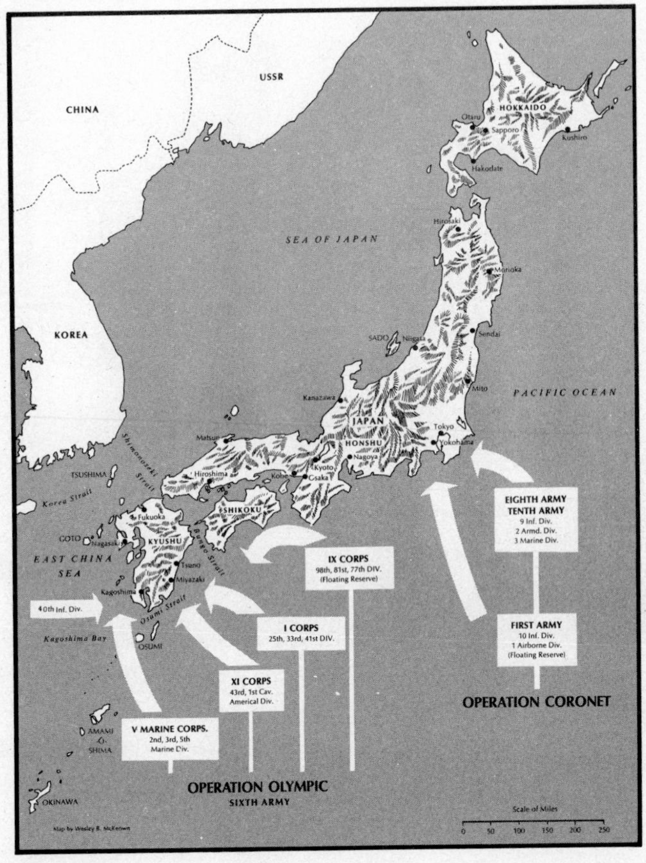

181.
Invasion of Japan *was expected to inflict fearful American casualties.*

Yokohama 9/6/45
Religious symbol amid ashes + corrugated iron roofing left after our fire raid.
B-11-3

182.
Left:
Fire raids *destroyed virtually all of Yokohama.*

183.
Hiroshima—1945: *A pencil drawing showing the horror of Hiroshima by the American artist Standish Backus, Jr.*

184.
The signing *is over. "These proceedings are closed" has been intoned by Douglas MacArthur, and now the Japanese delegation leaves the U.S. battleship* Missouri *after surrendering "unconditionally."*

185.

186.

"All the News That's Fit to Print"

The New [Y...]

Copyright, 1945, [...]

VOL. XCIV..No. 31,980.

Entered as Second-Class Matter, Postoffice, New York, N. Y.

NEW YORK, WED[...]

JAPAN SURREND[...] EMPEROR ACCE[...] M'ARTHUR SUPR[...] OUR MANPOW[...]

HIRING MADE LOCAL

Communities, Labor and Management Will Unite Efforts

6,000,000 AFFECTED

Draft Quotas Cut, Services to Drop 5,500,000 in 18 Months

By LEWIS WOOD

Special to THE NEW YORK TIMES.

WASHINGTON, Aug. 14—All manpower controls over employers and workers were abolished tonight, the War Manpower Commission announced, enabling employers to hire men where and when they pleased.

The end of the war threw on the Government the difficult task of trying to readjust perhaps 6,800,000 war workers into new employment. Nevertheless, the WMC said, all its facilities would [...] to help [...] find new

Third Fleet Fells 5 Planes Since End

By The Associated Press.

GUAM, Wednesday, Aug. 15—Japanese aircraft are approaching the Pacific Fleet off Tokyo and are being shot down, Admiral Chester W. Nimitz announced today.

Five enemy planes have been destroyed since noon today, Japanese time, or 11 P. M. EWT.

Gen. Douglas MacArthur has been requested to tell the Japanese that American defense measures require the Third Fleet to destroy any Japanese planes approaching United States warships.

GUAM, Wednesday, Aug. 15 (U.P.)—When Admiral Halsey received word of Japan's capitulation today he sent this message to his fliers:

"It looks like the war is over, but if any enemy planes appear shoot them down in friendly fashion."

SECRETS OF RADAR GIVEN TO WORLD

Its Role in War and Uses for

ALL CITY 'LETS GO'

Hundreds of Thousands Roar Joy After Victory Flash Is Received

TIMES SQ. IS JAMMED

Police Estimate Crowd in Area at 2,000,000—Din Overwhelming

By ALEXANDER FEINBERG

Five days of waiting, of rumor, intimation, fact, distortion—five agonizing days following the first indication of a Japanese surrender, days of alternately rising hopes and fears—came to an end for New York, as for the nation and the world, a moment or two after seven o'clock last night. And the metropolis exploded its emotions, harnessed for the most part during the day, with atomic force.

"Official—Truman announces Japanese surrender."

[...] were the magic words, [...] the [...]

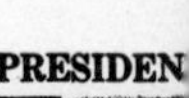
PRESIDEN[...]

Mr. Truman readi[...] Secretary of State Ja[...] to right) are Maj. Gen[...] Davis, Economic Stabi[...]

ork Times.

LATE C:TY EDITION

Thunderstorms, warm, humid; clear and cooler tonight. Fair tomorrow.

Temperatures Yesterday—Max., 84; Min., 71
Sunrise today, 6:06 A. M.; Sunset, 7:56 P. M.

York Times Company.

.Y, AUGUST 15, 1945. THREE CENTS IN NEW YORK CITY

RS, END OF WAR!
TS ALLIED RULE;
EME COMMANDER;
R CURBS VOIDED

NOUNCING SURRENDER OF JAPAN

sage in the White House. Seated are Admiral William D. Leahy, des and former Secretary of State Cordell Hull. Standing (left ming, head of the Federal Works Administration; William H. W. Snyder, Reconversion Director; James Forrestal, Secretary

YIELDING UNQUALIFIED, TRUMAN SAYS

Japan Is Told to Order End of Hostilities, Notify Allied Supreme Commander and Send Emissaries to Him

MACARTHUR TO RECEIVE SURRENDER

Formal Proclamation of V-J Day Awaits Signing of Those Articles—Cease-Fire Order Given to the Allied Forces

By ARTHUR KROCK

Special to THE NEW YORK TIMES.

WASHINGTON, Aug. 14—Japan today unconditionally surrendered the hemispheric empire taken by force and held almost intact for more than two years against the rising power of the United States and its Allies in the Pacific war.

The bloody dream of the Japanese military caste vanished in the text of a note to the Four Powers accepting the terms of the Potsdam Declaration of July 26, 1945, w

ARMY AIR FORCES

ARMY AIR FORCES

MEDITERRANEAN ALLIED AIR FORCE

U.S. STRATEGIC AIR FORCE

FIRST AIR FORCE

SECOND AIR FORCE

THIRD AIR FORCE

FOURTH AIR FORCE

FIFTH AIR FORCE

SIXTH AIR FORCE

SEVENTH AIR FORCE

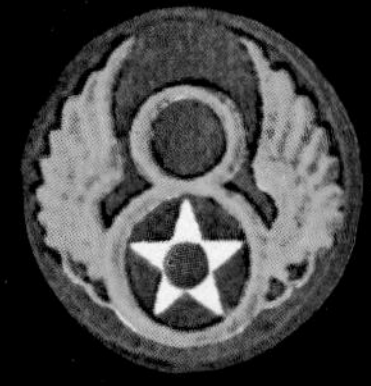

EIGHTH AIR FORCE

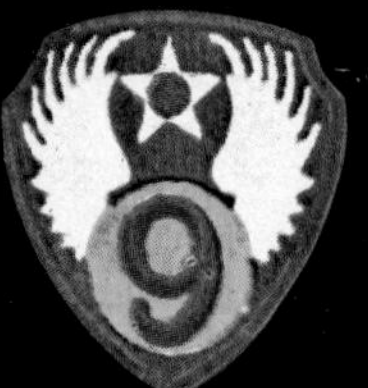

NINTH AIR FORCE

TENTH AIR FORCE

ELEVENTH AIR FORCE

TWELFTH AIR FORCE

THIRTEENTH AIR FORCE

FOURTEENTH AIR FORCE

FIFTEENTH AIR FORCE

TWENTIETH AIR FORCE

ARMORED DIVISIONS

1st

2nd "HELL ON WHEELS"

3rd "SPEARHEAD"

4th

5th "VICTORY"

6th "SUPER SIXTH"

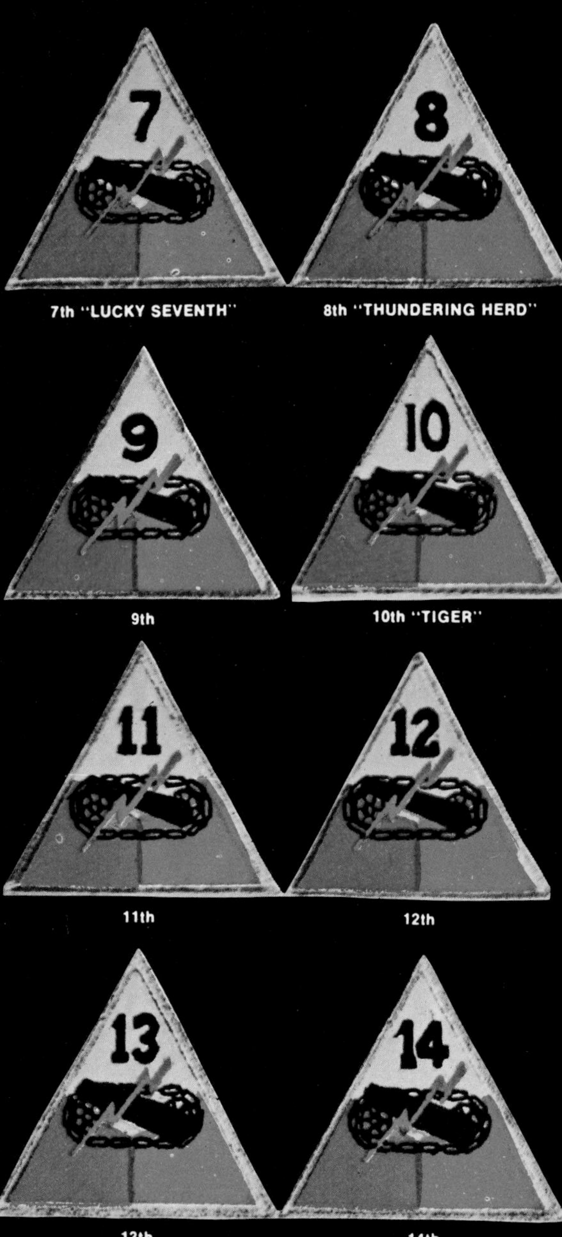

7th "LUCKY SEVENTH"

8th "THUNDERING HERD"

9th

10th "TIGER"

11th

12th

13th

14th

ARMY
SERVICE FORCES

ARMY GROUND FORCES

ARMORED CENTER AND UNITS

AGF REPLACEMENT DEPOTS

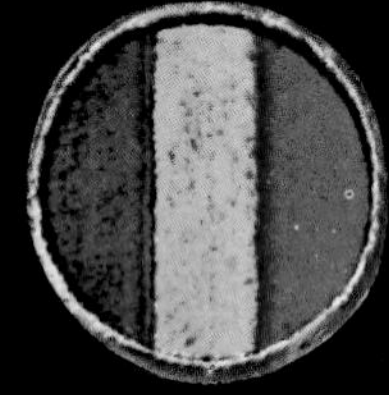

REPLACEMENT AND SCHOOL COMMAND

ANTIAIRCRAFT COMMAND

AIRBORNE COMMAND

ARMY SERVICE FORCES

PORTS OF EMBARKATION

1st SERVICE COMMAND

2nd SERVICE COMMAND

3rd SERVICE COMMAND

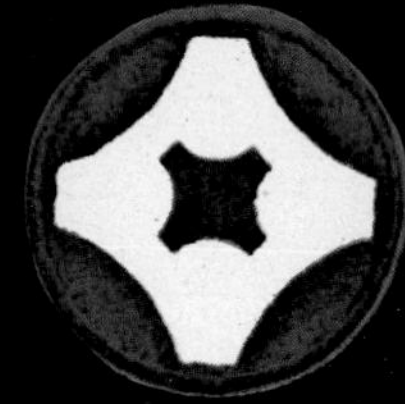

4th SERVICE COMMAND

5th SERVICE COMMAND

6th SERVICE COMMAND

7th SERVICE COMMAND

8th SERVICE COMMAND

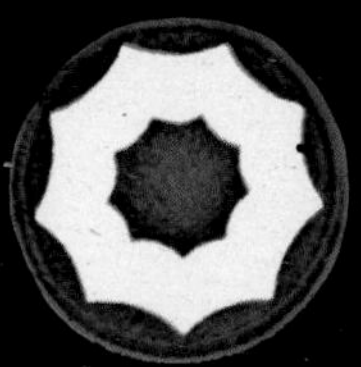

9th SERVICE COMMAND

NORTHWEST SERVICE COMMAND

MILITARY DISTRICT OF WASHINGTON

ASF TRAINING CENTER UNITS

ARMY SPECIALIZED TRAINING PROGRAM

ARMY SPECIALIZED TRAINING PROGRAM RESERVE

DEPARTMENTS

ANTILLES DEPARTMENT

ALASKAN DEPARTMENT

PANAMA CANAL DEPARTMENT

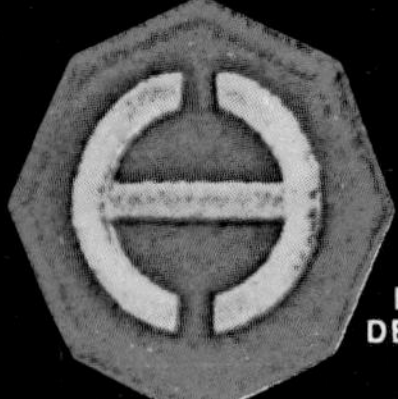

HAWAIIAN DEPARTMENT

SPECIAL INSIGNIA

1st SPECIAL SERVICE FORCE

U.S. MILITARY ACADEMY

ALLIED FORCE HEADQUARTERS

COMBAT TEAM 442

TANK DESTROYER UNITS

PERSIAN GULF SERVICE COMMAND

RANGERS

ARMY PERSONNEL AMPHIBIOUS

ARMY PERSONNEL

CORPS

I CORPS

II CORPS

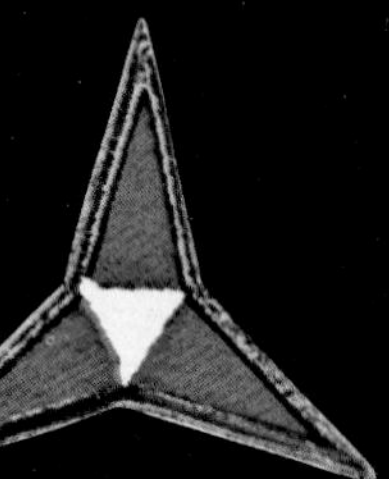

III CORPS

IV CORPS

V CORPS

VI CORPS

VII CORPS

VIII CORPS

IX CORPS

X CORPS

XI CORPS

XII CORPS

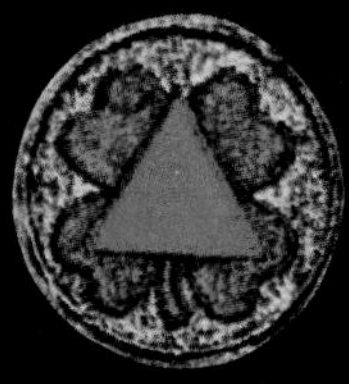

XIII CORPS

XIV CORPS

XV CORPS

XVI CORPS

XVIII AIRBORNE CORPS

XIX CORPS

XX CORPS

XXI CORPS

XXII CORPS

XXIII CORPS

XXIV CORPS

XXXVI CORPS

DEFENSE AND BASE COMMANDS

ATLANTIC BASE COMMANDS

EASTERN DEFENSE COMMAND

ANTIAIRCRAFT ARTILLERY COMMAND, WESTERN DEFENSE COMMAND

ANTIAIRCRAFT ARTILLERY COMMAND, EASTERN DEFENSE COMMAND

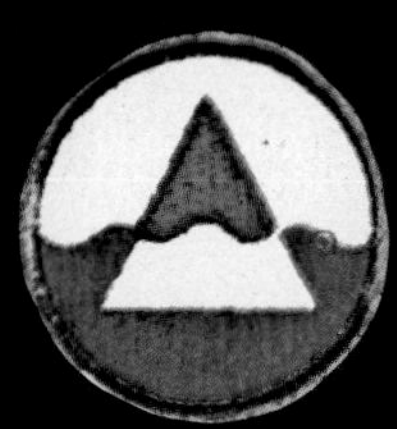
ICELAND BASE COMMAND

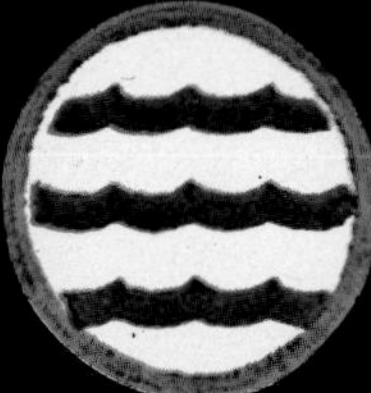
GREENLAND BASE COMMAND

BERMUDA BASE COMMAND

LABRADOR, NORTHEAST AND CENTRAL CANADA COMMAND

CARIBBEAN DEFENSE COMMAND

THEATERS

EUROPEAN THEATER OF OPERATIONS

U.S. ARMY FORCES SOUTH ATLANTIC

HEADQUARTERS SOUTHEAST ASIA COMMAND

CHINA-BURMA-INDIA THEATER

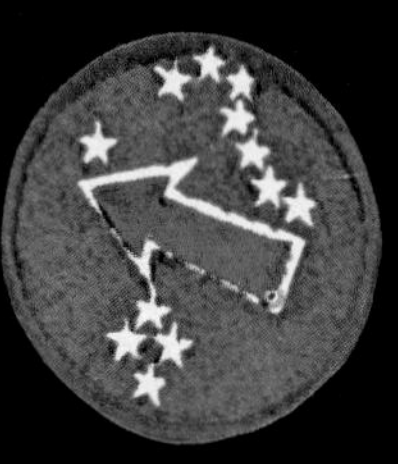

U.S. ARMY FORCES PACIFIC OCEAN AREA

U.S. ARMY FORCES IN MIDDLE EAST

NORTH AFRICAN THEATER OF OPERATIONS

cave complexes had to be taken hole by hole. So interwoven were the sniper holes and tunnels that the Japanese could run underground from one hole to another and begin firing before the marines could get close enough to flush out the first. In all, Iwo had 800 pillboxes and 3 miles of tunnels, and Kuribayashi had planned 18 miles. The 8-square-mile little island cost the United States 26,000 casualties, of whom 6,821 were dead. (Commentators always hasten to add, though, that by the end of the war 24,761 flyers and crewmen off the B-29s had saved their lives by using Iwo's airfields for emergency landings in their shot-up planes.) Japanese losses were 23,000, only 216 of them prisoners. And even before the fighting finished, B-29s were landing on the island, on March 4. And on April 7, ten days after the last shooting, 108 P-51 Mustangs took off for Tokyo to escort B-29s in a daylight raid for the first time.

Okinawa was a different kind of a fight, but it was just as costly. In fact, it was the bloodiest fight of the Pacific war. Total American battle casualties were 49,151. The United States lost 763 aircraft and 36 ships sunk; another 368 ships were damaged. The Japanese lost 110,000 men, counting conscripted and drafted civilians. Ten major kamikaze attacks were sent against Okinawa, using up 1,465 planes; and the total number of individual suicide sorties was 1,900. Japanese losses in aircraft were staggering: 7,800. The Japanese navy lost 4 ships damaged and 16 ships sunk, including the last great battleship *Yamato,* which was all they had left to lose; after Okinawa the Japanese navy was finished.

Ushijima had been ordered to hold out and fight a punishing campaign, and he did exactly that, with great skill. Like Yamashita on Luzon, he knew how heavily the odds were stacked against him and had no illusions about winning. His was a war of attrition, with the hope that if the Americans could be made to pay a price high enough, they would think twice before invading the main islands. Utilizing the southern half of the island where terrain was better suited to defense, he fought and withdrew, fought and withdrew, never letting the seven American divisions against him catch him out or encircle him, until at the very end, after his suicide, his remaining forces were bottled up in the very southernmost tip of Okinawa around Kiyamu and Mabuni. Only then, after their commander's death and split up into isolated pockets, did the Japanese begin to surrender, in small groups, for the first time in the war. In the end some 7,400 Japanese were taken prisoner.

As intended by both Ushijima and the Japanese High Command, American commanders and American privates stopped, stood up and looked around when the smoke cleared, and wondered.

If the defense of the Japan home islands, with their immensely greater area and enormously greater population, was going to take on the character of the defense of Okinawa, where and when and at what cost was it going to end?

The Last Yard

Not many Americans seem to have learned about it then, and not many know it today, but actual detailed plans for the invasion of Japan were actually worked up by the various staffs involved. Lost in the massive flood of publicity over Hiroshima and the abrupt end of the war, very little attention was paid to them at the time. And as far as I know no major work about them has ever been published since.

As far back as the Joint Chiefs' directive of October 3, 1944, on the invasion of Luzon, Iwo and Okinawa, authorization was given for the invasion of southern Japan sometime in the fall of 1945. On April 3, 1945, when the fighting on Iwo was barely finished and the invasion of Okinawa barely begun, the Joint Chiefs instructed MacArthur to begin detailing his plans for the invasion of southern Kyushu Island not later than November 1, and to begin general planning for the main invasion, which would take place on the Kanto plain to the east of Tokyo in March, 1946.

In preparation for the invasion, the command structures in the Pacific theater were to be reorganized. There was to be no supreme commander as in Europe. MacArthur was to command all army forces, and Nimitz was to be the naval commander. A little later, "Tooey" Spaatz was brought out from Europe to have overall command of the air forces which would control the air power for the invasion. On May 25, after the respective staffs had worked on the plans, MacArthur and Nimitz were ordered officially to invade Kyushu on November 1, 1945, and the main island Honshu on March 1, 1946. The two operations were to be called "Olympic" and "Coronet," respectively.

It stands to reason that staffs and planning specialists always have to work far ahead of the events as they are happening on the ground. But the thought that the United States actually came that close to a bloody, all-out invasion of Japan proper is chilling. The loss of life on the U.S. side alone, never mind the Japanese, would have more than tripled, quadrupled the combined losses of Hiroshima and Nagasaki. Japanese losses would have sent it sky high. That the planners were aware of the near certainty of this bloodbath is clear in the number of divisions they allotted to the invasion: twenty-eight. With more to follow, as reinforcements and replacements were needed.

It was known and gossiped about everywhere in the Pacific, and at home in the United States among the troops training for the invasion, that the United States expected and was prepared to lose the first three waves, something like one hundred thousand men, just getting ashore and in the first few days.

Corporation war had reached the point where even the term "corporation" didn't seem to apply anymore. Perhaps "conglomerate war" would have to be the new term.

Air Force Major General Curtis E. LeMay (he of SAC ill-fame of later years) who had arrived from Europe in January '45 to take over Twenty-first Bomber Command on Saipan, Tinian and Guam in the Marianas, was convinced that the war could be ended without invading Japan. LeMay thought air power and strategic bombing alone could force a Japanese surrender. The Joint Chiefs, however, did not believe an unconditional surrender could be obtained without a successful invasion, and saw both sea blockade and intensive strategic bombing only as means of aiding, and softening the cost of, the invasion.

LeMay had some sound reason for his conviction. He was a tough, hard-driving commander. The very qualities which later in Denver were to make him such an anathema to the doves and peaceniks of a later era stood him in good stead at this particular time of his career. The XXI Bomber Command had been getting very poor results over Japan with its ill-organized high-level pinpoint-precision raids when LeMay was ordered out to take it over and shape it up. He immediately instituted a harsh training program in formation flying and other operational techniques, which apparently were sorely needed and which did not make him popular. But after sending the big planes over Japan sixteen times, his results were little better than his predecessor's. It was at this point that LeMay conceived the phenomenally successful "Tokyo fire raids."

Everything about these raids contradicted standard practice. The B-29 was designed to carry out high-level precision daylight bombing. This time they would come in low, five to seven thousand feet, and they would come at night. They would go in singly, one at a time, and not in protective formation. They would carry only incendiary and no high-explosive. They would carry no guns or ammunition.

LeMay was staking his entire future on this change of tactics, but he was reasoning carefully. Japanese radar was terrible, the worst in existence, so antiaircraft fire was no such problem as over Germany. Few Japanese night-fighter interceptors existed, and they were equally bad. More B-29s had been shooting each other than the Japs had ever touched. Without guns and all the weight of their ammo, more weight in firebombs could be carried.

Later on March 9 (Iwo was still fighting, Okinawa not yet begun) the Superforts took off for the first of these experimental raids of LeMay's. The success went beyond even LeMay's wildest dreams, and immediately became history. A total of three hundred twenty-five aircraft had reached the target. The target itself was a three by four mile area in the heart of Tokyo, a crowded congested area of the city filled with home industries and "shadow" factories—small hidden plants dispersed and not easily detected. When it was over, nearly sixteen square miles of the main section of Tokyo had been wiped out. Along with it went twenty-two industrial targets that had been marked for pin-point precision bombing, but had never been hit. Returning crews reported being tossed thousands of feet upward by thermals from the fire as they came in to bomb. At least one Superfort was flipped over on its back out of control by updrafts of heated air, and very nearly crashed. Tokyo did not suffer a true firestorm such as Hamburg and Dresden had, but the mixture of napalm and oil bombs plus a strong wind, plus the wood and bamboo construction of the buildings, caused a raging rolling fire that was unquenchable. The official casualty figures were put at 83,700 dead and 41,900 injured, but they were almost certainly far too low. A million persons were rendered homeless, presenting an impossible task to the Home Defense organizations. And there was no question of the terrible effect on morale. In one night Tokyo had suffered a greater disaster than any city on earth, greater than London or Berlin or Hamburg or Dresden, greater even than Hiroshima and Nagasaki which were to come. The stories of the ordeal were horrendous. Flames roiled hundreds of feet high in a rolling wall of fire moving toward the buildings. Running people ignited in the streets from the heat as though from spontaneous combustion, and raced on as screaming balls of fire. Others suffocated from the heated air. People who took to the shelters found no safety and were roasted as if in ovens. Afterward charred bodies were found piled up three and four deep on the bridges and roads and in the canals, where they had tried to escape the flames. Even their enemies could not wish this on them, but the enemies were not there, they were high above in the sky or far away, and Pearl Harbor had come home finally to the Japanese people, a thousandfold.

And, in the terms of the new corporation war, the American loss ratio was calculated at 1.4 per cent. This compared very well with the 3.5 per cent figure for all B-29 raids and the 5.7 per cent for January.

So LeMay had ample proof of his faith in strategic bombing of Japan. One after the other the bombers hit Nagoya, Osaka and Kobe, on March 11, March 14, and March 16, and Nagoya a second time on March 19. If Nagoya suffered slightly less because of its terrain features and a lack of wind, all three cities were devastated. The normally laconic LeMay had revealed on the day of the first raid, while waiting for the news of it, what his real aim was: "If this raid works the way I think it will, we can shorten this war." And he was right, both tactically and strategically. Japan was finished as a warmaking nation, in spite of its four million men still under arms. But LeMay had forgotten one thing, and the Joint Chiefs in Washington were also right. LeMay had come from "civilized" Europe, but the Joint Chiefs had been dealing with the Japanese for years. Japan was not going to quit. Despite the fact that she was militarily finished, Japan's leaders were going to fight right on. To not lose national "face" was more important than hundreds and hundreds of thousands of lives. And the people concurred, in silence, without protest. To continue was no longer a question of Japanese military thinking, it was an aspect of Japanese culture and psychology.

And on Iwo on March 17, a day after the raid on Kobe, General Kuribayashi was still sending telegraph messages to his detached HQ on Chichi Jima Island and to Tokyo. At 0200 hours on March 17 he sent:

"From General Kuribayashi to all surviving officers and men. Battle situation come to last moment. I want surviving officers and men to go out and attack enemy until the last. You have devoted yourself to the Emperor. Do not think of yourself. I am always at the head of you all."

At midnight March 11 Kuribayashi and the four hundred army and navy personnel left to him, left his headquarters and shut themselves into a cave about one hundred fifty yards from his old cave HQ. On the night of March 23 Kuribayashi radioed one last message. "To all officers and men of Chichi Jima. Goodbye."

The last pocket to be destroyed on Iwo was the one at Kitano Point, which was declared secure on March 25. But that night more than two hundred Japanese charged out of the blackened shell-pocked nest of caves and charged among the sleeping men of the U.S. Fifth Pioneer Battalion. Led in person by Kuribayashi himself (although other sources say he committed *seppuku*) apparently, they fought and killed until all were dead.

Such courage was no longer just fanatical, it was insane. As in the final banzai charges at Saipan and Guam and Tarawa and Kwajalein, many of the Japanese privates appeared to be drunk, or drugged.

And in Tokyo servicemen and civilians were still trying to dig themselves out from under the destruction of the March 9–10 raid.

The Last Foot

Illustrations 181 and 182

The plans for Operation "Olympic" against Kyushu Island and Operation "Coronet" against Honshu Island are interesting. In concept, the Kyushu invasion was to establish a forward base for use in the invasion against Tokyo on Honshu later. Kyushu, being the southernmost of the large main islands, was about three hundred fifty miles from Okinawa. On its southern coast was an excellent fifty-mile-deep narrow bay called Kagoshima Bay after the city of Kagoshima at its upper end. This bay, which would be opened up to Allied shipping and through which would move most of the men and supplies for the Honshu invasion, and which would also serve as the navy's advance base, was the prime objective.

Walter Kreuger's U.S. Sixth Army was given the dubious honor of making the assault. Three corps of three divisions each would go in initially, and a fourth corps would stand offshore as reserve, after making a feint and simulated landing on Shikoku Island farther north to confuse the Japanese on X-Day minus 2,

October 30. Sixth Army's objectives were to clear the land areas around Kagoshima Bay, and then to form a stable solid line across the island north of the bay from Sendai on the west to Fukushima and Tsuno on the east. It would not attempt to capture and hold the entire island, and Sixth Army would hold this land line at all costs, while consolidation and buildup began behind it for the March invasion of Honshu at Tokyo.

Construction of airfields (and bases) was to begin immediately once the first bridgeheads were established. If the fourteen divisions assigned to Sixth Army could not capture and hold southern Kyushu, they were to be fed as reinforcements from the beginning of December three divisions a month, from those originally intended for Honshu. A lone division, the Fortieth Infantry, was to seize and hold a small group of offshore islands to the southwest on October 27–28 to protect lines of communication and secure advanced naval anchorages.

Kyushu Island was under the defensive wing of the Japanese Sixteenth Area Army, which as far as intelligence could make out had fourteen infantry divisions and two armored brigades. Just what fourteen American divisions could expect to happen to them, going up against fourteen Japanese divisions on home ground and amongst an alien, bitterly hostile enemy population, was not enumerated in the plans. But then, just about everybody knew what to anticipate. Most of them had been through it at least once, and many had been through it from Guadalcanal and Lae on up.

The naval designations were equally massive. Nimitz divided his forces into the Third and Fifth Fleets. The Third under Halsey was a collection of fast carrier groups plus their supporting battleships, cruisers and destroyers. Halsey's two main components were Towers' Second Carrier Task Force (T.F. Thirty-eight) and Vice-Admiral Rawlings' British Carrier Task

Force (T.F. Thirty-seven). Halsey was to operate against the Kuriles, Hokkaido, and Honshu.

The Fifth Fleet, under Spruance again, contained 2,902 vessels, and its main components were the First Fast Carrier Force under Sherman (T.F. Fifty-eight), the Amphibious Force under Kelly Turner (T.F. Forty) which would land the troops, the Gunfire and Covering Force (T.F. Fifty-four) for bombardment and fire support, and T.F. Fifty-six, responsible for minesweeping operations. The naval bombardment would begin eight days before the invasion, and continue until after the launching of the assault.

The "Coronet" plans for Tokyo and Honshu, naturally enough, were not quite so fully developed. Still, the planning was far enough along to know who was going to go in when, and where. In general, the attack would go in on the Kanto plain north of Tokyo. This was a level ground with good beaches, which would aid the Allied superiority in armor and mechanized vehicles. There were good harbors for logistics support, and the center of Japanese political and industrial life was situated here. The Joint Chiefs' planners hoped that a serious defeat here might convince the Japanese the war was lost.

Two U.S. armies were slated to go in. The First Army of two corps, under Courtney Hodges (who had come out from Europe), would go in at Kujikurihama beach and cross the Kanto plain. Eichelberger's Eighth Army with two full corps of infantry divisions, plus a corps of two armored divisions, was to go in at Sagami Bay just south of Tokyo Bay, and strike north and east to clear the long western shore of Tokyo Bay as far north as Yokohama. Simultaneously the armored corps would drive north to cut off Japanese reinforcements, and to isolate Tokyo. Hopefully, they could get as far north as Koga, and west to Kumagaya. Some of this armor would then be available to help First Army capture Tokyo, if needed.

"Coronet" never got much beyond this stage, although the assault troops were chosen and already in training. But "Olympic," against Kyushu, was well into its collecting and stockpiling stages before the war ended. What it must have been like to some old-timer buck sergeant or staff sergeant who had been through Guadalcanal and Bougainville and the Philippines, to stand on some beach and watch this huge war machine beginning to stir and move all around him and know that he very likely had survived this far only to fall dead on the dirt of Japan's home islands, hardly bears thinking about.

Whatever he thought, it almost certainly would not have been as bad as the reality. By April, 1945, the Japanese High Command had concluded that American forces already stationed in the Bonins and the Ryukyus would very likely invade Kyushu with between fifteen and twenty divisions in October of 1945, and then invade Honshu around March '46 with up to thirty divisions. The Americans would intensify their incendiary bombing and their blockade, and then concentrate on destroying the Japanese air forces. Consequently the Japanese issued a plan to decentralize command.

The home islands were divided into six more or less autonomous defense zones. Korea made a seventh. The most likely invasion areas, Kyushu and Tokyo, were given sixty-five infantry divisions, two armored divisions, twenty-five independent mixed brigades, three guards brigades, and seven tank brigades. This was over half the available forces. Arrangements were made for one area command to reinforce another if it became necessary. Continuous defenses were put under construction on the probable landing sites, but far enough back to be out of range of American naval bombardment. The coastal defense divisions were to contain the invaders in their beachheads, so that mobile assault divisions could then move up and annihilate the enemy. Across the country Japanese civilian populations were put into training. Imperial General Headquarters planned, if sufficient arms were not available, to arm them with bamboo spears.

At this same time (May and June of 1945) American ground forces were still fighting desperately to complete the conquest of Okinawa. The last organized resistance—on Hill 85, between Medeera and Makabe—was finally broken on June 21. It was that night that General Ushijima radioed his last message to Tokyo and then arranged for and carried out his *seppuku*. Even so, even after their commander's death, the mopping up of the Japanese forces was not completed until July 2.

The fighting had been the bloodiest and most desperate the veteran American troops had seen. Some Japanese, though, had surrendered. Out of seventeen or eighteen thousand, some seven thousand had given themselves up.

What would it be like on Kyushu? On Honshu?

MUSHROOM

Illustration 183

They were saved from finding out by the brilliant, literally blinding, blue-white flash which ignited the sky 2,000 feet above Hiroshima at exactly 17 seconds after 0815 hours on August 6 of that same year, 1945.

Actually, they had been saved some time before that. Only none of them knew it. The decision to drop the atomic bomb, so-called, had been made tentatively at a White House meeting on June 18, 1945. This was at the same meeting where President Harry S. Truman had likewise given the go-ahead to the Kyushu and Honshu invasions. George Marshall and the Joint Chiefs were convinced that Japan must be invaded to end the war. Truman accepted the Joint Chiefs' assessment.

In actual fact, Marshall's assessment wasn't so very different from that of the Japanese. The War Minister General Anami had proposed the solution that Japan must fight to the end defending the home islands. She still had two million combat troops under arms at home, and nine thousand kamikaze planes. If these could inflict sufficiently huge casualties on the United States, the Americans might be forced to negotiate a peace more favorable to Japan than "unconditional surrender." The hope was to avoid an Allied military occupation of Japan, as well as to preserve Japan's imperial system with the Emperor at its head as a divinity.

None of the Americans wanted a peace that would leave Japan intact to that extent. Nor did they want a still-intact army of two million combat soldiers in Japan. Truman and Marshall were intractable on that, and said so. But George Marshall was deeply distressed over the possible casualties from the further ground invasions. That day, he estimated for Truman that the United States would lose sixty-nine thousand casualties in a one hundred and ninety-thousand-man operation against Kyushu alone. It was almost certainly a conservative estimate.

At the June 18 meeting one other hope for enforcing a Japanese surrender, short of invasion, was put forward. The Manhattan Project finally would have two "atomic bombs" available for operational use by the end of July. One of these was the now-famous "Little Boy," a gun-assembly type weapon which would fire a plug of U-235 into a U-235 core, thus creating the necessary critical mass and an explosion, but an explosion of gigantic dimensions. The scientists were pretty confident this type of armament would work. The other, called "Fat Man," was an implosion-type weapon which used plutonium, and the specialists were less sure that it could be made to function. It was to be test-fired at Alamogordo in mid-July.

So the tentative decision depended on several factors.

Truman took this knowledge with him to the Potsdam Conference. At Potsdam on July 16 he received the news that the implosion weapon had been tested, and did work. On July 26 the Allies issued the Potsdam Proclamation calling for the "unconditional surrender" of Japan. The alternative would be "prompt and utter destruction." The proclamation, of course, did not tell the Japanese how to expect this destruction, and the Japanese almost certainly believed the proclamation to be pure rhetoric. Anyhow, they refused. Not only that, their refusal announcement sounded contemptuous. The word the Japanese Premier used was *mokusatsu,* which meant to "treat" something "with silent contempt." The same word also meant "kill it with silence," a much less insulting connotation, but the announcement angered the Allies. Truman gave the order to drop "Little Boy." At the time he was on board ship in mid-Atlantic on the return from Potsdam.

Now things moved swiftly. In actual fact, the delivery system for the bombs already existed, ready to go, at North Field on Tinian in the Marianas: the 509th Bomb Group had been trained and familiarized with dropping "special bombs." On his way to take command of Strategic Air Forces in the Pacific, "Tooey" Spaatz was told of the projected atomic strikes. Spaatz refused to drop the bombs simply on oral instructions. "My God, Mr. President, I can't drop a bomb like that on verbal orders. Put it in writing for me." At Tinian the cruiser *Indianapolis* delivered the U-235 needed to arm the "reliable" "Little Boy." (Four days later *Indianapolis* was sunk at sea by Jap submarines!) On August 2, Twentieth Air Force printed top secret orders for the drop. Because visual bombing was mandatory, and we needed to observe the explosion, bad weather caused delay until the sixth.

Curiously, at 0815 hours plus ten seconds, people on the streets of Hiroshima watched the single object fall from the high-flying enemy plane into their city near the Japanese Second Army headquarters.

"Suddenly," an eyewitness Japanese newspaperman told later, "a glaring whitish pinkish light appeared in the sky accompanied by an unnatural tremor which was followed almost immediately by a wave of suffocating heat and wind which swept everything in its path.

"Within a few seconds the thousands of people in the streets and the gardens in the center of the town were scorched by a wave of searing heat. Many were killed instantly, others lay writhing on the ground screaming in agony from the intolerable pain of their burns. Everything standing upright in the way of the blast—walls, houses, factories and other buildings—was annihilated and the débris spun round in a whirlwind and was carried up into the air. Trams were picked up and tossed aside as though they had neither weight nor solidity. Trains were flung off the rails as though they were toys. Horses, dogs and cattle suffered the same fate as human beings. Every living thing was petrified in an attitude of indescribable suffering. Even the vegetation did not escape. Trees went up in flames, the rice plants lost their greenness, the grass burned on the ground like dry straw." A heavy fire storm followed on the strange, alien winds. "By evening the fire began to die down and then went out. There was nothing left to burn."

Nagasaki followed quickly on August 9. The war was all but over.

Bugbear

As time passed, and the great elation and joy over victory and the end of killing tapered off, a great wave of revulsion and hatred for the United States swept over most of the world. No human or group of humans had the right to construct and use such a catastrophic weapon on another human or group of humans, was the accusation. It was as if some mythic generic fear had arisen in all humans. The potential destruction of all mankind was at hand, here and now, and the United States was the master villain for having created it.

Deep down, impossibly incapable of definition, was a conviction among humans that humanity with all its bloody history was not at all evolved enough as an animal to be allowed to play with such destructive power. But no one could state it that baldly and still point to any culprit except the race itself. No one wanted to admit that the race of which he was a member had been mapped out for and deserved extinction in the same way that the dinosaurs of the Mesozoic had overbred themselves into extinction. And so the United States was the culprit. This attitude was first proclaimed by postwar French intellectuals who were trying to work themselves back to some position of power after the failure of their country, and was echoed and picked up by British intellectuals across the Channel, and finally was picked up and espoused by American intellectuals also. A sort of mass guilt complex of American liberal thinking was created which, as the United States gravitated to world power and remained there, has never left American liberals. And all this time, the attitude was being used with telling effect by Russian propaganda as the cold war came on.

At Potsdam, when Truman told Stalin about the new weapon the United States had developed and was going to use, old Uncle Joe answered that he hoped the United States would "make good use of it." And on August 7, 1945, the day after Hiroshima, Stalin called in the five leading Soviet physicists and—putting them in the care of his famed secret police boss, Lavrenti Beria—ordered them to catch up with the American atomic achievements. This they did, and on July 10, 1949—six to ten years before Washington believed it possible—Russia exploded its first A-bomb.

In the United States the great debate about the hydrogen bomb was going on at white heat. J. Robert Oppenheimer, who had worked so hard on the uranium bomb only to suffer agonies of guilt about it afterwards, was preaching that the United States should abandon its efforts toward an H-bomb; and a great mass of America's liberal intellectuals were following his position. Dr. Edward Teller rose to take the opposite position, that we must develop our H-bomb if only in self-defense. Backed by the military and most of the politicians, Teller won and on November 1, 1952, the United States exploded a hydrogen bomb. On August 20, 1953, less than ten months later, Russia announced and tested its own H-bomb.

In the wave of hard feelings (almost an unavoidable instinctual reaction probably, and one which so many Americans shared) against the United States for building and using its uranium bomb, no one ever mentioned the obvious restraint and reluctance with which the United States did use it. In an all-out, total corporation war like World War II had become in five years of fighting, one would think that showed considerable and serious thoughtfulness and consideration.

There can be no doubt, for example, about how it would have been used had Germany developed it first, or Japan. Or even Russia. Or the French?

When one contemplates those possibilities and broods on them, it appears a damned lucky thing for the world and for humanity that America did develop it first.

While one can with reason claim the United States was responsible for the atom bomb and its first use, no one can honestly claim the United States is responsible for developing the human race.

SURRENDER NOW

Illustrations 184 and 185

There had been every reason for Japan to surrender in late June or early July. She had lost the Philippines, then Iwo Jima, then Okinawa. Her only remaining ally, Germany, had capitulated in May. Many members of the still pro-war party had hoped that the death of President Roosevelt on April 12 would weaken and soften the American drive and movement north. It hadn't. If anything, it seemed to have intensified it. The Japanese didn't know what they were up against. The United States could no more have stopped its massive war machine, backed by all its industrial might—the whole created and expanded, finally, for just this very purpose—than the earth could have stopped spinning eastward and gone into reverse. Or, for that matter, than the Japanese, given their cultural heritage, could have surrendered. Part of this sense of intensification, at least, was due to LeMay's air force.

LeMay's big B-29s, after literally running out of incendiary bombs in March, then being diverted to fly support missions for the Okinawa landings for two months, had returned to their savage incendiary attacks in May. LeMay and Spaatz had always believed Japan could be bombed into surrender from the air. Now the vicious fighting for the last island, and the enormous cost in ships and lives and maimed from Ohnishi's increased kamikaze attacks, had convinced LeMay he should go all out. From Washington the Joint Chiefs had forwarded permission, and were shipping out the necessary ordnance. The new campaign began with a 472-bomber raid on Nagoya again, which burned out a further 3.15 square miles of that city on May 14. Within a month the B-29s had hit all six of the major cities so badly the campaign was over. Tokyo, Nagoya, Kobe, Osaka, Yokohama, and Kawasaki. All were crossed off the industrial targets list. A third of Yokohama was burned out in a single night. On May 23 and May 25 Tokyo was hit twice. In the first raid for the loss of 17 bombers an additional 5.3 square miles of Tokyo were destroyed. On the second, for 26 of the big Superforts, an additional 16.8 square miles, the greatest area ever destroyed in a single raid, lay smoking and in ruins. Even a portion of the sacred Imperial Palace of the Emperor burned that night when the fires ran out of control, although the Imperial Palace had deliberately never been a target. Over half of the entire city of Tokyo now no longer existed.

And after that, LeMay had turned his bombers onto attacks on the smaller industrial cities. Sixty attacks, from June 17 to as late as August 14, in fact, fell upon some fifty-odd secondary cities, with crippling results. The devastation was immense. But still the Japanese leaders refused to surrender. By this time even the pitiless, hardened old professional LeMay was moved to a little compassion. Like so many others who had passed through their FINAL EVOLUTION LeMay had grown up on World War II and learned the hard way its Total War ethic. Taking a serious chance, he began dropping leaflets on the cities before the raids.

"CIVILIANS!" they read, "EVACUATE AT ONCE!" On the backs of them, they warned the local military of the coming raids, and pointed out to the people that there was nothing their military could do to protect them. And there wasn't. On August 1, for example, the city of Toyama with a population of 127,860 was almost totally burned out of existence. Ninety-nine point five percent of it was ashes.

At the palace the Emperor seemed powerless in the hands of the pro-war party, who still wanted to continue. Always before, and almost always after, the Emperor has been pictured simply as a powerless tool, a figurehead in the hands of Japan's war leaders. Lately, in the 1970s, several well-researched books have come out showing that the Emperor himself played a much greater part in the policy for war than was formerly recognized. Whether or no, the statute of limitations has certainly run out on him; and at the time both his ministers, for obvious cultural reasons, and U.S. leaders, for military and political reasons, wanted to maintain the portrait of his innocence. At any rate, when the Emperor finally decided in favor of "unconditional surrender," he certainly had the power to make his decision stick.

But the Emperor had not decided in favor of surrender at the time of the Potsdam Proclamation on July 26. And his Minister of War General Anami and Army Chief of Staff General Umezu, the navy chiefs Admirals Toyoda and Ohnishi, all still favored a fight to the end. Even the new Premier Admiral Suzuki (who made the big error over the word *mokusatsu*), who had been chosen expressly to find a way to honorable peace, got up in the Japanese Diet and made an impassioned speech for a desperate last-ditch stand. The main strength of the army remained intact, and the air force had been dispersed to preserve itself. The army leaders still believed they could repulse an invasion. "What should be remembered in carrying out the general decisive battle is adherence to a vigorous spirit of attack" to "set the example for 100,000,000 compatriots," was how they put it.

Not until the second atom bomb had been dropped on Nagasaki did the Emperor finally come forward with the full force of his authority on the side of peace, to accept the Allies' Potsdam Proclamation. Even then, some members of the cabinet and many of the younger army officers wanted to go on fighting. But the atom bombs, by suddenly upgrading the war in a totally new, qualitative way, had given the Emperor the out he needed to accept the Allied terms. He remained firm.

Even so, there was still haggling. The military leaders wanted three other reservations, beyond the one that the Emperor's status be preserved. First, they asked to avoid an Allied military occupation of Japan. Second, they wanted to try their "war criminals" themselves. Third, they asked to disarm their own troops rather than surrender directly to the Allies. General Anami explained that this last could be taken to mean that the Japanese forces had not actually been defeated. They had simply stopped fighting on orders, to preserve the homeland.

Again the Emperor stepped in. He agreed with the peace party against the army. The only request in accepting the Allied proposition would be to ask that the Emperor's position be safeguarded. Cables were sent off to Switzerland to that effect.

A reply came back from Secretary of State Byrnes explaining that the Allies would accept nothing but an "unconditional surrender," and that this meant the Emperor would be subject to the Supreme Commander for the Allied powers. Another furor rose up in the cabinet. What did "subject to" mean? Next day, on August 14, someone pointed out that the Byrnes cable obviously meant the institution of the Emperor would not be abolished. Anyhow, had not the Japanese Emperors often been "subject to" the *shoguns?* Again Hirohito intervened, and said he would accept the Joint Declaration of the Allies. That night he recorded the historic message that would be broadcast at noon of August 15, announcing the surrender.

For the first time in history the people of Japan heard the voice of the Emperor. Listening to it, many of the common people prostrated themselves before their radios, pressing their foreheads to the floor. In front of the Imperial Palace elderly people came to kneel and weep and pray.

But even with this announcement, many still did not want to give up to the alien foreigners. A small group of younger officers attempted a *coup d'état* to capture the Emperor and make him change his mind, but were thwarted. An incipient rebellion at Atsugi airfield, led by a navy Captain Kozono, was also put down. And a final kamikaze attack occurred, after the Emperor's broadcast. Admiral Ugaki, who had commanded the destructive waves of kamikaze attacks at Okinawa, decided to lead one final kamikaze against the enemy at Okinawa, in spite of the Emperor's plea for acceptance and control of emotion. Ugaki had intended to go in in three planes; but when news of his proposed immolation went out, instead of three planes there were eleven waiting for him on the airstrip. The entire command was following him.

Four of the airplanes were forced to return with engine trouble. The other seven continued on, toward Okinawa, but were never heard from again, never found. In a final radio message Ugaki stated he was about to "crash into and destroy the conceited enemy in the true spirit of *bushido*" because he alone was "to blame for our failure to defend the homeland and to destroy the arrogant enemy." A short final message was flashed that the admiral's plane was diving on a target and the other six were following him. But no Allied ships or forces reported any attacks by kamikaze, nor were any of them hit. Nor were the planes ever found. The distraught Admiral seems not to have stopped to think that his attack, if it had succeeded, might have caused resumption of hostilities with a rain of atomic bombs on his homeland cities. Luckily, it didn't.

On August 30, the first American occupation forces landed at Yokosuka. And on Sunday, September 2, the formal surrender documents were signed on board the U.S. battleship *Missouri* in Tokyo Bay, with Douglas MacArthur presiding. The old ham actor, who was to become in effect almost the supreme ruler of Japan for a number of years, had his last word. As he closed the big folio cover over the signed surrender papers, that eminent Shakespearean actor proclaimed, "These proceedings are closed."

And the long march home for Americans, scattered all across the globe of the earth for years, could finally begin. At least, it could begin for those who did not have to stay, or did not choose to stay, to serve in the various occupation armies. An astonishing number did choose to stay.

Responsibility, But For What?

So much has been written, and orated, and sermonized about the symbolic qualities of the atomic bomb and Hiroshima and the mushroom cloud, that it is difficult to separate out the military and political factors of its creation and use.

About the only thing that can be said without dispute is that had the United States not used its A-bomb the invasions of Kyushu and Honshu would have had to be carried out. At great cost. But even that has been disputed.

As for the A-bomb, probably no other nation had the technological facilities to develop it; we didn't ourselves, and had to create them as we went along, and it took us six years to develop one. Possibly Germany might have developed one. But we bombed their heavy water installations in Norway, and together with the British bombed out their research plants in Germany itself. It was Albert Einstein who first brought the United States the news in 1939 that the Germans were working on an atomic bomb, and suggested we had better build one first.

Politically, there seems to have been just about every reason to go ahead and use it. Harry Truman in his memoirs and to his dying day cheerfully accepted full responsibility for ordering its use, and said he considered it a military weapon and that was that. Japan had attacked us without any military provocation, and without warning. Japan had conducted her war in an incredibly savage way. And after the unconditional surrender of Germany, and the uncovering of the political cruelties and brutalities and genocide which had taken place within the German borders, could anything less than unconditional surrender be accepted from the Japanese?

Militarily, there was never any doubt that the atom bomb could and should be used. If only in counting casualties, there was clear reason to use it. The near ruin of Hiroshima (ironically, little of its war production potential was touched) and the partial destruction of Nagasaki were a small price to pay for an end to the war which must have exacted, at a minimum, five times as many casualties, and have taken months and perhaps two years to accomplish. In terms of destruction alone, the total annihilation of both cities (which was not accomplished in either case) was small compared to the destruction that would have taken place all over Japan had the war continued and the U.S. invasions been carried through.

Militarily and politically, it is impossible to point out reasons or make a sound argument for not using the A-bomb.

But at any rate the long war, for those who had fought it, as well as for those who had gotten rich off it, was over.

An End to It

Illustration 186

How did you come back from counting yourself as dead?

The plans called for nine million Americans to be demobilized between June, 1945, and June, 1946. The slow demobilization was necessary. Not only were large numbers required for the armies of occupation until they could be replaced, but the sheer physical logistics of transport made it necessary to string out the return. And what would happen to the happily humming economy, buzzing along, if you suddenly dumped nine million men on the job market? Already the "veterans" were a problem, even before they got to be "veterans." Many home-front assembly-line workers feared for their jobs, as the huge numbers of "vets" flooded back into the country.

If the "vets" were a problem to the economy and to the society as a whole, they neither minded nor cared. All they wanted was to get there: home. The combat men—the new "professionals"—of course got priority, or were supposed to. Out of the nine million very few had ever put their lives on the line, and fewer still had ever heard a shot fired in seriousness. There was a lot of payola under a lot of tables, but in general the plans were followed pretty closely. If out of nine million men a few tens of thousands got home earlier than they should have, who was going to worry about it, except the men they had got themselves squeezed in front of? And among such huge numbers, who would hear or listen to such a small number of voices? In Europe they started coming home even before it was finished in the Pacific.

Housing was a problem. President Truman begged the public to find living space for the veterans. Getting your old job back, or getting a new one, was less of a problem. And the civilian world went merrily on in its happy, dizzy whirl of prosperity in a booming economy. Articles appeared in women's magazines with titles like "What You Can Do to Help the Returning Veteran" and "Will He Be Changed?" *Good Housekeeping* said, "After *two or three weeks* [my italics] he should be finished with talking, with oppressive remembering. If he still goes over the same stories, reveals the same emotions, you had best consult a psychiatrist. This condition is neurotic." *House Beautiful* recommended that "home must be the greatest rehabilitation center of them all" and showed an apartment fixed up for some homecoming general. *Ladies' Home Journal* asked, in 1945, "Has your husband come home to the right woman?"

The answer, of course, was no. How could any woman be the right woman for a man who had just spent one year or two years as essentially a dead man, waiting, anticipating having his head blown off or his guts torn out? Even if she was the same woman he left (and most were not; how could they be?) she was not the right woman for such a man.

Instead of talking about it, most men didn't talk about it. It was not that they didn't want to talk about it, it was that when they did, nobody understood it. It was such a different way of living, and of looking at life even, that there was no common ground for communication in it.

It was like a Ranger staff sergeant I met in St. Louis years ago told me, "One day at Anzio we got eight new replacements into my platoon. We were supposed to make a little feeling attack that same day. Well, by next day, all eight of them replacements were dead, buddy. But none of us old guys were. We weren't going to send our own guys out on point in a damnfool situation like that. We knew nothing would happen. We were sewed up tight. And we'd been together through Africa, and Sicily, and Salerno. We sent the replacements out ahead." He gave me a sad smile, "But how am I going to explain something like that to my wife? She'd think it was horrible. But it was right, man, right. How were we going to send our own guys out into that?" We had some more drinks, got pretty drunk in fact, then he went home to his wife. Who, I am sure, was angry at him for getting drunk.

Another time an infantry sergeant who had fought in the Bulge told me how his platoon had taken some prisoners west of St. Vith. "There were eight of them, and they were tough old-timers, buddy. Been through the mill from the beginning. It was about the fourth or fifth day, and we needed some information. But they weren't talking, not those tough old birds. You had to admire them. So we took the first one off to the side, where they could see him, and shot him through the head. Then they all talked. They were eager to talk. Once they knew we were serious. Horrible? Evil? We knew all about Malmédy, man, and Stavelot. We needed that information. Our lives depended on it. We didn't think it was evil. Neither did they. But how am I going to tell my wife about something like that? Or my mother? They don't understand the problems." We went on getting drunk, and talking, until he felt he was ready to go home.

Slowly, bit by bit, it began to taper off. Men still woke up in the middle of the night, thrashing around and trying to get their hands on their wives' throats.

Men still rolled out from a dead sleep, and hit the dirt with a crash on the bedroom floor, huddling against the bed to evade the aerial bomb or the artillery shells they had dreamed they heard coming. While their wives sat straight up in bed in their new frilly nightgowns bought for the homecoming, wide-eyed and staring, horrified. An old buddy would have roared with laughter. There is no telling what the divorce rate was then, in the early year or two. Certainly a lot higher than was ever admitted.

A number of men I knew slept with loaded pistols or unsheathed bayonets under their pillows for a number of months. Just made them feel more comfortable, they said shamefacedly, but it sure scared the shit out of their wives. And their wives' psychiatrists.

The DE-EVOLUTION OF A SOLDIER. It was longer in coming in some than in others. Some never did lose it, and some—a few—went off to the booby hatch. But not the vast majority. The majority, as they had survived the process of evolving into soldiers, now began to survive the process of de-evolving.

There was nothing the good old government could do about that. As with Uncle Sugar's expensive, astonishingly rich, lavish care which was being expended on the wounded and maimed, so with Uncle Sugar trying to fix things up for the returnee. Omar Bradley was put in charge of Veterans' Affairs, to modernize it and clean up its graft. Not only was the government sending everybody who wanted back to college, but it was sending anybody at all to college, anybody who asked, on their GI Bill of Rights. So much so that girls and civilian men who wanted to go had to score enormously high on the preschool exams, in order to get in. There simply wasn't room for them. But the government had never set up any DE-EVOLUTION OF A SOLDIER center, to match its induction centers. When you went in, they had the techniques and would ride you all the way to becoming a soldier. They had no comparable system when you came out. That you had to do on your own.

And with the de-evolving, as with the evolving, the first sign of change was the coming of the pain. As the old combat numbness disappeared, and the frozen feet of the soul began to thaw, the pain of the cure became evident. The sick-making thoughts of all the buddies who had died. The awful bad luck of the maimed. The next thing to go was the professionalism. How could you be a professional when there was no more profession? The only way was to stay in The Profession. And some, quite a few, did.

About the last thing to go was the old sense of *esprit*. That was the hardest thing to let go of, because there was nothing in civilian life that could replace it. The love and understanding of men for men in dangerous times, and places, and situations. Just as there was nothing in civilian life that could replace the heavy, turgid, day-to-day excitement of danger. Families and other civilian types would never understand that sense of *esprit,* any more than they would understand the excitement of the danger. Some old-timers, a lot of them, tried to hold onto the *esprit* by joining division associations and regimental associations. But the feeling wasn't the same, and never would be the same, because the motivation—the danger—was gone. Too many people lived too far away, and had other jobs and other interests, and anyway the drive was no longer there, and the most honest in their hearts had to admit it.

After all, the war was over.

When the veterans began to spend two nights a week down at the local American Legion, the families and parents and wives could heave a sigh of relief. Because they knew then that, after all, it—the war—was truly over.

Pass in Review!

How many times they had heard the old, long-drawn-out, faint field command pass down the long length of vast parade grounds, fading, as the guidons moved out front.

So slowly it faded, leaving behind it a whole generation of men who would walk into history looking backwards, with their backs to the sun, peering forever over their shoulders behind them, at their own lengthening shadows trailing across the earth. None of them would ever really get over it.

Artists' Biographies

I wish to pay tribute to the many artists who gave the world a pictorial record of WWII. Some gave their lives in the effort.

Because of the restrictions of space and the necessity to comply with the requirements of illuminating the text, I was unable to include some of the best art of the period in this book. To those artists whose work is not included I apologize.

A special appreciation goes to Colonel Egbert White, who was responsible for starting both *Yank* magazine and *Stars and Stripes* of WWII, and to Colonel Franklin Forsberg, whose faith carried *Yank* over many rough spots. My particular thanks go to Anne Weeks, our Washington consultant, author of *The History of Yank, The Army Weekly.* And thanks to Hy Steirman.

Art Weithas

GEORGE BAKER, is the creator of "Sad Sack," the most beloved cartoon character of WW II. Born in Lowell, Massachusetts, his earliest ambition was to be a ball player. In 1937, he went to Hollywood to work for Walt Disney and was inducted into the Army in '41. When a cartoon of his won a contest sponsored by the *New York Times* he was selected by *Yank, The Army Weekly,* to become staff artist. "Sad Sack" became the personification of the Army's little guy, the hopeless underdog with all of his frustrations. Baker died in 1975. He was a fine humanist and a great draughtsman.

STANDISH BACKUS, JR. is known primarily as a painter and illustrator. He was born in Detroit, Michigan and he received his B.A. from Princeton University and studied art in Germany at the University of Munich. He is well known for both murals and watercolors. Besides his work during World War II as a Navy Combat Artist, Backus went to the South Pole with the Byrd Expedition during the "summer" season 1955–56. He lives and works in Montecito, California.

ROBERT BENNEY, born in New York City in 1904, was educated at Cooper Union, Art Students League, and the National Academy of Design in New York City. He painted portraits of John Barrymore, Chiang Kai-Shek, Franklin D. Roosevelt and other prominent individuals. He produced paintings of army medical activities for Abbott Laboratories in 1944–45, and he has also done illustrations for the American Tobacco Company, *Argos,* Chrysler Corporation, *Collier's,* Standard Oil Company, *True* and Western Electric Company.

FRANKLIN BOGGS was born in Warsaw, Indiana, in 1915. He won two European traveling fellowships from the Pennsylvania Academy of Fine Arts. His paintings have been exhibited in many leading museums. As a war artist-correspondent for Abbott Laboratories in 1944, he portrayed Army Medical Department activities in the southwest Pacific.

CHESLEY BONESTELL is a member of one of the oldest California families. He is an architect, engineer, and above all an artist who specializes in creating scenes of the unknown from scraps of the known, i.e., paintings of worlds beyond the planets. His work has appeared in many magazines and books.

FRANK BRANDT worked on the *New York Daily News* prior to his induction into the army, and later became a member of the *Yank* staff as a cartoonist. After discharge, he contributed cartoons to many major publications, later becoming a successful art director and T.V. producer. He is now living in California.

HOWARD BRODIE, born in Oakland, California, in 1915, attended the California School of Fine Arts and became a veteran combat illustrator of three wars. As an enlisted man in World War II, he was first assigned by *Yank* to Guadalcanal and Europe. Later he was awarded a Bronze Star medal for his coverage of the Battle of the Bulge. When the Korean

War broke out he was sent to the scene by *Collier's* and he was in Vietnam several times to sketch combat action for various magazines and the Department of Defense. He has served as staff artist for San Francisco newspapers and has engaged in a variety of assignments including a weekly feature for Associated Press News Features, and pictorial coverage of special news events such as the Watergate hearings. His sketches are included in the permanent collections of the Library of Congress, New Britain Museum of American Art, Connecticut and San Francisco Olympic Club.

EMMANUEL BROMBERG, originally from Chicago studied under Boardman Robinson, the muralist at the Art Students League in New York. As an enlisted man he was selected by the Army Corps of Engineers to make a pictorial record of the war overseas, serving in England, Normandy and Germany. Some of his works are represented in the Army Historical collection in Washington, D.C.

GRIFFITH B. COALE, the first official Navy Combat Artist, was born in Baltimore, Maryland in 1890. Study in Munich and Paris preceded Coale's World War II art work. Besides his combat art, he established a reputation as a gifted muralist, executing a number of commissions for public buildings in and around New York City and other places. His portraits of well known Americans hang in the Maryland Historical Society and the Johns Hopkins University. Coale died in 1950.

TOM CRAIG was born in Upland, California, in 1909. He studied biology at Pomona College and agriculture at the University of California, and began painting while in college. He won many awards for his artwork. Craig served as a war artist for *Life* magazine in Italy. After the war he taught at Occidental College in Los Angeles and illustrated the Manual of Southern California Botony. He is a member of the Laguna Beach Artists Association and the Philadelphia Watercolor Society.

MARSHALL DAVIS is an extremely sensitive draughtsman. He occupied his spare time in the army recording the mundane aspects of soldiering, and worked as a contributing artist for *Yank*. After his discharge he became a prominent illustrator and a teacher at the Famous Artists School in Westport, Connecticut, where he now lives.

OLIN DOWS was one of the 12 enlisted men selected by the Army Corps of Engineers to make a pictorial record of the war overseas. Besides recording the war, he distinguished himself as a soldier in France and Germany. He is represented in the Army Historical collection in Washington, D.C.

KERR EBY was born in Japan in 1889, of Methodist missionary parents. Eby sketched scenes of both World Wars I and II. His famous book, *War,* was a result of his sketches of France during World War I. He was with the Marines when they landed at Tarawa and spent three weeks in a foxhole on the front line of Bougainville, rough-sketching the jungle fighting. A complete collection of his work up to 1932, including trial proofs, is housed in the New York Public Library. Mr. Eby died in 1946.

CARL ERICKSON dominated the field of fashion for over 35 years. An absolutely honest draughtsman, he drew only from life. Erickson was born in Joliet, Illinois, in 1891 and studied at the Chicago Academy of Fine Arts before moving to New York City. His drawings and paintings are authentic because he knew his subjects and their world. His taste and beautiful draughtsmanship reveal him to be an artist of permanent importance. Mr. Erickson died in 1958. In 1959, the Brooklyn Museum held a retrospective showing of his drawings.

KEITH FERRIS was born in Honolulu, the son of a career air force officer. He attended Texas A & M, George Washington University, the Corcoran School of Art and studied in Europe. As a freelance illustrator he specialized in aviation and aerospace art. He received the Citation of Merit, Society of Illustrators in 1966. Ferris has 19 paintings in the Air Force art collections and has had one-man shows at the Aerospace Art Hall of the National Air and Space Museum, the Smithsonian Institution and the Society of Illustrators of which he is a member.

LOREN RUSSELL FISHER was a student at the Fort Wayne Art School and the John Herron Art School in Indiana. In 1940, at the age of 27, he received the John H. Lazarus Fellowship to the American Academy in Rome from the Metropolitan Museum of Art. In World War II, as a member of the Combat Art Section, Corps of Engineers, he traveled and sketched in the Philippine Islands, Netherland Indies, Federated Malay States, Burma, India, China, and Japan.

TOM FLANNERY became a member of the *Yank* staff in London and contributed many humorous, biting cartoons. He is now staff cartoonist for the *Baltimore Sun.*

ALBERT GOLD, a native of Philadelphia, Pennsylvania, was born in 1916. He graduated from the Pennsylvania Museum School of Industrial Arts, having studied both commercial and fine arts. His paintings have been exhibited in many national and international exhibitions and are included in public and private collections such as the Library of Congress, New York Public Library, Philadelphia Museum of Art and Pennsylvania Academy of Fine Arts. During World War II he served as artist-correspondent for three years in England, France and Germany. He taught at the Philadelphia Museum School and served as Director, Department of Illustration, Philadelphia Museum Collection of Arts. He currently illustrates books and magazines and is a member of Artists Equity and the American Association of University Professors.

ROBERT GREENHALGH was born in Chicago, Illinois, in 1915. He studied at Illinois Wesleyan University and graduated from the University of Missouri. He joined the staff of *Yank* magazine in New York and later was assigned to the Pacific Theater in 1943, covering Guam, Bougainville and the raids on Wake Island. Greenhalgh received the Award of Distinctive Merit from the Art Directors' Club for a drawing done on Bougainville. He returned to the U.S. to cover President Franklin D. Roosevelt's funeral. Following his discharge from the army he remained in New York to continue his art career. His illustrations have appeared in many national magazines.

JOSEPH HIRSCH was born in Philadelphia, Pennsylvania, in 1910. He attended the Pennsylvania Museum School of Art where he studied with George Luks. During World War II he painted army medical activities in Europe and the Mediterranean Theater for Abbott Laboratories. His work appears in the collections of the Corcoran Gallery, Boston Museum, Philadelphia Museum, University of Arizona and the Library of Congress. His paintings have been shown in most of the leading American museums. His most recent one-man show was held at the Forum Gallery, New York in October-November 1974.

MITCHELL JAMIESON, one of the country's foremost watercolor artists, was born in Kensington, Maryland and attended the Abbott School of Fine and Commercial Arts and the Corcoran School of Art in Washington, D.C. Having already established himself with many noted commissions, he began his duty in 1942 as an official combat artist depicting the navy in its operations from the North African campaign to the South Pacific. His combat paintings have been extensively reproduced by *Life, Fortune* and other national magazines. Mr. Jamieson is now painting in his studio near Washington, D.C.

LESLIE LANE was born in England, studied at Chelsea College of Fine Arts in London; the Ontario College of Art, Toronto; the Art Students League in New York and the Ecole S-de Beaux Arts in Paris. He joined the U.S. Army in 1943 and served in the European theater of war assigned to paint scenes and impressions of the war for American archives. He also painted the American cemeteries of Europe. This collection is known as "The Land of Rest" and has been widely exhibited and lauded by critics.

WILLIAM LAWRENCE was born in 1915 in Rumson, New Jersey and studied at the Art Students League, New York City. As a Marine artist and proficient boatman, he enlisted in the U.S. Coast Guard in 1942 and became a Chief Boatswain's mate. He was awarded the Silver Star and citation for action in the invasion of Sicily and Salerno. In the Pacific he covered the assaults of Iwo Jima and Okinawa, and received a letter of congratulations from Admiral Nimitz. He now lives in Red Bank, New Jersey.

TOM LEA, a native of El Paso, Texas, was born in 1907. He studied at the Art Institute of Chicago and with the Chicago muralist, John Norton. From 1941 to 1945 he served as a war artist for *Life* magazine recording military activities in the North Atlantic, Pacific and Solomon Islands. He returned to El Paso to work as a painter, illustrator and muralist. Also a prolific writer, he has written seven books, of which two, *The Brave Bulls,* and *The Wonderful Country,* were produced as motion pictures. He collected numerous awards for both his writing and painting and his artwork is represented in many public collections. A retrospective of his work in 1971 included ten World War II paintings from the United States Army Collection.

FLETCHER MARTIN, born in Colorado in 1904, presently resides in Woodstock, New York. Since his first one-man exhibition of paintings at the San Diego Fine Arts Gallery in 1934, he has exhibited in all the leading American museums and in Europe, South America and Africa as well. He received many painting awards and his work is in numerous public collections including the Metropolitan Museum of Art and Museum of Modern Art in New York. During World War II, as artist-correspondent for *Life* magazine he covered the North African and Normandy campaigns. His work has been reproduced in *Life, Time, Newsweek, Art News, Art Digest* and other magazines.

BILL MAULDIN is probably the most famous cartoonist-writer to come out of WW II; receiving the Pulitzer Prize during the war for his work as the creator of Willie and Joe, the cartoon characters that appeared in *Stars and Stripes.* He drew the infantryman truthfully because he himself was one, fighting through the Sicily and Italian campaigns where he received the Purple Heart. He later wrote *Up Front* and other books. Born in New Mexico, he studied at the Chicago Academy of Fine Arts. Mauldin now resides in Chicago where he is attached to the *Chicago Sun.*

ROBERT McCALL was a scholarship student at the Columbus School of Fine Art. In 1941 he enlisted in the Army Air Force. His off duty hours were spent painting pictures of planes. His involvement with aerospace grew out of this work. He illustrated the ad campaign for the film *2001,* and has done numerous illustrations for *Life* magazine, *National Geographic* and for many books. The illustration in this book came out of his meticulously researched series of the paintings for *Tora, Tora, Tora,* a film on the story of Pearl Harbor. He lives on Moonlight Way, Paradise Valley, Arizona, which must be as close to heaven as you can get.

BARSE MILLER, born in New York City in 1904 studied at National Academy of Design in New York, Pennsylvania Academy of Fine Arts in Philadelphia, and Salon d'Autome in Paris. He is represented in numerous museum collections. He taught art in California; the University of Vermont and Academy of Fine Arts, Queens College, in New York. In 1942 he was commissioned by *Life* magazine to produce a series of paintings depicting the West Coast defense areas to tell the story of America's supply lines. That same year he joined the army and as a combat artist in the Corps of

Engineers was assigned to General MacArthur's headquarters. He covered army activities in New Guinea, the Philippines, Japan and North China. After the war he continued his painting and teaching career.

GEORGE PAYNE was born in Oakland, California in 1913. He studied at the Art Center School of Los Angeles and at the Art Institute of Chicago. He has worked as an art director, designer and illustrator in Chicago, Cleveland and New York. Payne served in the maritime service in the North and South Atlantic, the Mediterranean Sea and the Indian Ocean during WW II. Now semiretired, he resides in New York City and specializes in painting marine subjects.

OGDEN PLEISSNER, born in Brooklyn, New York, in 1905, studied at the Art Students League in New York City. In World War II he served in the air force and later as artist-correspondent for *Life* magazine. His paintings hang in many national museums and art galleries throughout the United States including the Metropolitan Museum, Brooklyn Museum, Minneapolis Museum, Toledo Art Institute and National Academy of Design in New York. He has won numerous awards and prizes and was elected to the National Academy of Design and to the Royal Society of Art in London. He also holds memberships in the National Arts and Salmagundi Clubs.

EDWARD REEP, born in New York in 1918, grew up in California and graduated from the Art Center College of Design in Los Angeles. He served as an army artist in Africa and Italy during World War II. In 1947 he won a Guggenheim Fellowship for creative painting and since then, while teaching painting in art schools and colleges, he has won many prizes, exhibiting his work throughout the United States. His paintings have appeared in numerous books and magazines and he is the author of *The Content of Watercolor*, published in 1969. He completed a three-week tour in Germany as a volunteer army artist in 1971 and is currently artist-in-residence at East Carolina University.

NORMAN ROCKWELL'S paintings have depicted and entertained America for over five decades. He sold his first cover illustration to the *Saturday Evening Post* in 1916. Presidents Eisenhower, Kennedy and Johnson have sat for his portraits. As his personal contribution during World War II, he painted the famous "Four Freedoms" posters. His "Freedom of

Speech" painting is in the collection of the Metropolitan Museum of Art. His work and career are described more fully in *Norman Rockwell, Illustrator* and *Norman Rockwell: My Adventures as an Illustrator,* an autobiography.

JOHN RUGE was born in 1915 in Faribault, Minnesota. In 1925 his family moved to New York. He later enrolled in the Art Students League in 1933. At the age of 21, he sold his first cartoon to *Collier's.* Ruge worked as a cartoonist and illustrator for all the prominent magazines of that time. He entered the army in 1942 and transferred to *Yank* as Pacific combat art-correspondent, covering air strikes from the Maaiana, the Iwo Jima campaign, Okinawa and later Tokyo during the occupation. He received the Art Directors' Club Award of Distinctive Merit for one of his combat drawings. After discharge, he resumed his career of cartooning and illustrating. His work has appeared in *Look, Playboy,* the *American Legion* and many other national magazines. Ruge is married to the painter Jane Chenoweth.

ALEXANDER RUSSO is known for his ability to work in a number of painting mediums including oils, watercolor and silk screen. He was born in Atlantic City, New Jersey, in 1922. He studied at Pratt Institute, Swarthmore College, Bard College and Columbia University. He has been a Guggenheim Fellow, awarded a Fulbright grant and a number of other prizes and awards. His works are on display around the world. Today he is Associate Professor of Painting and Drawing at the Corcoran School of Art and Hood College.

ALLEN SAALBURG was born in Rochelle, Illinois, in 1899. He studied, worked and exhibited in New York and Paris. In the 1920s he did freelance work for magazines and in advertising. His work has appeared on the covers of *Fortune* and the *Saturady Evening Post.* From 1934–36 he was in charge of the W.P.A.'s mural project for the New York City Park Department. In 1938 he had an exhibit at the Whitney Museum in New York. Saalburg was awarded the Cross of Honor and Patriotic Service Cross in 1942 by the United States Flag Association for painting *Flag Over Mt. Vernon.* He is renowned as one of America's finest silk-screen painters of documented American folk art and recognized as a foremost American magic realist painter. His work is represented in many museum collections and the U.S. Air Force Historical Art Collection in Washington, D.C.

JES SCHLAIKJER, a resident of Washington, D.C., was born in 1897 and spent his youth on a ranch in South Dakota.

During World War I he enlisted in the army and went overseas. He remained in France after the war to study art at the Ecole des Beaux Arts. Later he returned to the United States and studied at the Art Institute of Chicago. As an official War Department artist during World War II he painted a series of inspirational posters. He was elected to membership in the American National Academy.

JOHN SCOTT was born in Camden, New Jersey, in 1907. He was inducted into the Army Engineers in April 1942 and later, in 1943–44, served as an artist-correspondent for *Yank* magazine, covering the Normandy advance and the breakout into Germany. He now specializes in hunting and fishing illustrations for magazines and advertisements.

DWIGHT SHEPLER, a native of Everett, Massachusetts, was born in 1905. He studied at the Boston Museum of Fine Arts School and Williams College. His works are in the Boston Museum of Fine Arts, Williams College, Borough Museum of Dartmouth, England, the Harvard University Graduate School and others. He has done numerous murals and some sculpture for institutes around the world. Besides exhibits at many of the representative galleries in the U.S., Shepler has had a number of one-man shows.

SIDNEY SIMON was born in Pittsburgh, Pennsylvania, in 1917. He studied at Carnegie Institute of Technology, Pennsylvania Academy of Fine Arts and University of Pennsylvania. In 1943 he was assigned to General MacArthur's headquarters and covered all major operations in New Guinea and the Philippines, including the signing of the peace on the U.S.S. *Missouri.* He received numerous painting and sculpture prizes and has exhibited in the Whitney Biennial and Corcoran Biennial. His works are in public and private collections.

LAWRENCE BEALE SMITH was born in Washington, D.C., in 1908. He attended the Art Institute of Chicago and graduated from University of Chicago. He has received numerous painting awards and his work is in many permanent museum collections including Harvard University, John Herron Museum, Indiana, Addison Gallery, Andover, Massachusetts, the Library of Congress and the Encyclopedia Brittanica Collection. As a combat artist for Abbott Laboratories he covered army medical activities in England and France during World War II. He is a member of Phi Beta Kappa and Delta Kappa Epsilon societies.

HARRISON STANDLEY was born in San Francisco, California, in 1916 and graduated from Stanford University. He attended Pomona College, Los Angeles, and the Academie de la Grande Chaumiere in Paris. During World War II he served as artist-correspondent for the army in Iceland, England, and France. After the war he returned to Paris, married a French woman, and continued his art career.

JOSEPH STEFANELLI was born in Philadelphia, Pennsylvania, in 1921. He studied at the Pennsylvania Academy of Fine Arts and the Art Students League in New York. As a staff artist for *Yank* magazine in World War II he covered the landings at New Guinea, Leyte, Luzon, Borneo and Jolo Islands. With the first Cavalry Division he entered Manila on the first day of liberation. After the war he resumed his art studies at the Pennsylvania Academy and produced illustrations for books and magazines. Stefanelli's works are represented in numerous museums and collections and has been the recipient of many awards including a Fulbright in 1958–59.

RALPH STEIN was born in New York. He became a successful cartoonist for major publications and in advertising. He enlisted in the army to become a staff member of *Yank* as cartoonist and ordnance authority. He has since written numerous books and articles on classic old cars, cameras and guns. Stein's most recent book is *The History of the Pin-up,* which is proof of his versatility.

NORMAN THOMAS was creator of the Coast Guard World War II Memorial. He has had a distinguished art career, including four years of wartime service as combat artist. Born in Dedham, Massachusetts, he attended the Portland School of Fine Arts, Maine and the National Academy of Design in New York City. He enlisted in the Coast Guard in 1942 and covered assignments in Greenland, Kwajalein, Saipan, Leyte and Iwo Jima. Mr. Thomas now resides, paints and maintains a gallery in Mexico City.

JOAQUIN ALBERTO VARGAS was born in Peru in 1896. He is best known as the creator of the Varga Girl. Educated in France and Switzerland, he left Europe at the outbreak of World War I. He came to New York and in 1920 began an eleven-year association with Florenz Ziegfeld as a poster artist. He later married Anna Mae Clift, a Follies Girl. After a stint with various Hollywood studios, he returned to New York in 1940 and began working for *Esquire* magazine. He was known as *the* pin-up artist of the Second World War. In 1945, Vargas was honored by the Treasury Department for his work during the war years. In 1953, he received the medal and brevet of knighthood in the Order of the Sun from the Peruvian government. He is now a contributor to *Playboy* magazine.

ED VEBELL was born in Chicago. He started his career as a professional illustrator at 18. Inducted into the army and serving in Africa, he was picked up by *Stars and Stripes* and served as artist-correspondent in Africa, Italy and France. After discharge, he spent two additional years in Paris free-lancing. In 1947 he returned to the U.S. and picked up his career as illustrator of sports and military subjects. One of the top illustrators, Vebell brings the same intensity to his art work as to his other major interest—fencing. One of the top epee men in the country, he represented the United States on three olympic teams.

ARTHUR WEITHAS was born in New York City, where he attended the Art Students League. He later became art director for top advertising agencies. In 1942 he enlisted in the army to serve as head art director for *Yank*. He received the Legion of Merit for his work as art director and artist-correspondent in the Pacific. He saw action in the Philippines and on Corregidor. An extremely versatile artist, he has received awards in editorial, advertising, packaging, television and fine arts. Mr. Weithas has had several one-man exhibitions and is a member of The Art Directors' Club and The Society of Illustrators.

HUNTER WOOD was born in 1908 in Babylon, Long Island. He is the son of the well known marine painter Worden Wood. Schooled in New Jersey, he entered the New York State Merchant Marine Academy. He enlisted in December 1941 in the U.S. Coast Guard as a navy combat artist. He had charge of a landing detail in the North African invasion. He saw the British carrier *Avenger* blow up and pulled survivors of the U.S. transport *Leedstown* out of the Algerian surf. Wood's pictures hang in many American and foreign collections.

Picture Credits

Army insignia—
Courtesy of U.S. Army, Office of the Chief of Information
New York Times front page 12/8/41 © 1941 by The New York Times Company. *Reprinted by permission*

Illustration numbers

1 Griffith Bailey Coale, *Courtesy of U.S. Navy Combat Art Collection*
2 *Courtesy of the artist,* Robert T. McCall
3 Ezaki Kohei, Captured Japanese Art, *Courtesy of U.S. Army Center of Military History*
4 K. Sato, Captured Japanese Art, *Courtesy of U.S. Air Force Art Collection*
5 Mukai Junichi, Captured Japanese Art, *Courtesy of U.S. Army Center of Military History*
6 Miyamoto Saburo, Captured Japanese Art, *Courtesy of U.S. Army Center of Military History*
7 © 1944 by George Baker, *Courtesy of the artist,* George Baker
8 K. Nakamura, Captured Japanese Art, *Courtesy of U.S. Air Force Art Collection*
9 Griffith Bailey Coale, *Courtesy of U.S. Navy Combat Art Collection*
10 Robert Benney, *Courtesy of U.S. Navy Combat Art Collection*
11 *Courtesy of the artist,* Robert F. Greenhalgh
12 *Courtesy of the artist,* Marshall Davis
13 Albert Gold, *Courtesy of U.S. Army Center of Military History*
14 A. Hierl, Captured German Art, *Courtesy of U.S. Army Center of Military History*
15 Lanzinger, Captured German Art, *Courtesy of U.S. Army Center of Military History*

WW II

16 Adolf Hitler, Captured German Art, *Coutresy of U.S. Army Center of Military History*
17 Helmut Jensen, Captured German Art, *Courtesy of U.S. Army Center of Military History*
18 Wilhelm Petersen, Captured German Art, *Courtesy of U.S. Army Center of Military History*
19 Schmitz Westerholt, Captured German Art, *Courtesy of U.S. Army Center of Military History*
20-23 Howard Brodie, *Courtesy of U.S. Army Center of Military History*
24 Unknown Marine artist, *Courtesy of Marc Jaffe*
25-27 © 1944 by George Baker, *Courtesy of the artist,* George Baker
28 Howard Brodie, *Courtesy of U.S. Army Center of Military History*
29 Varga, *Reprinted by permission of Esquire Magazine.* © 1943 by Esquire, Inc.
30 Robert F. Greenhalgh, *Courtesy of U.S. Army Center of Military History*
31 *Courtesy of the artist,* Joe Stefanelli
32 Georg, Captured German Art, *Courtesy of U. S. Army Center of Military History*
33 Griffith Bailey Coale, *Courtesy of U.S. Navy Combat Art Collection*
34 Carl Erickson, *by permission*
35 Kerr Eby, *Courtesy of U.S. Navy Combat Art Collection*
36-38 John Ruge, *Courtesy of U.S. Army Center of Military History*
39 Al Melinger, *Courtesy of U.S. Army Center of Military History*
40 John Baldwin, *Courtesy of U.S. Army Center of Military History*
41 Leo Salkin, *Courtesy of U.S. Army Center of Military History*
42 Bill Newcombe, *Courtesy of U.S. Army Center of Military History*
43, 44 Ralph Stein, *Courtesy of U.S. Army Center of Military History*
45 Frank Brandt, *Courtesy of U.S. Army Center of Military History*
46 Tom Flannery, *Courtesy of U.S. Army Center of Military History*
47 Tom Flannery, *Courtesy of U.S. Army Center of Military History*
48-53 *Courtesy of the artist,* Robert F. Greenhalgh

54 Norman Thomas, *Official U.S. Coast Guard Photo*
55 *Courtesy of the artist,* Robert F. Greenhalgh
56 *Courtesy of the artist,* George N. Payne
57 Carl Erickson, *by permission*
58, 59 Albert Gold, *Courtesy of U.S. Army Center of Military History*
60-64 Kerr Eby, *Courtesy of U.S. Navy Combat Art Collection*
65 Franklin Boggs, *Courtesy of U.S. Navy Combat Art Collection*
66 Norman Rockwell, *Reprinted with permission from The Saturday Evening Post.* © 1945 The Curtis Publishing Company
67 Allen Saalburg, *Office of War Information, No. 44-PA-191 in the National Archives*
68 Jess Schlaikjer, *Courtesy of the U.S. Army Center of Military History*
69 *Courtesy of the artist,* Robert F. Greenhalgh
70 UPPER—Kerr Eby, *Courtesy of U.S. Navy Combat Art Collection*
70 LOWER—*Courtesy of the artist,* Robert F. Greenhalgh
71-73 Kerr Eby, *Courtesy of U.S. Navy Combat Art Collection*
74 Charles Shannon, *Courtesy of U.S. Army Center of Military History*
75-76 *Courtesy of the artist,* Robert F. Greenhalgh
77 Wesley B. McKeown
78 Miyamoto Saburo, Captured Japanese Art, *Courtesy of U.S. Air Force Art Collection*
79-82 Kerr Eby, *Courtesy of U.S. Navy Combat Art Collection*
83-85 Tom Lea, *Courtesy of U.S. Army Center of Military History*
86-90 Kerr Eby, *Courtesy of U.S. Navy Combat Art Collection*
91 *Courtesy of the artist,* Leslie Lane
92 Edward Reep, *Courtesy of U.S. Army Center of Military History*
93 Tom Craig, *Courtesy of U.S. Army Center of Military History*
94 Tom Craig, *Courtesy of U.S. Army Center of Military History*
95-97 Drawings copyrighted 1944 by United Features Syndicate, Inc. *Reproduced by courtesy of* Bill Mauldin

WW II

98 Ogden Pleissner, *Courtesy of U.S. Army Center of Military History*
99 William Caldwell, *Courtesy of U.S. Army Center of Military History*
100 Edward Reep, *Courtesy of U.S. Army Center of Military History*
101 Edward Reep, *Courtesy of U.S. Army Center of Military History*
102, 103 Edward Reep, *Courtesy of U.S. Army Center of Military History*
104 Franklin Boggs, *Courtesy of U.S. Navy Combat Art Collection*
105-108 *Courtesy of the artist,* Albert Gold
109 Harrison Standley, *Courtesy of U.S. Army Center of Military History*
110, 111 Dwight C. Shepler, *Courtesy of U.S. Navy Combat Art Collection*
112 Emmanuel Bromberg, *Courtesy of U.S. Army Center of Military History*
113 Robert Benney, *Courtesy of U.S. Army Center of Military History*
114 Joseph Hirsch, *Courtesy of U.S. Army Center of Military History*
115 Edna Reindell, *Courtesy of U.S. Army Center of Military History*
116 Mitchell Jamieson, *Courtesy of U.S. Navy Combat Art Collection*
117 Alban Wolf, Captured German Art, *Courtesy of U.S. Army Center of Military History*
118 Dwight C. Shepler, *Courtesy of U.S. Navy Combat Art Collection*
119 Hunter Wood, *Official U.S. Coast Guard Photo*
120 Mitchell Jamieson, *Courtesy of U.S. Navy Combat Art Collection*
121 Wesley B. McKeown
122 Mitchell Jamieson, *Courtesy of U.S. Navy Combat Art Collection*
123 Mitchell Jamieson, *Courtesy of U.S. Navy Combat Art Collection*
124 Alexander Russo, *Courtesy of U.S. Navy Combat Art Collection*
125 Dwight C. Shepler, *Courtesy of U.S. Navy Combat Art Collection*
126 Mitchell Jamieson, *Courtesy of U.S. Navy Combat Art Collection*

WW II

127 Mitchell Jamieson, *Courtesy of U.S. Navy Combat Art Collection*
128 Albert Gold, *Courtesy of U.S. Army Center of Military History*
129 Wesley B. McKeown
130 Albert Gold, *Courtesy of U.S. Army Center of Military History*
131 Fletcher Martin, *Courtesy of U.S. Army Center of Military History*
132 Olin Dows, *Courtesy of U.S. Army Center of Military History*
133 Edward Reep, *Courtesy of U.S. Army Center of Military History*
134 Harrison Standley, *Courtesy of U.S. Army Center of Military History*
135 Jacob, Captured German Art, *Courtesy of U.S. Army Center of Military History*
136 Lawrence Beall Smith, *Courtesy of U.S. Army Center of Military History*
137 John Scott, *Courtesy of U.S. Army Center of Military History*
138 Floyd Davis, *Courtesy of U.S. Army Center of Military History*
139 Karl Raible, Captured German Art, *Courtesy of U.S. Army Center of Military History*
140 Hagenkotter, Captured German Art, *Courtesy of U.S. Army Center of Military History*
141 Keith Ferris, *Courtesy of U.S. Air Force Art Collection*
142 Ogden Pleissner, *Courtesy of U.S. Army Center of Military History*
143 Lawrence Beall Smith, *Courtesy of U.S. Air Force Art Collection*
144, 145 Kerr Eby, *Courtesy of U.S. Navy Combat Art Collection*
146 Dwight C. Shepler, *Courtesy of U.S. Navy Combat Art Collection*
147 *Official United States Air Force photographs*
148 Albert Gold, *Courtesy of U.S. Army Center of Military History*
149 Wesley B. McKeown
150 Olin Dows, *Courtesy of U.S. Army Center of Military History*
151 Emmanuel Bromberg, *Courtesy of U.S. Army Center of Military History*

WW II

152 Albert Gold, *Courtesy of U.S. Army Center of Military History*

153-159 Howard Brodie, *Courtesy of U.S. Army Center of Military History*

160 *Courtesy of the artist,* Howard Brodie

161, 162 Dwight C. Shepler, *Courtesy of U.S. Navy Combat Art Collection*

163-167 Joe Stefanelli, *Courtesy of U.S. Army Center of Military History*

168 Barse Miller, *Courtesy of U.S. Army Center of Military History*

169 Sidney Simon, *Courtesy of U.S. Army Center of Military History*

170 Dwight C. Shepler, *Courtesy of U.S. Navy Combat Art Collection*

171 M. Susuki, Captured Japanese Art, *Courtesy of U.S. Air Force Art Collection*

172 *Courtesy of the artist,* Art Weithas

173 Loren Russell Fisher, *Courtesy of U.S. Army Center of Military History*

174 *Courtesy of the artist,* Edward Vebell

175 William G. Lawrence, *Official U.S. Coast Guard Photo*

176, 177 John Ruge, *Courtesy of U.S. Army Center of Military History*

178 Chesley Bonestell, *From the Marine Corps Art Collection*

179, 180 John Ruge, *Courtesy of U.S. Army Center of Military History*

181 Wesley B. McKeown

182 Standish Backus, Jr., *Courtesy of U.S. Navy Combat Art Collection*

183 Standish Backus, Jr., *Courtesy of U.S. Navy Combat Art Collection*

184 Standish Backus, Jr., *Courtesy of U.S. Navy Combat Art Collection*

185 Barse Miller, *Courtesy of U.S. Army Center of Military History*

186 Howard Brodie, *Courtesy of U.S. Army Center of Military History*

New York Times front page, 8/15/45 © 1945 by The New York Times Company. *Reprinted by permission*

REFERENCES

The American Heritage Picture History of World War II, C. L. Sulzberger, American Heritage, New York, 1966.

History of the Second World War (magazine), Marshall Cavendish, London.

The Sad Sack, George Baker, Simon & Schuster, New York, 1944. By permission of the William Morris Agency, Inc. Copyright © 1944 by George Baker.

Terror From the Skies, Tragic Victories, Outraged Skies, copyright © 1971 by Edward Jablonski and *Wings of Fire,* copyright © 1972 by Edward Jablonski. By permission of Doubleday & Co., Inc., New York, and by permission of the author and the author's agents, Scott Meredith Literary Agency, Inc., 580 Fifth Avenue, New York, New York 10036.

Up Front, William H. Mauldin, World, New York, 1945.

World War II, E. Bauer, Orbis Publishing Ltd., London.

Yank, The Army Weekly, New York.

INDEX

INDEX

INDEX

INDEX

INDEX

INDEX

INDEX

INDEX

INDEX

INDEX

INDEX